D1547305

Technology Infrastructure
and
Competitive Position

Technology
Infrastructure
and
Competitive Position

Gregory Tassey

Kluwer Academic Publishers

Distributors for North America:
Kluwer Academic Publishers
101 Philip Drive
Assinippi Park
Norwell, Massachusetts 02061 USA

Distributors for all other countries:
Kluwer Academic Publishers Group
Distribution Centre
Post Office Box 322
3300 AH Dordrecht, THE NETHERLANDS

Library of Congress Cataloging-in-Publication Data

Tassey, Gregory.
    Technology infrastructure and competitive position / Gregory
Tassey.
        p.   cm.
    Includes bibliographical references.
    ISBN 0-7923-9232-9 (acid free paper)
      1. Technology--United States.   2. Competition, International.
I. Title.
T21.T33   1992   92-1291
338.9'7306--dc20   CIP

About the Author

Gregory Tassey is senior economist for the National Institute of
Standards and Technology in Gaithersburg, Maryland. Prior to
assuming that position, he was Chief of Economic Policy Research for
the Experimental Technology Incentives Program in the Department
of Commerce. Since receiving the Ph.D. from George Washington
University in 1978, he has conducted strategic planning and
microeconomic analyses of technology-based industries and the
government policies that affect them. His research has been
published in economics, business, and policy research journals; he is
co-author of *Strategies for Technology-Based Competition* (Lexington
Books) and co-editor of *Cooperative Research and Development: The
Industry-University-Government Relationship* (Kluwer Academic
Publishers).

All opinions expressed in this book are those of the author and do not
represent official positions of the Department or Commerce or the
National Institute of Standards and Technology.

To my wife and daughter:
they love me more than
economics, which enabled
this book to be completed

Table Of Contents

Chapter 4
RESEARCH CONSORTIA   107

Chapter 5
INDUSTRY STRUCTURE AND INVESTMENT IN TECHNOLOGY INFRASTRUCTURE   139

Chapter 6
STRATEGY AND STANDARDS   169

Acknowledgements

The broad scope of this book means that varied sources had to be used. Many of the most valuable were individuals in government and industry, both in the United States and elsewhere. Too numerous to name, they all have a common bond -- the desire to find better ways of combining government and industry assets in the pursuit of economic growth. A debt is due to the staff of the National Institute of Standards and Technology, who provided numerous insights into both technological and industry trends. Without their contributions, this book would not have been possible. Al Sher provided expert consultation on graphics, including the design of the cover. A special thanks is due Elaine Bunten-Mines, whose intellectual stimulation and moral support over many years have been invaluable.

List of Figures

List of Tables

Preface

A number of nations, including the United States, have demonstrated a superb ability to solve *systems* problems, when the problem is *technical*. The ultimate example is NASA's lunar landing program in the 1960s. The U.S. space program spends a significant portion of its resources on systems integration, so that a large number of hardware components work together physically and functionally to achieve the mission objective.

Unfortunately, similar systems approaches have been rejected to varying degrees for economic growth policy. These rejections are throwbacks to the Adam Smith-type characterization of a "private" market, in which *individual* greed -- alias the "invisible hand" -- single-handedly succeeds in forcing efficient use of available resources.

Today, the concept of the private market still holds and, in fact, remains the prime mover of economic efficiency. However, as in other areas of human existence, learning has taken place. This evolutionary process has led to, among other things, an increasing division of the systems problem into specialized components. In some cases, this specialization results in a highly segmented economic structure or "non-system" that malfunctions. In other cases, the economic system survives and prospers because the *interaction* among components is not ignored.

Another part of human learning is the development and use of technology. A major consequence is that the static economic market of Adam Smith's time is no more. For today's market participants, dynamic efficiency has become at least as important as the static efficiency requirements of *The Wealth of Nations*. This is not to say that Adam Smith ignored the impact of change on economic markets. Rather, change was slow enough so that it did not have a major impact on day-to-day economic activity.

Today, however, technology coupled with the globalization of markets have made change an integral part of economic strategy -- even the primary component. In addition to the impacts of these two factors on private economic behavior, nations around the world have attempted to help their economies adapt to dynamic markets through provision of a variety of so-called "public economic goods".

As has always been the case, some nations are doing a better job of facilitating adaptation than are others. One of the major differences in the observed approaches to economic strategy has been the degree to which economies recognize the existence of public and private elements of industrial technology, identify these elements in an operational sense, and provide them efficiently and in the correct time periods.

Some nations have steadfastly refused to acknowledge the multi-dimensional systems character of technology-based economic activity, choosing instead to rely on the over-simplified "free market" approach to achieving efficiency. Much worse, others have tried to isolate their domestic markets from foreign competition. Yet, other nations have at least partially accepted the heterogeneity of industrial technology and the consequent need for both public- and private-sector roles in providing it.

This last group has just begun to focus on the fact that the emerging economic "system" is one in which the elements cannot remain separate to a significant degree and that the interfaces between elements cannot be partial or rigid. A few of these nations are even rapidly pursuing the evolutionary path to a true systems strategy. In the latter case, not only are the multiplicity of technology elements identified with their public and private sources recognized, but an awareness of the dynamic character of the economic system drives the provision *and* integration of these elements.

Thus, in the 1990s, the major factors determining competitive position are the degree to which nations will adapt to the dynamics of global competition by altering (1) the structure and behavior of the private sector, (2) the content of economic infrastructure, particularly the technology components, and (3) the efficiency with which the public and private sectors can provide this infrastructure. This last factor is the key to the efficiency of a modern economic system. Without it, the most dynamic of private sectors will eventually be thwarted by a large number of barriers that force poor investment decisions and inappropriate industry structures.

In this context, the rationales for undertaking this book are (1) interest in technology-based growth policies is growing worldwide as technology becomes an increasingly important factor in economic competition; (2) in spite of the increased efforts in many nations to develop more effective industry strategies and government policies, most of these endeavors have been *ad hoc* exercises rather than derived from a comprehensive set of principles that would impart increased efficiency to the decision making process; and, (3) these increased efforts to develop national strategies have created an awareness of the need for frameworks that assist strategy and policy formulation.

Relatively little argument remains with respect to whether or not significant external technical elements exist that affect the competitiveness of the private corporation. Just as roads, bridges, railroads, and other infrastructure are essential to traditional commerce, so are these technical elements essential to the high-tech economic world. Elements such as generic technologies, infratechnologies, standards, scientific and technical information, and testing methodologies comprise a complex technology infrastructure.

Thus, one of the most critical issues in technology-based competition is the type and magnitude of technology-related support that should be provided to private firms. More specifically, issues are beginning to be considered such as (1) at what stages in the technology-life cycle are different infrastructure elements most useful; (2) what mechanisms are most efficient for developing and disseminating these elements; and, (3) what are the divisions of responsibilities between industry and government for providing technology infrastructure.

This book addresses these three issues by drawing upon a wide range of sources. Many of these are government and industry data that are either unpublished or not widely circulated or known. Other sources are the results of industry surveys that the author has either directly participated in or commissioned. Finally, in addition to assessments of the more widely read literature, numerous documents from a number of national governments relating to technology infrastructure policy are utilized.

The scope of the book is broad, covering such elements of technology infrastructure as "pre-competitive generic technology", various types of industry standards, measurement infratechnologies, scientific and technical information, etc. Thus, it will provide an integrated view of technology infrastructure for corporate managers, academic researchers, and government policy makers.

Trends which affect both the amount and type of investment in technology infrastructure are analyzed. These include the effects of direct foreign investment, the use of various types of research consortia, and industry structure changes such as shifts in the degree of horizontal and vertical integration. The various technology infrastructure elements are integrated into a conceptual framework to indicate how these elements interact with, complement, and substitute for one another. Finally, this framework and the subsequent analysis are tied together and related to the more global economic growth issues and trends.

The first two chapters provide an overview of technology-based competition and the related growth policy issues facing industrialized nations in the 1990s. Some of the points made here will not be new to the dedicated student of this general topic. However, an attempt is made to provide a fairly comprehensive characterization of technology-based competitiveness and to do so in a way that conveys the *systems* character of the problem -- the only way to approach economic growth policy, if long-term efficiency is to be achieved. These two chapters also provide an historical perspective, focusing on strategy and policy trends that lead up to the present and future demands for technology infrastructure.

In Chapter 3, a conceptual model of the technology-based economic process is developed that emphasizes the roles and impacts of the various elements of the supporting infrastructure. Responding to the increased attention now being given to technology-based growth policy, an appendix to this chapter provides definitions of relevant terms that are frequently used and more frequently misused.

The next four chapters analyze specific elements of technology infrastructure and how these elements interact with industry strategy and structure, including important trends such as foreign direct investment, horizontal and vertical integration, and new management strategies (total quality management, etc.).

The last two chapters address the interaction of corporate and government roles for providing technology infrastructure, some funding issues, and mechanisms for cooperative planning and implementation.

1 The Economic Roles of Technology Infrastructure

"People never blame themselves for their misfortunes, until they have exhausted every alternative"

Mark Twain

As markets have become more global and as more nations have become globally competitive, the interactions of economic systems and their broader social and political structures have become more intense. Along with the "globalization of markets" has come a steady increase in the complexity of the nature of economic activity. Part of this trend is explained by the fact that technology has become a dominant competitive force.

In addition to more reliance on technology *per se*, the ways in which technology is used as a competitive weapon have diversified enormously. In particular, emphasis is now being placed on such strategies as productivity, quality, speed in getting new products to market, and after-sale service to buyers. These strategies are being directed not only at increasingly complex technology-based products but at systems of products whose components must function together flawlessly.

The vastness of these changes and the tremendous demands on nations to adopt new ways by which their economic systems are viewed and managed have overwhelmed social and political structures. In recent years, the growing perception that the United States has serious long-term (structural) economic problems has led to an avalanche of "analyses". The vast majority of these efforts has singled out a particular element of the economic system as the "major" problem. Examples are the "cost of capital", the "ability to turn science into marketable technologies", "lack of cooperation between government and industry", an "inadequate and out-of-date educational system", etc.

Such analyses are useful for identifying inefficiencies within the particular element. However, a fundamental requirement for effective competitive behavior is a concept or a philosophy, including a vision of long-term direction, that addresses *all* of these elements simultaneously and allows roles to be assigned to the various major components of the technology-based economic system.

Failure to proceed in this manner has led to piecemeal and painfully slow approaches to redirecting economic strategy. In the United States, while individual actions taken to date have had some merit, in the aggregate the results have not been particularly productive. All major indicators of the competitiveness of the U.S. economy continue to read at or below the *average* for the industrialized nations against whom the United States competes. Some improvement occurred in the 1980s, but by and large this trend was due either to short-term measures such as "cost-cutting" and "restructuring", or to a depreciating dollar (which itself is a symptom of economic problems).

One positive trend was a significant change in philosophy by U.S. industry towards global competition. In 1980, the chief executive officers of most U.S. companies only had one desire with respect to interactions with government: "get out of the way and let us do our job". This led in the early 1980s to tax reductions and deregulation, among other things. This "hands-off" attitude, which included isolation not only from government but also from universities and other private firms, has in a few short years undergone a major shift toward increasing partnerships with domestic and foreign firms, more substantive relationships with universities, and, in the most radical about face of all, increasing cries for substantive, cooperative programs with government.

Progress toward this last objective has, however, been particularly frustrating for industry managers increasingly pressed by foreign competition. William J. Spencer, President and Chief Executive Office of the United States' first, and to date only, major industry-government research and development (R&D) consortium (SEMATECH) stated industry's increasing frustration:

> "Our big problem is that we lack visionary leadership in all the key positions in government. If you look at what's fueling economic growth in the Pacific Rim and in Europe, it's an alliance between business, industry and the government. Here, there is a lot of mistrust that everyone has for everyone else."[1]

A number of explanations can and have been brought forward to explain this situation. However, these analyses do not address the major conceptual change that must occur in the U.S. approach to fostering global competitiveness. In fact, where past analyses have attached strategic and policy recommendations to the end of problem-focused treatments, they have lacked the systems-level context and thus have ignored the complementary, recursive, and mutually-dependent character of the major elements of a modern economic system. The problems of under-performing industrialized economies will not be solved by singular or sequential approaches to industrial strategy or policy development.

The beginnings of an evolutionary movement towards a "systems" approach to economic strategy and policy are fortunately becoming evident. In an excellent report by the Manufacturing Studies Board of the National Research Council [1991], the emphasis was not on discrete technologies that have been the focus of previous technology-based policy initiatives. Rather, so-called "disembodied" technologies were emphasized. These latter technologies include such entities as process models, methods, techniques, etc., that are not embodied in a piece of equipment or a product. Instead, they are used to *integrate* products, both hardware and software, into efficient economic systems.

---

[1]   *Washington Post*, January 27, 1991, p. H4.

At the level of the individual firm, the NRC report states that "firms that use advanced manufacturing technology will thus be distinguished less by their manufacturing processes than by the integrated system that drive those processes". Moreover, "the changes that attend the development and deployment of advanced manufacturing technology involve the availability of *information* and the *integration* of that information with business functions to achieve various kinds of *intelligence*".

This and other analyses of trends in manufacturing technology provide insights into an emerging economic system that not only integrates the heretofore separate activities within the firm, but also integrates the activities of several firms in a "production chain".[2]

The key points to be made are that the generation of various kinds of information and their integration is occurring more and more in a multi-firm environment, and, thus, many of these elements of economic activity take on an infrastructure character. Moreover, specific technologies and their integration into larger systems today require such great efficiency in the R&D process that their early phases of development as well as their subsequent compatibility with other products create new infrastructure requirements. Most nations have only begun to adapt to these new and important technology infrastructure demands.

A Changing Framework for Growth Strategies

The reasons for major underinvestment in technology infrastructure revolve around a failure to understand and provide for the elements of a technology-based economic system that exist outside the traditional boundaries of the private firm. In the following chapters, these *technology-infrastructure* elements will be portrayed as part of an overall systems approach to economic strategy in which the identification of institutional roles is very important. Moreover, the

---

[2]   The term "production chain" refers to the vertical industry structure by which raw materials are turned into components, these components are used to produce more complex products, and finally systems of products are formed to perform services. An example would be silicon, which is turned into silicon wafers, which are turned into integrated circuits, which are used to produce computers, which are used in data processing systems.

dynamic interactions between the corporate strategy and the institutions that provide technology infrastructure will be represented as an equally important driver of economic efficiency.

Two fundamental premises for a competitive, technology-based economy will be developed: (1) a modern economy is a *system* of diverse and interacting elements, including both public and private entities, and (2) to function efficiently this system must embody certain behavioral and organizational constructs that *integrate* economic activity, not only in a "total-organization" mode but in a broader "multi-enterprise" structure.

Such a global statement is necessarily abstract, but, as the pages that follow will hopefully demonstrate, the choices among alternative behavioral and organizational strategies can be made specific and functional in character. In particular, the pervasiveness of technology, not only for intrafirm strategy but for inter-firm interactions, leads to a set of diverse needs for technology infrastructure -- the "lubricator" of the modern economic system.

The Role of Technology in Economic Strategy

The culmination of technological change in the 19th century was the development of mass production technologies with the consequent realization of scale economies. These process technologies drove economic growth and dominated global economic competition among industrialized nations for almost the entire 20th century. However, as this century draws to a close, fundamental and far reaching changes have begun to occur that are greatly altering the requirements for sustained domestic economic growth and global competitiveness. The major *agents of change* are technology and the ways by which technology is put to economic use.

The first of these two agents, technological change, while increasingly rapid and widespread, did not begin to significantly alter economic strategies and the nature of economic competition until about the mid 1970s. Prior to this point, new products were designed for and integrated into the long-standing mass-production environment. Competition was based almost entirely on the attributes of the product itself, with cost reductions achieved largely through the realization of scale economies in production.

However, in the last half of the 1970s, it became increasingly clear that the proliferation of product technology -- particularly the ability to engineer slight variations in a generic product -- was creating a demand for custom and semi-custom products. Such demand was anathema to the mass-production specialists who had ingrained in them the singular objective of producing ever larger volumes of identical products.[3]

In addition, the relentless rise in the number of technology-based competitors around the world led to higher rates of product obsolescence, increasingly thwarting the realization of economies of scale from these rigidly-configured production processes. The progressive shortening of the so-called "technology life cycle" reached such an extent in the 1980s that in some industries, such as semiconductors, several cycles had to overlap one another.[4] This put tremendous strains on the conventional linear model of technology-based economic activity. In fact, stubborn pursuit of the "old ways" lead to certain economic death.

The first answer to this dramatic shift in the nature of competition became evident in the late 1970s. The automation of the manufacturing process began to allow *flexibility* in terms of product variety within the same physical production setup. Thus, smaller production runs have become increasingly cost-effective. The net result of these technological impacts has been the dawning of an era of competition based more on *economies of scope* than on economies of scale.

Along with increased flexibility to achieve product variety within the same production structure came the ability to fine-tune individual product attributes with a high degree of precision. This capability not only made rapid and flexible response to changing demand possible, but the same automated manufacturing technology allowed greater *product quality*. Moreover, the achievement of many

---

[3]   In the mass production era, the typical production line was characterized by *generalized* machine tools configured in a *rigid* and *specialized* format. Even small product design changes were expensive and time-consuming to implement.

[4]   In 1991, semiconductor manufacturers, for the first time, found themselves facing the prospect of producing and marketing three generations of memory circuits simultaneously -- 4K, 16K, and 64K dynamic random access memory (DRAM) chips.

small design changes demanded by increased customization of products required not only more efficient product research and development (R&D), but also much more precise control of the production process. Achievement of better process control offered increased productivity, while at the same time reducing the volume of any specific product produced -- a concept totally antithetical to the mass production era.

The second agent of change derived from the first. The evolution in economic strategy away from high-volume, relatively stable product structures toward flexible manufacturing systems, with emphasis on small but rapid and precise product changes, was only the first level of adaptation in the way technology was to be used. Rapid and precise change requires close coordination between the R&D, production, and marketing operations within the firm -- a marked departure from past behavior.

Under an economies-of-scale strategy, time was not of the essence. And, with volume the main driver in reducing unit costs during production, R&D simply handed a product design over an "organizational wall" and was hardly heard from again. At the other end, marketing personnel often did not hear about a new product until it was given to them to sell.

This organizational segmentation is being brought to an end by radical changes in the use of technology. Although one can debate the precise number and substance of the requirements for global competitiveness, six will be asserted here: *technological innovation, design and process flexibility, quality, productivity (cost), speed-to-market, and marketing/service.*

At the traditional level of the firm, these requirements or factors can only be met, especially simultaneously, through virtually total integration of the corporate organization. Thus, heretofore separate functions are being forced to communicate, cooperate, and generally function in a much more cohesive manner than was even conceived of just several decades ago.

In one direction, this radical change goes all the way down to the individual employee. Under the mass-production paradigm, workers were given limited, highly-repetitive tasks. The philosophy was that productivity could be increased by perfecting a few regimented functions. Meaningful communication among workers, especially workers with different functions, was minimal.

The new global competition has radically changed this philosophy. Communication is not only promoted but is considered a prime indicator of corporate vitality. To improve communication, management layers are being deleted and individuals are being given much more freedom to make decisions. This trend has, in turn, greatly increased the demands on the educational infrastructure beyond that attributable to increased technological complexity.

At a second level, the entire corporate entity -- long a closed and impenetrable fortress -- is becoming much more open to external interactions. Even the largest corporations typically contribute only a fraction of the total value added embodied in the products they sell. Subcontracting, joint ventures, participation in research cooperatives, cross-licensing and other external arrangements have become a way of corporate life. External arrangements occur at all stages in the economic process: R&D, production, and marketing. These interactions with outside "partners" must be just as rapid and efficient as the internal ones.

In the mass-production era, exchanges among firms consisted primarily of physical goods. Today, although goods still change hands through formal market transactions, the majority of exchanges consist of *information* and *services* of various types. The efficiency of such exchanges is driven by communications and data processing technologies. These systems technologies are based on new and rapidly changing "products" (semiconductor, optical, and other "enabling" technologies), but even more radical is the type of information infrastructure that these products make up.

At the product level, the proliferation of new technologies has resulted in a virtual explosion of product variety with more to come. While these trends offer tremendous benefits to the consumer and to the producers who successfully adopt the new technologies and associated organizational strategies, they pose a nightmare for the infrastructure that must facilitate the entire economic process.

Variety all by itself creates problems for infrastructure. In the mass-production era, product change was slow and relatively simple. A few standards, evolving slowly, enabled efficient marketplace transactions to take place. Today, with rapid-fire product change, with complex inter-firm partnerships, with transactions taking place not only in finished products but in technology as well, and with these transactions often taking place electronically over long distances, the ability to execute them efficiently has become a serious problem.

Beyond the marketplace transaction, the efficacy of technology-based infrastructure in scientific and engineering information along with the common channels for its transfer and diffusion has become a major determinant of global competitiveness. As a result, demand is increasing for a technology-based infrastructure that is as fast, flexible and adaptable, as one hopes will be the case for the industry structure it supports.

The Elements of Technology Infrastructure

Traditional economic infrastructure is widely recognized as having a significant role in facilitating long-term economic growth. Beginning in the 19th century, the construction of railroads and canals greatly enhanced the economic development of the United States. Cost-effective access to natural resources in one region by manufacturers in others enabled efficient combinations of inputs resulting in low-cost production. Equally important, these transportation networks expanded regional markets into national ones, leading to economies of scale in production and further cost reductions. As technology has become increasingly important as an economic strategy, a major technology-based component of this economic infrastructure has evolved.

This *technology infrastructure* consists of science, engineering, and technical knowledge available to private industry. More specifically, it includes generic technologies, infratechnologies, technical information on practices and techniques, and standards for such diverse areas as the physical and functional interfaces between components of a product system, performance test methods, and quality assurance. It also includes less technically-explicit areas such as information relevant for strategic planning and market development, forums for joint planning and collaboration, and assignment of intellectual property rights. Like traditional infrastructure, it is widely and uniformly used.

Technology infrastructure can be produced within individual firms, but more often it originates outside the single-firm environment. It can be disseminated directly (in "raw" form through person-to-person contact or publications), codified in standards, organized in "programs" (quality assurance techniques), etc. An important characteristic is that it depreciates slowly, but requires considerable effort and long lead times to put in place and maintain.

A variety of institutions provide this type of infrastructure -- public, private, and public-private combinations. Its provision is directed, organized, and delivered largely by organizations other than the individual firms that ultimately use it. The sources of financing are equally varied. The three major funding options for providing the underlying technology base are direct funding of individual firms, indirect funding (tax incentives) of individual firms, and funding of other institutions, particularly research consortia and government laboratories.

For example, a specific growth policy objective, such as advancing generic technology, can be achieved through government laboratory research, direct funding of individual firms or industry consortia, or specific tax incentives.[5] In addition to funding the production of technology infrastructure, provision must be made for technology transfer.

Technology infrastructure is used in all stages of economic activity. It improves the efficiency of research and development (R&D), production, and market transactions. In fact, many of the most advanced elements of these three categories of economic activity could not be conducted at all, let alone efficiently, without specific technology infrastructure. For example, many research methods could not exist without attendant measurement techniques and scientific data bases. Advanced automation technologies could not function without measurement techniques and process control models. Automation systems could not achieve cost efficiency without interface standards.

Moreover, technology infrastructure itself serves as the basis for many of the newest and potentially commercially important economic infrastructure. For example, broadband fiberoptic networks, which will be the infrastructure for future multi-media communications, will only work once a number of technical standards

---

[5] Unfortunately, these alternatives are usually discussed separately, rather than as alternatives, which is not efficient policy analysis. See Tassey [1991].

are in place. These standards, in turn require complex technical foundations.[6]

A comprehensive analysis of the functions of technology infrastructure should include the strategies of domestic corporations, the strategies of their foreign competitors, and the relevant government growth policies among industrialized nations. Collectively, these determine the roles for technology infrastructure. Such global role analysis must be followed by assessments of the functions of specific corporate strategy and policy mechanisms that define and implement the designated roles. Finally, the institutions must be studied that fund technology research, conduct this research, transfer the research results, and provide related technical information and services.

A Brief History of Technology Infrastructure Policy

With a few notable exceptions, namely agriculture and aerospace, the U.S. Government provided little technology infrastructure prior to World War II. However, during World War II, the possibilities for a government role in industrial technology development became evident.

Perceiving this fact, President Roosevelt asked Vanevar Bush to head a study of the potential of such programs for peacetime goals. Bush and his colleagues produced the now-classic *Science -- The Endless Frontier*. This report established a charter for government support of basic research and science education and hence provided a national science policy. After considerable debate, the National Science Foundation was established in 1951 to support basic scientific research. Bush and his co-authors viewed support of science as the first step in a "chain of endeavor that leads to industrial advance".

---

[6] Such technology-based economic infrastructure can be extremely expensive. With respect to broadband fiberoptic networks, the Microelectronics and Computer Technology Corporation (MCC), one of the first industry-level research consortia in the United States to be stimulated by the 1984 National Cooperative Research Act, plans to spend approximately $1 billion over the next three years for its "First Cities" program, which is intended to accelerate the development of such a network.

However, for the next 15 years, *science* infrastructure was the sole objective of civilian policy.

In the 1960s and 1970s, investment in civilian *technology* infrastructure expanded significantly, but it was highly mission-oriented. Besides agriculture, space exploration, energy independence, environment quality, housing, transportation, and health -- all having what economists call "public good" attributes -- no other civilian technologies, including the many with purely commercial potential, received significant government assistance. No philosophical basis evolved for government support of civilian technologies generally. That is, commercially-focused technologies were not considered to have public good attributes.

Some important commercial technologies did receive considerable indirect assistance through "spin-offs" from research support by the Department of Defense, notably semiconductors and computers. Large procurements by DoD also were instrumental in establishing production economies of scale that translated into efficiency gains in subsequent commercial applications.

However, in 1958, the launching of Russia's *Sputnik* sent shock waves through the technology establishment. Although not a commercial technology effort, it demonstrated that other nations besides the United States could mobilize resources and achieve major technological advances. One U.S. response was to create in 1962 an Assistant Secretary for Science and Technology in the Department of Commerce to provide a link to technology-based industries and to encourage S&T applications in civilian markets. This position complemented the President's Science Advisor's responsibilities in basic science. Two years later, the Congress passed the State Technical Services Act, to provide technology transfer assistance in a format modelled after the successful Agricultural Extension Service. Neither of these efforts had any significant impact.

In the 1970s, the perception spread that the substantial increase in mission-oriented R&D support over the past decade or so was not having acceptable levels of economic impact. In 1972, the White House commissioned a study of civilian R&D programs. The resulting Magruder Report spawned several small programs to promote more effective civilian use of Federal technology.[7] But one year later, President Nixon abolished the Office of Science and Technology Policy (OSTP) in the White House and hence the role of the President's Science Advisor. It took Congress three years, until 1976, to re-create OSTP.

Thus, in the more than 30 years since *Science -- the Endless Frontier*, relatively little change occurred in civilian technology infrastructure policy for economic growth. The defense and space programs "spun-off" modest amounts of technology with civilian applications, although with declining economic impact in the last 20 years. In terms of a public technology infrastructure role with at least partial commercial objectives, the two most significant events were the creation in the 1970s of the National Institutes of Health and the Department of Energy.

The 1978-79 period might be viewed as an "awakening" with respect to the inadequacies of civilian technology policies. The first broad-based review of policies affecting industrial innovation was undertaken by the Department of Commerce at the request of the Carter Administration. A number of Congressional hearings were held on innovation, productivity, and technology transfer. In 1980, Congress passed the Stevenson Wydler Act which made technology transfer a part of the mission of all Federal agencies carrying out R&D.

In 1981, the incoming Regan Administration decentralized what S&T program management existed. However, in response to increasing concerns over the competitiveness of U.S. industry in global technology-based markets and pressure from U.S. industry, the Regan Administration initiated a series of domestic policy reviews in the 1982-84 period. These reviews had little direct impact on policy but served the very useful purpose of exposing top-level industry officials

---

[7] The most notable of these was the Experimental Technology Incentives Program (ETIP) located at the National Institute of Standards and Technology (then the National Bureau of Standards). ETIP was given a small amount of funds to induce other Federal agencies to "experiment" with changes in their existing policies. These changes were designed to increase rates of innovation in the private sector as a result of an agency's activities, while still accomplishing the agency's primary mission. For a small program, ETIP had some remarkable successes over a five-year period (1974-79). The program was terminated in 1982 due to mismanagement and a general lack of appreciation for its innovative approach. See Tassey [1985].

to the broad set of competitiveness issues facing the economy and, equally important, to the policy development process.

In 1984, Congress passed the National Cooperative Research Act, which facilitated collaboration among technology-based firms, including potential future competitors, in the conduct of early-phase technology research. Thus, 40 years after the establishment of a national science policy, the United States took its first significant step towards a broad-based civilian *technology* infrastructure policy. Well over 100 private consortia filed under the Act before the first consortium with significant government funding (SEMATECH) was proposed in 1987. By 1990, approximately 200 filings had occurred, but most were relatively small in terms of resources committed.

The Technology Transfer Act of 1986 contrasted significantly with its predecessor, the Stevenson-Wydler Act of 1980. The 1986 Act's substantive provisions reflected the increased concern over U.S. competitiveness. This Act significantly increased incentives to and the capabilities of Federal laboratories to commercialize technology.

More specifically, the Act encouraged Federally-owned and operated labs to form Cooperative Research and Development Agreements (CRDAs) with private firms.[8] A significant aspect of CRDAs is the ability of the Federal lab to negotiate, as part of the agreement, the assignment of intellectual property rights to participating firms. By 1991, five years after passage of the 1986 Act, about 400 CRADAs had been signed, mostly by laboratories under the Department of Defense, National Institutes of Health and the Department of Commerce (primarily the National Institute of Standards and Technology).[9]

The Act also established royalty sharing for Federal scientists and engineers whose research results in patentable technology. Cash awards were provided for technology transfer efforts and a Federal Laboratory Consortium (FLC) was formally established to facilitate dissemination of technological information.

In 1988, Congress passed the Technology Competitiveness Act. This Act created the National Institute of Standards and Technology

---

[8]   Contractor-operated Federal labs were given similar authority two years later.

[9]   See for example, Maggs [1991].

(NIST) by the taking the laboratory research role of the National Bureau of Standards and adding to it the other two basic categories of mechanisms for providing technology infrastructure. One of these is a technology research funding mechanism, the Advanced Technology Program (ATP). The ATP is the civilian counterpart to the Defense Advanced Research Projects Agency (DARPA), which has had a very successful record in funding the early-phase development of a number of defense technologies, some having significant economic impact.

The second new category of technology infrastructure mechanisms was aimed at technology transfer. Two different mechanisms were established here -- the Manufacturing Technology Centers (MTCs) and the State Technology Extension Program (STEP). The former are consortia of state and local governments and universities, started with grants from NIST, whose purpose is to transfer manufacturing technology and techniques to small and medium firms in their regions. STEP is modelled after the Agricultural Extension Service and thus seeks to provide technical assistance to small businesses at the local level. Finally, the Act created within the newly-established Technology Administration of the Department of Commerce the Clearinghouse for State and Local Initiatives in Productivity, Technology and Innovation, which provides a database on some 1400 state-run programs promoting technology-based economic development.

Thus, the 1980s saw an increasingly concerted effort to bring U.S. technology infrastructure up to a level necessary to compete in technology-based global markets. All three categories of government technology infrastructure mechanisms were now in place: civilian technology-oriented laboratory research, civilian technology-funding, and formal technology transfer.

However, as of 1990, these mechanisms were funded at very low levels and considerable debate continued over their precise roles, methods of coordination among Federal agencies, and the sharing of these roles with private-sector responsibilities for providing technology infrastructure. Moreover, the interactions of the individual roles with each other and with proprietary technology investment activity by industry were still poorly understood. In other words, technology-based competition was still addressed element-by-element, with little thought given to the interfaces of these elements -- the ways by which a technology-based economy functions as a *system*.

Chasing the Japanese Model

One of the devices used by defenders of the status quo, which includes minimal technology infrastructure, is the charge that the Japanese, although successful, have a model of economic growth that is highly skewed relative to most industrial nations and particularly the United States. However, this position does not stand up to objective analysis. Several decades ago, Japan could still be labeled as a developing economy in the sense that it had at best a modest technology base and a relatively small capital stock. As those deficiencies have been emphatically eliminated, the Japanese have evolved their model of technology-based competition, including the roles of the technology infrastructure, to a form that has many attractive attributes.

In the past, the Japanese made more extensive use of what might be called "interventionist" industrial policy tools -- i.e., policy mechanisms applied selectively and intensively on an industry-by-industry basis. Measures such as industry-specific tax credits, differential antitrust policy, control of investment, regulation of patent policy and technology transfer were widely used. Even more aggressive were trade measures -- tariffs, quotas, and standards -- which were used extensively, and successfully, in the 1950s and 1960s to protect infant industries. By the end of the 1960s, the Japanese Government had laid the foundation for a rapidly growing industrial economy.

These examples of Japanese Government industrial policy are frequently cited. What is less well known, but more relevant for the topic of technology infrastructure, is the fact that during the 1950s and 1960s, when the Japanese economy was still capital-poor, efforts to increase productivity centered on improving the organization of production. This strategy was adopted because most Japanese firms could not afford state-of-the-art production equipment, so they concentrated on what economists call "disembodied" technologies -- the methods, techniques, procedures that squeeze the maximum productivity out of a given level of technology embodied in available production equipment.

Analyses of manufacturing processes indicate that approximately 70 percent of a product's cost is "locked in" during R&D. Thus, simply paying attention to product design from the standpoint of how that product can be produced reliably and at low cost can greatly increase productivity. This approach, which is now called *concurrent engineering (CE)*, and other organization-dependent manufacturing strategies such as *just-in-time (JIT)* inventory management and *total quality management (TQM)*, have been embraced and greatly advanced by the Japanese well ahead of western economies.

During the 1970s, with increased command of manufacturing process technology and a swelling supply of low-cost capital, Japan increasingly shifted support toward knowledge-intensive industries, characterized by high-risk, long-term R&D with product as well as process technology objectives. Consequently, growth policy and the subsequent strategies for technology infrastructure shifted toward support of a technology *production* (as opposed to *acquisition*) strategy. The more blatant protectionist measures of the previous decade gave way to more subtle R&D-related forms of assistance.[10]

Most important, these new strategies have included a more subtle but complex and sophisticated technology infrastructure, which is being supplied through a continually evolving set of institutional mechanisms. Belatedly, western economies have begun to realize that similar strategic responses are required.

The Need for Expanded Technology Infrastructure

A major issue facing the United States more than most nations is the need to changeover from a mission-oriented technology infrastructure (defense, space, energy, etc.) to one that supports a broad range or "portfolio" of emerging and strategic technologies with direct *commercial* applications. The United States has traditionally been second to none in developing systems technologies to achieve specific missions:

---

[10]　Japanese firms became both more able and willing to conduct R&D. As a result, national R&D grew at an average annual rate of 11 percent during the 1980s. Simultaneously, budget pressures and increasing independence on the part of Japanese industries led to a substantial decrease in the use of direct and "control-oriented" government policies.

"We have immense capability in this country, if you think of it in
terms of technological know-how, technological applications, and
the invention of effective gadgetry."[11]

Where a specific mission to achieve some public good is
undertaken, the systems management problem is both recognized and
generally effectively executed. A single management hierarchy with a
relatively limited set of final objectives has been a U.S. strength. This
was evidenced in the superbly efficient effort to put a man on the
moon and in numerous weapons systems that performed so well in the
war with Iraq.

But, as Robert M. White, Department of Commerce Under
Secretary for Technology put it, "The government cannot play the
systems management role in commercial enabling technologies that it
plays in defense and space projects".[12] Instead, this role must be
implemented jointly by industry and government. Thus, the
conceptual model for technology-based infrastructure to be developed
in Chapter 3 is based on a *systems* concept of both private and public
sector behavior. The distinguishing feature is that industry and
government must *together* manage this system. In this mode, as co-
managers of the economic system, industry and government will have
to collectively deal with the major changes in the technology
infrastructure required for a nation to be competitive in the global
economy of the 1990s.

For example, the need for information infrastructure is
becoming ubiquitous in the modern economic system. Research has
shown that *all* stages in the process of creating and using technology
benefit from networking and communication -- the very essence of the
systems approach.

Even the first step in the process of technological change,
invention, which is often thought of as the product of individual genius,
typically draws heavily on technical developments by others. Thomas
Edison's invention of the incandescent light bulb depended on
Herman Sprengl's work on the use of vacuums, advances in electricity

---

[11]   Michael Dertouzos, Director, MIT Laboratory for Computer Science,
and Chairman of the MIT Commission on Industrial Productivity.

[12]   Address at the second annual meeting held by the Council on
Superconductivity for American Competitiveness, September 14, 1990.

by Oersted, Ampere, and Faraday, and collaborations with others in engineering the physical configuration of the light bulb and the selection of materials.

As inventions move toward the marketplace (i.e., as they become *innovations*), the complexity of the systems problem increases. *Connections* by James Burke [1978] describes the broad range of complementary assets, both technical- and market-related, that are required for successful innovation. He emphasizes that success requires knowing both the technology and the needs of potential users, and to acquire this information one must communicate and network with the varied sources of the required information.

As corporate strategy moves beyond single-stage strategies (such as a focus on innovation) to a *total organization productivity* approach, the systems management requirements increase in complexity. Corporate strategies are now being built around such systems concepts as *total quality management, concurrent engineering, and total productivity management.* These "systems" strategies are much more difficult to design and implement than former linear management concepts. In recognition of this trend, only a portion of the criteria for the Malcolm Baldrige National Quality Award emphasizes technical-based strategies for improving quality such as reduced product defect rates. Other criteria focus on planning, human resource utilization, and the degree and comprehensiveness of customer interactions.

From the end of World War II until the 1980s, industrialized nations succeeded by emphasizing *one* stage of the technology-based growth process. Nations developed comparative advantages in technology and innovation (United States), product improvement and production efficiency (Japan), and quality and niche market development (Germany). In each case, the technology infrastructure was narrowly defined to emphasize support of these focused strategies.

During the 1980s, however, the continued growth of the competitive importance of technology coupled with increasingly intense global competition began to force nations toward *multi-stage* growth strategies. Japan began planning for an "information society" 20-30 years into the future and set about creating both the private and public sector resources to pursue this complex systems technology. European countries finally made real progress towards economic integration, not just to create a single, large market, but to combine *complementary technology assets* that would enable them to realize the economies of scale and scope inherent in the increasingly complex technologies that would drive global competition in the 1990s and beyond.

One of the major elements of European unification is the establishment of a technology infrastructure that seeks to efficiently provide the complete range of elements of emerging systems technologies. Prior to this change in strategy, most European countries, in part by attempting to specialize in individual technology elements, were steadily falling behind the Japanese and Americans.

The United States had a different problem. Its domestic market was large enough to allow a range of related technology elements to be efficiently developed. However, its past successes had made it complacent, *and* this dominance in technology had led it to rely almost entirely on the dynamics of private sector competition to create and market new technologies. In this situation, not only was interaction between industry and the technology infrastructure largely random and uncoordinated, but the latter was primarily oriented toward particular missions, especially defense, rather than commercial markets broadly.

The Evolution of National Economic Strategies

The future of the world's economies will depend on how they choose to compete on the basis of technology over the next several decades. Technology has become an increasingly important factor in the economic growth of nations, but its impact will continue to increase for several reasons: (1) more nations are using technology as a major element of their economic growth strategies, (2) in addition to the magnitude of technology's impact, its evolving character is causing major changes in both the structure and behavior of most industries, and (3) the simultaneous breaking down of national boundaries in an economic sense is making most markets global.

Because these trends are already redistributing wealth, nations are increasingly asking what economic strategies will be required to attain desired rates of economic growth in this new environment. In particular, the battle ground will be the microeconomic level. Macroeconomic strategies will clearly remain different across economies over the next several decades, but the integration of national economies will force a convergence. The European community is only the first example. Thus, the opportunity for competitive advantage lies at the microeconomic level, where both industry strategy and government policy will have more freedom to be creative.[13]

For example, at the early stages in a technology's development, considerable underinvestment occurs, the degree being a function of a number of factors, including corporate strategy and industry structure. Research consortia have been proposed as an efficient device for overcoming at least some of these underinvestment phenomena. However, corporate participation in such consortia have lagged behind many estimates of that required to accelerate technology development through its early phases. Economists point to "free riding" as an explanation of the reluctance of industry to fund cooperative research. Corporate strategy analysts point to "American individualism" as a factor in the stubborn adherence to "market monopoly" strategies.

Others have tended to play down the importance of early-phase technology research, or, at least, the need for significant changes in present policies. One reason cited is the fact that the cost structure for the typical R&D process approximates an "inverted pyramid". In fact, the cost of development can be a factor of ten more than early-phase research. This has led to a neglect of the importance of early-phase technology research and the role of research consortia.[14]

---

[13]   Of course, macroeconomic policies are extremely important in that they create the "environment" which affects the quantity of investment, for example. The cost of capital frequently has been cited in the United States as a severe barrier to the competitive position of technology-based firms, with respect to financing both R&D and subsequent productive capital formation. In this regard, the United States has put itself in a serious bind. From the end of World War II until the early 1980s, the U.S. economy carried debt in the consumer, business, and government sectors that ranged from 1.3 to 1.4 times the gross national product. Ignoring the productivity of the uses to which this debt was put, the total amount at least seems to have been manageable. But, by the end of 1990, that ratio had soared to nearly 1.9 time GNP, the largest since the 1930s. Such a burden will hamper any policy thrust to increase *long-term* productive investment in the domestic economy.

[14]   See for example, Porter [1990b, pp. 635-637] and Council on Competitiveness [1991].

However, as subsequent discussion will show, the lower expenditure patterns for what we will call "generic technology" research in no way diminish the importance of this critical phase in the R&D stage of a technology's life cycle. Generic technologies have important leveraging effects on subsequent rates and patterns of R&D and capital investment, market penetration decisions, and hence economic growth. Significant underinvestment can cost a nation the chance to enter a "window of opportunity" and claim a portion of the economic benefits over the life cycle of a particular technology.

Insufficient recognition of the heterogeneous nature of the R&D process has led to dysfunctional policy. One aspect of this malfunctioning -- the inability to place generic technology in its proper context relative to other phases of technology development and, more specifically, to determine a rationale for the nature and magnitude of government support -- derives from a broader problem. This problem is the lack of an accurate model of technology-based economic activity. Without such a model as a point of departure, roles for providing the needed infrastructure will not evolve. As a result, growth policies have lurched from one crisis to another. In fact, in the United States in particular, only when a problem area becomes bad enough to reach "crisis levels" does some action result.

At such points, one of two tracks has been typically followed. In some cases, a single policy mechanism is latched on to and overused. Tax policy is a good example. During the "productivity crisis" of the late 1970s and early 1980s, a tax incentive was proposed for almost every conceivable barrier to technology-based growth. The R&D tax credit, in particular, is one of the most over-analyzed policy mechanisms.

In other cases, the opposite extreme occurs. Every conceivable policy instrument is thrown into the hopper. The various HDTV proposals brought forth in 1989 are an example of this latter approach. Implementation of such attempted overkill is, of course, terribly inefficient. Fortunately, such attempts typically die of their own weight. However, after all the furor dies down, no effective process is in place to address the real policy problem.

No matter how good the policy process, a problem is that companies respond differently to a particular policy initiative because they pursue distinctly different strategies. Their strategic foci greatly influence how they organize their internal R&D efforts and, more recently, how they choose to interact with outside sources of technology, including infrastructure. In the 1990s, both innovator and imitator strategies will require broad and rapid access to technology infrastructure.[15]

To access external sources of technology, U.S. firms have begun to adopt more efficient internal technology transfer strategies, based primarily on regular person-to-person contact. Most large high-technology firms use the hub-and-spokes organizational structure. The hub is the central corporate laboratory, where projects typically aim to achieve completion within a three- to seven-year time frame. The spokes represent the applied R&D operations of the line-of-business units or divisions, where projects typically have a one- or two-year horizon.

The concept behind such organizational strategies is precisely what is to be discussed here for the economy as a whole. U.S. corporate management has realized the existence of economies of *scope* and *scale* (especially with a time dimension). They therefore fund a central, long-term research operation that can capture the efficiency gains from providing technologies that have utility for several operating divisions or from conducting long-term, early-phase research.[16]

A national economy works on the same general model, only at a higher plane in terms of scope, time-frame, etc. However, until recently, at least, this conceptual model has only begun to evolve in a number of nations, including the United States. The mention of government participation in early-phase technology research -- the analog to the role of the central corporate laboratory within the scope

---

[15]   See Link and Tassey [1987] for a summary of different corporate strategies in technology-based industries and an analysis of the implications for government policies. Although as many as four generic technology-based strategies were viable in the 1970s and 1980s, the changing nature of global competition may be paring these down to two: "innovator" and "fast follower". In manufacturing at least, "slower imitators" and those firms that rely almost entirely on "service-oriented" strategies may be increasingly trampled by the every-shortening technology and accompanying product life cycles.

[16]   As will be discussed in Chapter 7, the economic rationales for dividing up R&D between a central research laboratory and the R&D operations of business units are approximately the same as those for dividing resources between internal corporate R&D and external mechanisms, such as joint ventures, consortia, and government laboratories.

of overall corporate research objectives -- has brought tirades of objections under the label of "industrial policy", as if such a role for government is the harbinger of economic control.

In fact, industrial nations increasingly accept the general premise that government has a major responsibility for contributing to a viable technology infrastructure which includes the results of early-phase ("pre-competitive") research. These nations do not use the *same* model for dividing up responsibility between government and industry for providing technology infrastructure. The overriding requirement is to have a model that *works*.

In the face of trends in the strategies of nations around the world, several aspects of the new levels and formats of global competition make the content and timing of strategic planning decisions extremely important. First, because innovation is the launching point for technology-based competition, research and development has become a focal point of national competitive strategies. This intense competition at the R&D stage is increasingly shortening the technological life cycle--that is, the time available to convert basic scientific knowledge into products and processes.

Second, novel management practices and techniques are being introduced which can significantly increase the efficiency of the R&D-production interaction, thereby reducing the time required to reach commercialization. Third, once innovations and subsequent improvements are entered into the marketplace, the rate of market penetration becomes the determining factor in long-term success. Market share in technology-based markets is determined by *realized* performance/price ratios. That is, the successful firms and national industries will be those that not only produce *potential* performance improvements through technological advance, but that also introduce these advances rapidly at high quality and reliability levels, *and* do so at low cost.

Furthermore, most technology-based products do not function in isolation, but are components of more complex products or elements of systems of products. Physical and functional interfaces therefore are becoming increasingly important in determining the total cost to the user of adopting a technology. Hence, the availability of these interfaces in the form of standards affect purchase decisions. The complexity of new technologies makes decisions to adopt them difficult even for technically sophisticated users. Thus, nations (and therefore their domestic industries) with the ability to assure customers that performance specifications have been met and that these products will "fit seamlessly" into their internal production systems will increase market shares at the expense of industries in other countries that have not invested in the technology infrastructure supporting such investment decisions.

Finally, not only are increasing numbers of technology-based products part of large and complex systems, but the firm itself can no longer be an island. It must instead regard itself as part of an economic system with major dependencies on other institutions for complementary assets that it cannot efficiently produce. The new strategy variables which increasingly determine competitive position underscore this point. For example, "flexibility" is often regarded as a purely technological problem, or at best an organizational problem *within* the firm. In fact, no firm can become truly flexible by itself. At a minimum, it must cultivate a network of both suppliers and customers with similar strategic objectives. This fact, in turn, has implications for the technology infrastructure -- both in terms of the types of competitively-neutral technologies and services provided to industry and the technology transfer mechanisms.

In summarizing these trends, one might characterize the 1980s as the decade in which the six major competitiveness variables were increasingly targets of U.S. corporate strategy. But these variables were attacked independently to a significant degree. The Japanese, on the other hand, had perceived the critical importance of an *integrated* strategy in which all strategy variables are adjusted over time in an iterative manner. Just-in-time delivery, concurrent engineering, and total quality management are prime examples.

Competition in the 1990s will be based to a large extent on extensions of this *systems* approach to corporate strategy and then to an industry-level or multi-enterprise strategy. At the firm level, R&D, production, and marketing will have to be coordinated in ways that seemed unimportant just a few years ago. In addition, the diversity and magnitude of multi-firm cooperation is increasing, thereby forcing similar integration across corporate boundaries and between corporations and government. These varied channels of integration and hence cooperation will have to be timed to rapidly changing global markets in which sources of new technology will be increasingly varied. As a result, the technology infrastructure underlying a particular nation's economy will have more roles to play and the timing of its provision will be more critical than ever before.

In particular, emerging technologies are the economic lifeblood of an advanced society. Higher standards of living in industrialized nations are reflected in higher wage structures. In most cases, these nations have exhausted most or all domestic supplies of essential raw materials. Thus, technology is the one available long-term comparative advantage, whether the application be manufactured products or services based on these products.

Expanding global competition precludes the historical "random chance" or "benign neglect" approaches to the emergence of economically beneficial technologies. Instead, industry and government must cooperatively identify emerging technologies and determine the infrastructure and other requirements for rapid commercialization.

Summary

A number of factors have combined to retard the competitive positions of the United States and other industrialized nations over the past several decades. In particular,

o   the increasing number of technology-based economies is causing *increased competition and a shortening of the time* in which a domestic industry can make the decision to invest in a new technology and have a chance that the investment will pay off;

o   competitor nations have adopted larger roles for consortia and government laboratories in order to *increase the efficiency of early-phase (generic) technology research* and thereby overcome the unattractive risk-reward ratios that are typical of early-phase technology research;

o   these nations have recognized that the *emerging technologies* that will control future economic growth are *"systems" technologies*, in that they are collections of many, sometimes technologically diverse, components that must work "seamlessly" together; and

o most of these nations have or are in the process of approaching these "systems" problems by *increasing the resources devoted to the establishment of interfaces and other technical infrastructure*, that are essential before private investment will be forthcoming for the individual components.

However, the combination of increasing speed and complexity of technological change as an economic weapon has so distorted the risk/reward calculation on many investment opportunities that substantial underinvestment by individual firms around the world has resulted. Nations are dealing with this problem by defining larger portions of the typical industrial technology as either "pre-competitive" or "competitively neutral". The operational significance of such terms is that these elements of an industry's technology are being developed outside the traditional boundaries of the firm.

Pre-competitive technology research, primarily at the generic technology phase of R&D, is increasingly undertaken by industry-government consortia or in government laboratories with subsequent transfer to the private sector. Competitively neutral technologies, such as a test method or a standardized approach to quality assurance, affect the *efficiency* of every stage of economic activity, not just R&D but production and marketing as well.

The economic leverage gained by defining these technological elements as "infrastructure" and therefore providing them outside the traditional firm in consortia or government laboratories is tremendous. The Japanese have greatly shortened technology life cycles and more widely and rapidly diffused the research results through the extensive use of research consortia. Their extensive national laboratory system is largely oriented toward supporting Japanese industry's *commercial objectives*. Some European nations already have well-developed national laboratory systems and others will access the technology infrastructure now being produced through European integration. In the United States, on the other hand, the vast majority of the annual $18-$20 billion budget of Federal laboratories is mission-oriented, with most of the resources currently committed to defense, space, and other technological areas with only tangential commercial objectives.

The legitimate policy questions do not include should the current technology infrastructure role be expanded; that issue should be beyond argument. Rather, the current questions are what particular set of institutions and what levels of resources are required to provide the generic technologies and the supporting infratechnologies that a technologically-competitive nation needs in the time frames required by the pace of global competition.

A few recent analyses have continued to argue that the United States and other nations do not have severe competitiveness problems and that economic revival will take place as part of the normal business cycle. If the United States, or any industrialized nation, insists on maintaining view that continued decline relative to other industrialized nations is not an immediate worry or that current economic philosophies and strategies are adequate, the following chapters as well as other writings that propose new, aggressive growth strategies are a waste of time.

Nations that persist in remaining attached to increasingly out-of-date economic philosophies, which among other problems are too narrowly focused with respect to the roles of technology, are resigning themselves to a scenario whereby their industries will progressively decline. This decline will reach a state in which these nations can do no better than exist as "off-shore" manufacturing sites for the knowledge-producing economies of the world.

Momentum is a very important concept in economic growth analysis, and it works in both the positive and negative directions that changes in competitive position do take. The idea that a nation can simply wake up one day, throw a switch, and return to a competitive posture is absurd. The world economy is littered with examples that support this point.

2 Strategic Issues in Technology-Based Competition

"The first step toward improvement is to face the facts"

Oliver Wendell Holmes

Certain basic concepts for successfully conducting human activity are timeless. Yet, societies periodically lose their grasp of them and suffer considerable pain until they are rediscovered. As *relative* quality, productivity, and thus the overall competitiveness and standards of living of a number of major industrialized nations' economies, particularly the U. S. economy, eroded in the three decades, 1960-1990, increasingly intense scrutiny has been applied to success stories in other industrial nations. Yet, in spite of these analyses and considerable debate, major disagreements have only increased with respect to the causes of economic decline and especially over the remedies.

Over the two centuries since Adam Smith invented western economic thought, the philosophical pendulum has always returned to the premise that free markets and free trade are the best system for not only maximizing national economic efficiency but global efficiency as well. This belief in the efficiency of the free market has caused no small amount of consternation in the face of Japan's virtually unsurpassed rates of growth since World War II.

After all, the Japanese do not adhere to the principles of maximum competition as defined by western, especially U.S., philosophy. In addition, their industrial structure -- especially, the most successful elements -- is characterized by firms that are highly vertically and horizontally integrated. Such huge companies are themselves part of even larger networks of companies. The most frequently cited examples are the horizontally-integrated "megacompanies" or horizontal *Keiretsu*, which are interlocked structures with a bank at the center providing patient, low-cost capital to manufacturing and service firms. This strategic approach reduces the number of pure free-market interactions between buyers and sellers.

Equally confounding to western principles is the apparent rigidity of the Japanese labor markets that should by all tenets of economic efficiency result in lower, rather than higher, productivity. Wages are tied closely to seniority, salary structures are flat (much lower differentials between top and middle management, management and workers, etc.), promotions tend to be tied to seniority rather than to performance, labor mobility between companies is very low, and the idea of layoffs is horrifying to management.

Alan Blinder [1990] has said that "there is no comparable theory of Japanese capitalism [compared to American capitalism], but we need one if we are to formulate an intelligent economic policy toward Japan. The Japanese themselves seem less concerned with conceptualizations than with results."

However, it will be argued throughout this book that the Japanese do in fact have an exceptionally well-developed conceptual framework of economic growth and competitiveness. In fact, all technology-based economies must plan long-term strategies and policies based on an understanding of economic behavior, industrial structures, and the infrastructure that determine current and future world economic trends. In essence, what most nations still is need today is a better framework for understanding what over time determines "competitive position".

To begin to answer such fundamental questions, certain basic information must be available. The first level of such information is a set of indicators of competitive position. Without understanding where a domestic industry is positioned relative to competitors, subsequent growth strategy and policy analysis will not likely be productive. Such analysis may seem straightforward, but, in fact, many misinterpretations of competitive position abound.

Indicators of Competitive Position

The U.S. industry-sponsored Council on Competitiveness uses four summary indicators of a nation's competitive position: trade (share of world exports), productivity, investment, and the standard of living. Because the standard of living is the ultimate objective of a nation's economic activity, it really stands alone as an indicator of competitiveness. Growth in the standard of living is highly correlated with the growth in value added, which summed over all domestic industries, yields *gross national product (GNP)* or, alternatively, *gross domestic product (GDP)*. Value added is, in turn, determined largely by the first three of the Council's summary competitiveness indicators, which are second in line to the standard of living, will be discussed first.

Table 2-1

U.S. Growth Since 1972 Relative To Other Nations
**(an Index value of 100 represents
the average growth rate for Summit Seven)**

Competitiveness Indicator	U.S. Index
Trade (1972-90)	94.5
Investment (1972-87)	91.3
Productivity (1972-86)	90.1

Source: Council on Competitiveness and the WEFA Group (Wharton Econometrics Forecasting Associates)

Relative competitive position can only be truly assessed over extended periods of time. Therefore, Table 2-1 compares the United

States to the average performance for the leading (so-called "Summit Seven") industrialized nations in trade, investment, and productivity over recent 14 to 18 year periods. The indices show that the United States has lagged even the *average* growth rates for this group of nations.

These indices, which use the latest internationally comparable data available, represent trends for an entire economy over several business cycles, implying that U.S. competitiveness problems represented by its low ranking is *structural* rather than cyclical. Recent data indicate that the U.S. position may be improving with respect to productivity and trade. The trade index rose for the fourth consecutive year in 1990, but is still below the average growth rate for the Summit Seven. Moreover, a good portion of this improvement has been due to a depreciating dollar. The impact of short-term factors such as currency shifts must not be allowed to distract growth strategy from addressing the longer term competitive forces.

The productivity indicator is particularly important because it is greatly affected by technological change.[1] Long-term trends for the United States and five of its major competitors are shown in Table 2-2. Other similar summaries of productivity growth rates over various time periods have been compiled, but these periods are particularly revealing because they coincide with significant technology-driven cycles.

The mid-1950s saw the emergence of other industrialized nations selling technology-based products, followed quickly by Sputnik and the intensive period of technology investment that it set off. This period ended in 1973, when a quadrupling of oil prices made obsolete a significant portion of the industrialized nations' capital stock. The next period, 1974-81, was one of adjustment to the greatly altered productivity of capital stocks caused by their relative dependency on energy. Some economies dealt with the required adjustments better than others.

This period effectively ended in the severe worldwide recession of 1981-82. One result of this recession was a closer examination by

---

[1]   See Link [1987, pp. 6-8 and 25-26] and Landau [1988]. The combined contribution of formal R&D and "learning by doing" experience to long-term productivity growth has been estimated by economists to be in the 75-80 percent range. In other words, fully three quarters of long-term productivity growth is accounted for by advances in knowledge.

most industrialized nations of the elements of industrial
competitiveness. It became increasingly clear that more
comprehensive and integrated growth policies were required. The
exact composition of this "competitiveness objective" and the degrees
to which industrialized nations should establish new strategies were
topics of increasingly intense debate.

The period 1982-86 was one of considerable growth worldwide,
stimulated by a number of factors. During this period, U.S.
productiyity growth became competitive. However, while other
nations were broadening their views of the factors driving
competitiveness, growth policy debates in the United States focused
largely on productivity (to the exclusion of quality, education, new
roles for technology infrastructure, etc.).

Table 2-2

Average Annual Percent Growth in Productivity
(Output per Hour in Manufacturing)

Years	*United States*	*Japan*	*France*	*Germany*	*Italy*	*United Kingdom*
1955-73	3.45	23.4	10.3	11.1	10.1	5.19
1974-81	1.54	6.73	4.75	3.63	3.72	1.50
1982-86	5.00	5.32	2.70	2.85	5.80	5.65
1987-89	4.72	5.55	4.96	3.92	2.89	5.00

Source: U.S. Dept. of Labor, Bureau of Labor Statistics, April 1991.

Moreover, this resurgence in U.S. productivity growth was
mainly the result of "restructuring" which involved more focused
corporate strategies and cost-cutting. In effect, these strategies tried
to squeeze more efficiency out of *existing* technology and an *existing*
technology delivery system. Technology development was undertaken
largely in the traditional sequential pattern within individual firms. In
other words, the longer-term technology-based growth requirements in

response to changes in global competition were not addressed in any substantive or systematic way, as they were in some other countries.

Between 1987 and 1990, the United States managed to maintain an annual rate of productivity growth that was the average for its major competitors. Unit labor costs in the United States dropped significantly relative to other industrialized nations after 1985, but this very positive effect on trade position was greatly aided by a significant depreciation of the dollar.

Table 2-3

Value-Added Productivity Trends
Percentage Changes, 1979-87

Country	Based on Value-Added	Based on Production
United States	3.7	4.0
Japan	5.8	2.7
Belgium	4.5	3.2
Denmark	1.0	2.2
France	1.8	2.2
Finland	4.7	4.7
Australia	2.3	2.0

Source: OECD [1990b, pp. 91-92].

Although labor productivity (the type shown in Table 2-2) is the most commonly used productivity measure, application to analysis at the microeconomic (industry) level suffers from the fact that it relates *gross* output to the labor input. Thus, labor productivity, and other productivity measures for that matter, reflect both the growth in value added contributed by the industry being measured *and* the valued added embodied in the intermediate goods that the industry buys from other industries.[2]

The Organization for Economic Cooperation and Development (OECD) has begun to construct a *value-added-based* labor productivity measure. National trends in this productivity measure for which comparable data are available are shown in column 2 of Table 2-3.

Quality improvements and the shift in overall product mix towards "downstream" or "up-market" products will tend to raise the overall value added in a particular industrial sector. When this happens across enough sectors, it is reflected in a gap between the two measures of productivity shown in Table 2-3. The data show, for example, that Japan has a growth rate of value-added productivity that is significantly above its production-based rate, likely reflecting that economy's steady and widespread movement to efficient investment in downstream products.

The "bottom line" of productivity growth along with the trade balance and investment (the three indicators in Table 2-1), is the standard of living -- the ultimate objective of all economic growth policy. In 1990, the Council on Competitiveness index for the U.S. standard of living stood at 85 percent of the average growth rate for the seven leading industrialized nations over the period 1972-90 -- the lowest level ever.

The standard of living has been typically measured as per capita Gross National Product (GNP). Because GNP is the sum of the value added by each industry, a rapidly growing GNP, especially in a large economy, requires a large number of competitive industries.[3]

Table 2-4 gives a long-term perspective on how national economies have fared relative to each other in terms of being able to sustain acceptable rates of growth in per capita value added. The last row gives a 40-year (1948-88) average annual growth rate for real output per person in each of the Summit Seven nations (except Canada). Among these largest industrial nations, the United States

---

[2]   Obviously, this is also a problem at the national level to the extent that imported goods are used as intermediate products.

[3]   Actually, GDP is an increasingly used alternative measure because it reflects value added within the *domestic* economy. GNP includes this measure plus a portion of value added by foreign affiliates.

has the worst performance. Even the much-maligned economy of the United Kingdom has performed better. In the succeeding two years (1989-90), the U.S. average annual growth rate was 1.7 percent. This continued slow rate of real growth badly trailed the average for the European Community (3.2 percent) and for Japan (5.8 percent).

Table 2-4

Growth in Real GNP/GDP: Selected Periods, 1948-1988
(average per capita percent growth per year)

Period	United States	Japan	West Germany	United Kingdom	France	Italy
1948-1973	2.2	7.8	5.7	2.6	4.3	5.0
1973-1981	1.1	2.7	2.0	0.7	2.1	2.2
1981-1988	2.0	3.2	1.9	2.7	1.3	2.0
1948-1988	1.9	5.9	4.2	2.2	3.3	3.9

Source: *Economic Report of the President*, 1989, p. 27. Note that data for some of these nations are stated in terms of Gross Domestic Product (GDP) rather than GNP.

Microeconomic Indicators of Competitive Position

Stopping with the above macroeconomic indicators of competitiveness would be incomplete. Michael Porter goes so far as to argue in his excellent book, *The Competitive Advantage of Nations* [1990b, pp. 9-10], that one should not even try to explain competitiveness at the national level. Instead, he recommends focusing on "specific industries or industry segments". Two categories of infrastructure are influential at the industry level: infrastructure generated by the industry itself (such as information flows, standards, etc.) and infrastructure generated by a broader set of institutions, including government.

However, a singular focus the industry level ignores the critically important economies of scope in many emerging technologies that have led to Japanese successes in technologies such as optoelectronics (which borrowed much of its process technology from semiconductors). In 1979, a MITI "vision" statement, followed by the formation of a research cooperative, launched the Japanese optoelectronics industry on a path to worldwide leadership.

The Japanese did not invent the term "fusion" technologies because they think each technology and industry operates independently of each other. The knowledge of potential uses of technologies in industries other than the originating one, including industries in distinctly separate sectors, is one of the many elements of technology infrastructure that display economies of scope and therefore experience private-sector underinvestment at the industry level.

Thus, Porter's statement that "we must abandon the whole notion of a 'competitive nation' as a term having much meaning for economic prosperity" ignores the economies of scale and scope captured by a system of national laboratories, research consortia, national data bases of both technical and market-relevant information, and a host of networks, extension services, and other technology transfer mechanisms that are multi-industry and even national in coverage.

It is therefore necessary to include the interdependence of industries in developing a complete set of indicators of competitive position. This step is especially important when assessing the roles of technology infrastructure, much of which has multiple-industry impacts.

The Information Technology Production Chain

The interdependency of technology-based industries and the consequent added importance of infrastructure can be seen by examining a total technology-based production chain, such as information technology. Beginning with materials and components and moving forward in the chain to products/devices and then product systems and finally to the services based on the underlying product structure, the value added at each step can be analyzed and the distribution of this value added among national industries assessed.

Figure 2-1 shows a portion of the production chain for information technology. The competitiveness of the markets for information systems (the product systems and the services based on them) are dependent on upstream devices such as computers and telecommunications equipment. These devices are, in turn, dependent semiconductors and optoelectronic components. Finally, increasingly complex and "engineered" materials greatly affect the productivity of these components.

Information Technology Production Chain

Figure 2-1

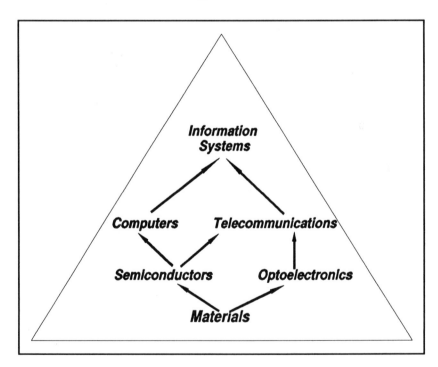

As Table 2-3 and the related discussion indicate, it is naive to
think that an industry producing one of the above elements in the
production chain can remain competitive over time in isolation from

Figure 2-2

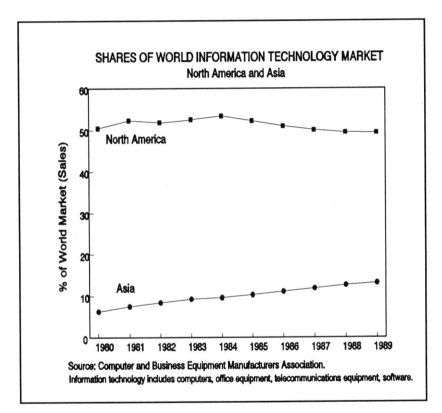

other industries active in the same production chain. To examine this
point, Figures 2-2 thru 2-6 show trends over the past decade in shares
of world markets (sales) for various levels in the "production chain"
for information technology. Figure 2-2 shows the market share trends
in North America (mainly the United States) and Asia (mainly Japan)

for information technology (defined as systems made up of computers, office equipment, telecommunications equipment, and software).[4]

North America is shown to have maintained a substantial, although declining, lead over the past decade, but the more important issue is whether this decline will continue. In this regard, a better indicator of future *shifts* in the competitive position of a domestic

Figure 2-2a

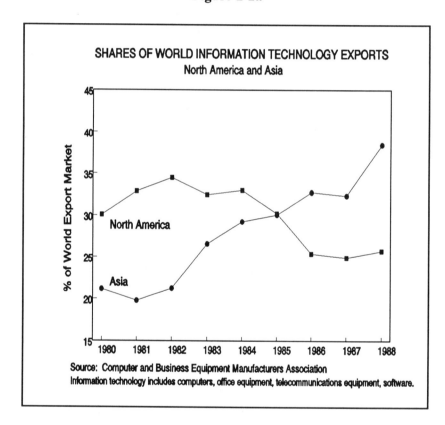

SHARES OF WORLD INFORMATION TECHNOLOGY EXPORTS
North America and Asia

Source: Computer and Business Equipment Manufacturers Association
Information technology includes computers, office equipment, telecommunications equipment, software.

---

[4]   A reason for portraying market share trends for "North America" and "Asia" is to better capture the regional distribution of production that is evolving. U.S. firms have significantly expanded production facilities in Canada and Mexico, while Japan has expanded into a number of Asian countries. These *economic zones* are becoming increasingly integrated, including the use of the same infrastructure.

industry is its share of global exports. This is because exports must compete directly with other nations' exports in third-country markets and overcome preferences in the home markets of competitors for domestic versions of the same products.

Figure 2a shows trends in shares of world exports. These data yield a different assessment of competitive position in information technology. While still leading in shares of total world sales (Figure 2-2), North American firms have clearly lost the lead in shares of world exports, with the "crossover" occurring in 1985.

Figure 2-3

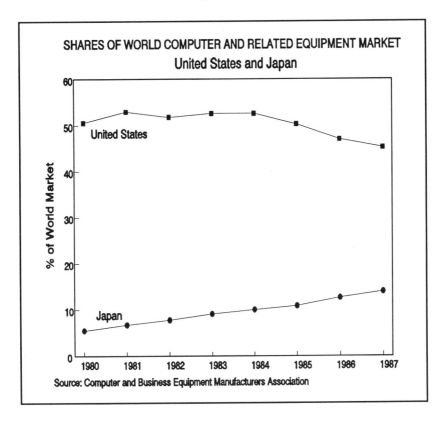

This pattern -- market share erosion in world trade preceding market share erosion in total production -- has occurred in a number of technologies. The implication is that world trade share may be a *leading* indicator of shifts in overall competitive position, reflected by world production share, which measures *current* aggregate economic position.[5]

Figure 2-4

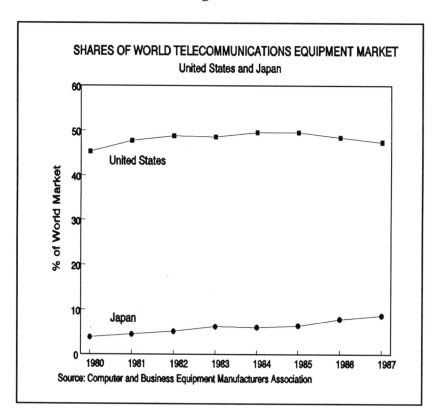

Moving one level back up the production chain, Figures 2-3 and 2-4 show the market share trends for several classes of equipment, computers and telecommunication equipment, that are major elements of information systems. In both cases, the United States has a substantial lead over Japan.

---

[5]   These crossover points and other indicators of competitive position trends depend greatly on how the terms "market" and "market share" are defined.

Figure 2-3a

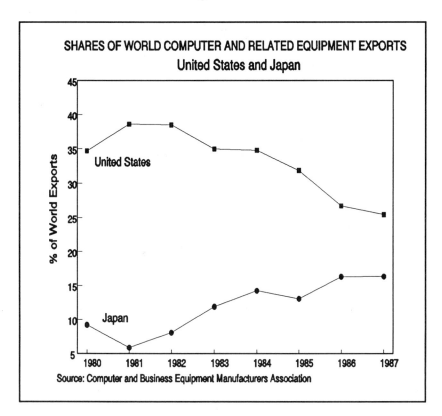

SHARES OF WORLD COMPUTER AND RELATED EQUIPMENT EXPORTS
United States and Japan

% of World Exports

United States

Japan

Source: Computer and Business Equipment Manufacturers Association

However, these margins are narrowing. One major reason is shown in Figures 2-3a and 2-4a; export share trends turned against the United States in both markets around 1982. Thus, although the large installed customer base acquired by virtue of being the market innovator can sustain sales for a time, the negative trends in export markets, where different versions of a product compete directly, indicate a decline in competitive position.

A number of analysts have made the point that a substantial "lead" in market share for a given domestic industry can be misleading if the components making up much of that industry's product come from foreign suppliers. In other words, if the components of computers come from Japan and if the computers themselves (along with other components of information technology, such as communications equipment) come increasingly from Japan, then, the argument goes, it is just a matter of time before the overall U.S. lead in information technology passes to Japan. It is this situation that has given rise to the term "hollow corporation", meaning that most of the value added embedded in the sales price comes from foreign sources.

Figure 2-4a

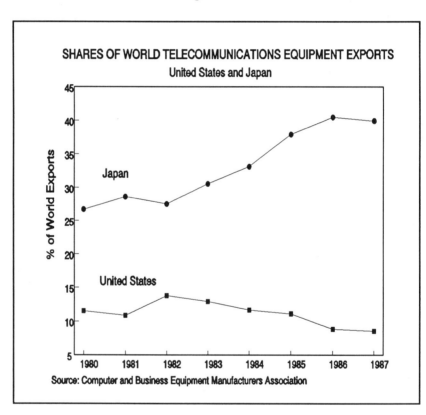

Not only does this "hollowing out" reduce the current potential domestic value added, but it makes the domestic industry more vulnerable to swings in global demand or shifts in competitive position by other nations. If the cash flow from single-product strategies declines, even temporarily, the lack of cash flow from other levels in the production chain will create a cash flow squeeze on the domestic industry that may prevent sufficient investment in the next generation of the underlying technology. To the extent that the nature of global competition and demand make this sort of scenario likely, diversified sources of cash flow (i.e., vertical integration) are warranted.[6]

Figure 2-5

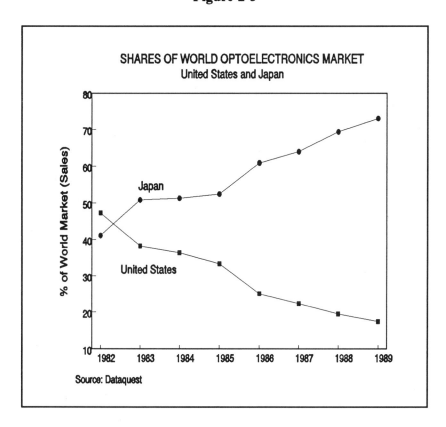

Moving yet one more level up the production chain to the component level, Figures 2-5 and 2-6 show that even the total market

---

6 Horizontal diversification will provide similar benefits. However, in some cases at least, such benefits will not be attainable to the same extent, as demand patterns are more correlated and related product lines are based on the same generic technology. Other strategic benefits from vertical integration will be discussed in succeeding chapters.

shares (sales) have turned against the United States. To some, this
level is the most important because these components can spawn or
"enable" a wide range of downstream products. Because of timing
benefits and occasional cash flow transfers to the development of
downstream products, being competitive at this level in industries with
short technology life cycles can be essential.

Figure 2-6

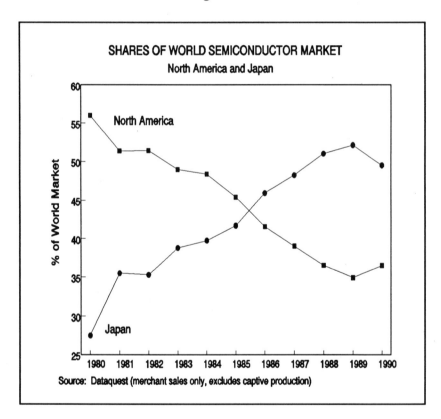

These last two graphs also can be used to help show how two
apparently unrelated technologies at the same level in the production
chain can affect one another. The semiconductor market share graph
(in terms of sales) reflects the fact that the success of the Japanese
effort in the late 1970s to attain world leadership in semiconductor

process technology resulted in a "crossover" in the mid 1980s in favor of Japan.

This success in semiconductors opened up the potential to accelerate market penetration in optoelectronics, whose process technology has major similarities. The United States never saw and certainly never pursued this opportunity for synergy or "fusion". The optoelectronics market share graph clearly shows the result of the differences in the two countries' strategies.

It is also interesting to note that the crossover occurred several years earlier for optoelectronics than for semiconductors. This is because optoelectronics was an infant market around 1980 -- the time when the Japanese were transferring or, to use their term, "fusing" semiconductor process technology to this new technological area. Thus, the United States did not have an established production base to be eroded away, as was the case in semiconductors where the crossover in terms of shares of world sales took until the mid 1980s.[7]

Growth Policy Issues

The key to long-term success for any economy is its ability to *adapt* to new technological, managerial, and organizational trends as the nature and opportunities of global competition create them. A large economy must even be a creator of these trends. Smaller economies are banding together to achieve just such goals. Thus, structural and behavioral change must be the core elements of any successful economy in a dynamic world marketplace.

Even though a struggle to develop the new institutional apparatus and to make new role assignments between industry and government for a more comprehensive competitiveness policy has finally begun, this process is still in its early stages. Such major changes, as they are established, will mean new roles and resources for some institutions and the reverse for others.

---

[7] Even one more step up the production chain could be presented as evidence of the serious problem of the "hollow production chain". U.S. semiconductor manufacturers are almost totally dependent on foreign materials suppliers for silicon and silicon wafers.

Different national growth strategies in the past have demanded different combinations of technology infrastructure, although, as Chapter 3 will argue, national strategies will converge in certain respects over this decade. Among industries, however, factors such as firm size, nature of the technology base, labor skills, structure of market demand, etc., will continue to create differential demands for technology infrastructure support.

A study by Daniel Luria of the Industrial Technology Institute [1990] finds that U.S. small and medium size companies, which are growing in importance as large companies increasingly subcontract production, are not keeping pace with their larger industrial customers in deploying new technologies and systems to enhance productivity. The U.S. manufacturing sector employs approximately 19 million people, with about 7 million working in large businesses -- some 6,000 establishments with 500 or more employees.[8]

The remaining 120,000 medium or small firms, employing 20 to 500 workers each, are "the core of the nation's industrial base". Luria estimates that such companies, which mainly supply the components and materials used by larger manufacturers, were 20 percent less productive than larger ones in 1967. This gap in value added efficiency has widened to nearly 30 percent over the past two decades. Luria concludes that "one reason that industrial productivity growth is faster overseas is that smaller firms in Northern Europe and Japan are technically more advanced than in the U.S."

Science and technology and the ability to apply these assets will play major roles in responding to the challenge to remain competitive in international markets. The need for technology infrastructure will be greater in the next two decades than at any time since the first great industrial revolution. Biotechnology is revolutionizing the agricultural, chemical, medical, and drug industries. Computers and automated manufacturing technologies are revolutionizing the goods producing industries. Computers, telecommunications, and optoelectronics are revolutionizing financial, information, and government services and operations. Ceramics, polymers, and composites are revolutionizing the materials industries.

However, in spite of this proliferation of technological

---

[8]   Companies employing less than 500 employees is the most commonly used Small Business Administration definition of a small business.

opportunity, a highly competitive U.S. economy in the 1990s cannot be projected. U.S. productivity, quality, and market share trends still lag the performance of major international competitors. Not only are the infrastructure policies not yet in place to support a competitive technology-based economy, but the aggregate resources being discussed for recently implemented or proposed infrastructure policies are inadequate.[9]

Now that competitiveness has become widely recognized as a major problem for the United States, criticism rains down. For example,

> "The U.S. government has not addressed the commercialization of technology as a public policy issue"
>
> > B.R. Inman and Daniel F. Burton[10]
>
> "To our knowledge, the United States has no policy development process"
>
> > Editor, *New Technology Week*

However, it is necessary to be much more definitive about policy and the policy process. Specifically, the United States is proceeding as if technology life cycles are still long, when, in fact, they have shortened dramatically. Our funding and conduct of early-phase technology research aimed ultimately at commercial markets are still inadequate. The externalities that exist are not being addressed.

Many production technologies have not adapted to the demands of global markets for increased quality, productivity, and flexibility. The critical elements of these process technologies exhibit significant "economies of scope" and are therefore not being developed by industry. That is, many new technologies have ranges of potential market applications that are greater than the set of markets targeted by the strategies of most, if not all, of the potential market participants. Firms therefore tend to underinvest, especially in the

---

[9]   Japan, with an economy two-thirds the size of the United States, invests more in R&D and capital formation.

[10]   "Essay: Technology and Competitiveness", *Scientific American*, January 1991.

early phases of the technology's development when uncertainty is high as to the eventual size and nature of specific market applications.

Even at the marketing stage, significant economies of scope exist. Many of the most important technologies for the 1990s, such as communications, distributed data processing, and factory automation, are *systems* technologies. Such technologies require significant infrastructure to assure private investment. For example, a communications system includes hardware (telecommunications equipment, computers, printers, etc.), software (operations, applications, and programming), and infrastructure (optical fiber, associated hardware, interfaces between all components, and conformance testing "suites" for assuring compatibility).

A major policy issue is to decide what is the "technology driver"; that is, what element (or elements) of the overall technology system will "pull" the other elements and thus realize the exceptional economic growth potential that these systems technologies offer. For example, many analysts believe that dynamic random access memory (DRAM) circuits are the "drivers" of all applications of semiconductor technology.

The Japanese believe that the infrastructure is the "technology driver" of the "information age". In addition to a large number of national laboratory research programs and government-industry research consortia, they are spending huge amounts of money on "wiring" their country with optical fiber cable. With the fiber widely installed, the risk to hardware and software providers that future markets of sufficient size will not develop is greatly reduced.

If the infrastructure is to be the technology driver, then the public and private sources of funds assume the risk that the demand for the ultimate services (in this case, information) will not grow as fast or become as large as forecast. In Japan, this decision to invest was pushed by Nippon Telegraph and Telephone (NTT), which was recently privatized but still dominates telecommunications strategies in that country. Their Integrated Network System (INS) is the key element behind the Japanese forecast that in 20-25 years approximately one-third of Japan's GNP will be derived from information technology-based services.

The comparable information infrastructure in the United States is Integrated System Digital Network (ISDN), but a more diverse industry structure and lack of a forceful policy thrust make the progress of ISDN difficult to predict. The debate over information technology in the United States has focused on (1) industry structure issues such as should the Regional Bell Operating Companies (RBOCs) be allowed to vertically integrate (that is, manufacture and sell hardware and software, including programming), and (2) specific applications of the generic technology such as high-definition television (HDTV).

These hardware, software, and infrastructure issues are not separable because they function as a system. Thus, a critical additional infrastructure element is a set of interface standards. Moreover, a technology's infrastructure is typically not homogeneous in that different elements display varying degrees of what economists call a "public good". For example, the trunk lines of optical fiber are more a public infrastructure than are the fiber links from these trunk lines to individual homes. Thus, it could be argued that any government support that is provided should be focused on the trunk lines, leaving the individual home hookups largely to industry.

Therefore, when government assistance is needed for some types of infrastructure design and definition, such help will be technical in nature, whereas, in other cases, the assistance will be financial and the removal of regulatory uncertainty. In other words, the range of possible government roles is both diverse and complex, thereby requiring considerable analysis and joint planning with industry.

In releasing the Office of Science and Technology Policy's (OSTP) FY 1991 budget request, the President's Science Advisor, Dr. D. Allan Bromley, stated

> "The sophistication and capital-intensive nature of modern technology require new ways of increasing cooperation between government and industry and of fostering communication on long-term technology goals."

The "Overview" to the Administration's FY 1991 budget stated that one of the two areas in which the Federal Government has traditionally supported R&D is

> "to meet broader national needs (e.g., basic research in all areas, measurements and standards R&D, health-related R&D)." This "R&D, for which the Government is not the principal market, includes both basic research and generic applied research. Federal investment in such R&D is warranted to capture the public good benefit."

With respect to the criteria for implementing this support role, the "Overview" states

o   "there should be 'externalities' associated with the R&D;

o   there should be benefits to broad segments of the economy simultaneously; and

o   the private sector is without sufficient incentives to capture enough of the benefits to make such R&D investments worthwhile. In such cases there should be private support (e.g., joint ventures or cost-sharing) commensurate with the expected benefits to the private parties."

In summary, some *general* rationales for government support of *technology* infrastructure are beginning to emerge, but understanding of the precise industry targets, mechanisms to be used, and expected economic benefits is still primitive.

Economic Impacts of Infrastructure R&D

The first question to ask is how important is this issue of competitiveness? Tables 2-1 through 2-4 give the answer. The second question to ask is whether technology is a major part of the answer to this competitiveness problem. The answer is given by a number of economic studies over several decades that indicate technology is responsible for more than one-half of per capita GNP growth experienced by the U.S. economy since the 1930s. More than one-third of the average annual growth in productivity over this same period is attributable to R&D and other knowledge production. Other economic studies have shown high rates of return for both private and public R&D.[11]

---

[11]   These studies have been conducted over several decades, but only recently have high-ranking government officials begun to cite them as a rationale for increased support of R&D. See Bromley [1991]. The total estimated contribution to

Table 2-5

Social Rates of Return from Technology Investments

Study	Technology Area	Source of R&D	Social Rate of Return (%)
Mansfield *et al.* [1977]	miscellaneous (18 innovations)	private	77
Tewksbury *et al.* [1980]	miscellaneous (20 innovations)	private	108
Peterson [1967]	poultry	public -- DoA	18
Griliches [1958]	hybrid Corn	public -- DoA	37
Griliches [1964]	agriculture, generally	public -- DoA	10-50
Charles River Associates [1981]	semiconductor -- three subareas	public -- NIST	63-181
Link [1991a]	optical fiber	public -- NIST	423
Link [1991b]	semiconductor -- electromigration	public -- NIST	117
Link [1991c]	electromagnetic interference	public -- NIST	266

Table 2-5 summarizes quantitative estimates from economic studies of the rates of return from several categories of technology infrastructure and compares them with two National Science Foundation (NSF) studies of rates of return from a cross-section of

the economy from "technical knowledge" is even higher. See footnote 1 to this chapter.

private-sector innovations. The rates of return from infratechnology research (conducted by NIST) are particularly high. The latter results are not surprising, given that NIST targets its research at specific industry infrastructure problems and builds a technology transfer strategy into each project.[12]

More generally, given that industry typically realizes much lower rates of return on capital investment, the high rates estimated for technology investments leads one to conclude that more resources should be allocated to investment in all categories of technology research.

The third question is what are the elements of the technology-based strategies needed to achieve desirable rates of economic growth in the 1990s and beyond. This last question is the most complicated and has spurred continuous debate, including comparisons among the strategies of industrial nations. The Japanese may not systematically estimate rates of return to the major elements of industrial technologies. However, they certainly have grasped the fundamental fact that each element is essential and must have its share of resources allocated to it in a timely manner. They have consequently developed the strategies to produce and effectively utilize these technology elements.

Summary

Any economy that loses dominant positions in such varied applications of major technologies as color Tvs, video tape recorders,

---

[12] The success of these infratechnology research programs depends in part on the availability of an underlying measurement science base. Thus, basic research conducted at universities, NIST, and other government laboratories is an essential precursor to achieving high rates of return in all technology research. A number of studies of the rate of return (measured as the contribution to productivity growth) from basic research have been conducted. Mansfield [1980] and Link [1981] estimated the rate of return to *company-funded* basic research be 178 and 231 percent, respectively. Link also estimated a rate of return of 117 percent for *government-funded* basic research. More recently, Mansfield [1991] estimated the rate of return to "academic research" that contributed directly to the commercialization of products and processes to be 28 percent (this latter number is smaller because of the relatively narrow scope of impact being measured and the relatively long lags to which a discount rate is applied).

telephones, machine tools, robots, memory circuits, optical disks, ceramic capacitors, etc., as has the United States, needs systematic examination of both government and industry strategic behavior. In particular, the loss of leads in the underlying generic technologies from which these and many other applications derive has serious implications for attaining future competitive positions.[13]

Much has been written about the degree and the causes of declining U.S. competitive position. The corporate strategy literature has grown exponentially in recent years, offering techniques for improving quality, productivity, flexibility, etc. But, far less has been written about government growth policy, especially in a systematic and usable manner.

One of the many requirements for useful growth policy constructs is recognition of the interdependency between the government and industry roles in developing and marketing new technologies. An algorithm is required for explaining these interdependencies and describing the respective roles in a way that allows a better understanding of the interfaces.

From an national economy's point of view, the adoption of breakthrough and continuous-improvement strategies by one or a few firms is not sufficient. Supporting such strategies is a positive step, but it does not incorporate explanations of why some economies have larger numbers of competitive industries than do others. In particular, at the multi-industry and national levels, growth strategies must recognize that the *quality, timeliness, and size of a nation's technology infrastructure is a critical factor in determining the overall competitive position of the modern technology-based economy.*

---

[13] The ongoing process of losing technological leadership has been documented in a number of cross-cutting assessments of emerging technologies by the Department of Defense, Department of Commerce, and the Office of Science and Technology Policy.

3 A Conceptual Model of Technology Infrastructure

"If one does not know to which port one is sailing, no wind is favorable"

Seneca
(Roman philosopher)

Conceptual frameworks do not themselves produce good strategy and policy. However, they provide an essential common ground for the subsequent economic and policy analysis and the communication of this analysis to the policy decision process. Consequently, this chapter presents a model for identifying and relating the basic elements of a technology infrastructure strategy.

In the past, the longer, more leisurely technology life cycles permitted a limited microeconomic policy structure based on a simple model of the technology change process. This model, represented in Figure 3-1, resulted in the premise that the only major funding role of government was to support basic research. Hence, it represented U.S. thinking that evolved in the post-war years and remained in place until very recently.

Figure 3-1

"Black Box" Technology Model

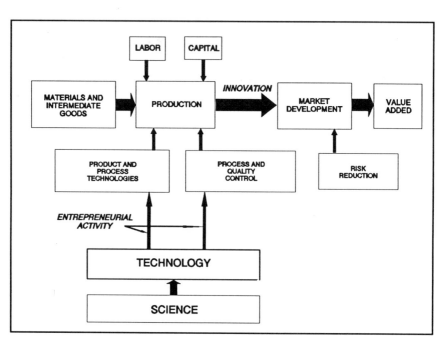

In this conceptual framework, technology is viewed as a "black box", i.e., a homogeneous entity which entrepreneurs create out of basic scientific knowledge. If this were the case, the required microeconomic policy roles for government would be limited to support for basic research, some of the measurement infratechnologies supplied by government laboratories, and certain types of technical information. This view of technology-based economic activity was reflected in the very slow and segmented evolution of science and technology (S&T) policies, as summarized in Chapter 1.

However, the reality of technology-based competition is demonstrated considerably better by Figure 3-2. Here, industrial technology is disaggregated into several components that reflect major elements of the process by which scientific knowledge is made progressively application-oriented.

One reason for this disaggregation is that each of these components exhibits different types and magnitudes of externalities. Thus, such a model helps understand and design microeconomic strategies that address the elements of an industry's technology. The four major elements of an industry's technology base -- generic *product* and *process* technologies, the supporting *infratechnologies*, and *management practice* will be analyzed in the following sections and succeeding chapters.[1]

Figure 3-2

Disaggregated Technology Model

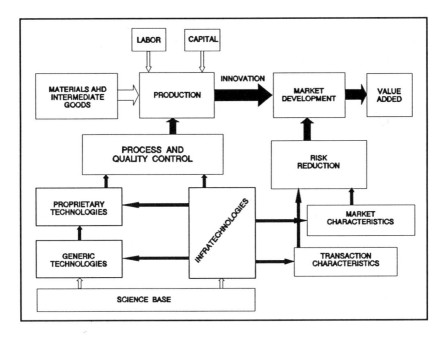

---

[1] These three terms along with many others frequently used in discussions of technology-based strategies and policies are collected together and defined in the Appendix to this chapter. The defined terms are proposals for this new area of technology-based growth policy analysis.

Generic Technology

Generic technology research is the first phase in *technology* R&D. Its objective is to prove that a product or process concept with potential market applications has merit. This phase ends approximately with proof of concept, which may be in the form of a laboratory prototype. Proving a concept in the laboratory is a long way from a commercially viable product, but the fact that this research is driven by an ultimate market objective is what qualifies it as technology research as opposed to scientific research. However, its distance from the market place and the attendant uncertainties with respect to the particular markets, their sizes, and the time to commercialization all combine to cause substantial underinvestment by individual firms.[2]

Once a technology concept has been proven in the laboratory, enough of these uncertainties have been reduced to warrant investment by individual firms in most, but not all, technologies. Thus, after the generic technology has been proven, a series of *proprietary* phases in the R&D stage ensue, eventually leading to commercialization.

Infratechnology

All phases of R&D, plus production and market development, are supported by a set of *infratechnologies*, as indicated in Figure 3-2. This element of technology infrastructure becomes embodied in or supports generic technology and its applications. It also provides the technical basis for standards, which directly affect process and quality control at the production stage and the efficiency of market

---

[2] In the United States, NIST's Advanced Technology Program defines generic technology as "a concept, component, or the further investigation of scientific phenomena, that has the potential to be applied to a broad range of products or processes. A generic technology may require subsequent research and development for commercial application". (See the Appendix to this chapter for a more detailed definition). In Japan, a set of criteria have evolved for identifying a technology as being in the generic phase of development: the technology has (1) the prospect of "productization", (2) high technical risk, (3) a significant number of potential market applications, and (4) a large aggregate (across markets) expected economic impact.

transactions through risk reduction. Infratechnologies fall into three categories:

o   scientific and engineering data that are used for conducting R&D and controlling production, especially in continuous process technologies (such as chemical production and petroleum refining);

o   measurement and test methods that are essential to conduct state-of-the-art R&D, monitor and control production, and execute market transactions (product acceptance testing); and,

o   practices and techniques, such as process control models, that allow various elements of the typical industrial technology to be organized and utilized efficiently.

As an example of the increasing pervasiveness of infratechnologies in the modern economic system, consider the varied roles of measurement:

(1) At the *R&D stage*, measurement science adds to the pool of basic knowledge that all scientists and engineers use. Scientific advances are often driven by state-of-the-art measurements, which open up new fields for investigation. For example, the trend in materials research is to "engineer" technologically-advanced ceramics, polymers, metal-matrix composites, etc., for increasingly differentiated applications. Design for these new custom materials is reaching the molecular or even the atomic level; that is, performance characteristics are being adjusted for specific uses by rearranging individual atoms and molecules. This level of design sophistication was hardly contemplated just a few decades ago, when materials for most products were highly uniform in composition and alterations in composition were quite crude, consisting only of gross changes in the proportions of the components.

To engineer advanced materials at the molecular and atomic levels requires measurement accuracy with respect to the properties of these materials that are orders of magnitude beyond that of just a few years ago. In fact, totally new measurement techniques are needed. Without these new techniques, much state-of-the-art R&D would not be possible. For example, research in new high-temperature superconductors has been impeded by the lack of a widely accepted measurement method for determining the current-carrying capacity of the superconductors. In the absence of such a method, researchers cannot readily compare and verify their findings.

Such measurement technologies, standards, and associated materials properties data make industrial research and development more productive by allowing industrial scientists and engineers to not only detect and analyze new technological principles, but also to communicate the results to the corporate decision making process.

(2) At the *production stage*, measurements, measurement methods, standards and data are crucial to quality assurance and process control. Modern production depends increasingly on ubiquitous, precise measurement. In the past, measurement for process control was mostly a static or "snap shot" activity, occurring mainly at the *end* of production. By contrast, many modern processes require continuous measurement and the ability to respond continuously to measurement change *during* production.

Because products are increasingly based on advanced materials, where defects even at the single-atom level can affect performance characteristics, their production requires measurement-intensive control. For example, accurate measurements of the thickness and electrical properties of the thin layers within integrated circuits are essential to controlling the quality to those circuits during manufacture. Accuracy good enough to distinguish the thickness of individual atomic monolayers will be required for the next generation of integrated circuits. The nation whose infrastructure provides this measurement capability will likely be the leader in semiconductor technology for this next generation.

Similarly, quality assurance was once mostly a matter of inspection at the end of the production line. Today, the emphasis is on making it right the first time. Machines are being programmed to measure their own performance attributes, to measure the attributes of the products being processed, and to adjust the production process automatically to account for deviations from some ideal.

It is not just the critical role of measurement infratechnologies in quality assurance and process control that make them important. They constitute an important element of overall production cost.

About 20 percent of the cost of producing optical fibers is measurement. About 25 percent of the cost of making silicon integrated circuits is attributable to measurements, and, similarly, about 25 percent of the cost of making microwave integrated circuits is measurement-related. Thus, their efficient use is important.

(3) Measurements, measurement methods, standards and data are also essential for **market penetration**. High levels of performance risk frequently accompany high technology products to market. Test methods, test structures and industry standards help new technologies "diffuse" or get into wider use faster by reducing these risks. Risk reduction also stimulates market growth by leading to higher sales which result in economies of scale in production, lower costs, and then even higher sales.

For example, power transformers used by electrical utilities must have extraordinarily low electrical losses, since those losses can cost the utility *more* over the lifetime of a transformer than its purchase price. Advanced measurement methods are necessary to detect these losses, and severe penalties can be exacted by the buyer for the seller's failure to meet agreed loss specifications.

The above three roles indicate that the overall economy benefits greatly from measurements, measurement methods, data, and standards. However, industry tends to underinvest in research related to measurement science and technology.

The rationale for a national measurements and standards infrastructure is based on this economic imperfection: a large number of both individuals and firms benefit from the same measurement science and technology; thus, the aggregate benefit to the economy is high, but these benefits are only realized through widespread and consistent use by market participants. This commonality and comprehensiveness of use of measurement-related infratechnologies and data give them a nonproprietary character which results in underinvestment by the private sector.

The development of measurement infratechnologies frequently require expensive equipment and highly skilled staff which have limited although essential benefits to a particular firm or industry. The measurement-related research of a firm or industry therefore may have insufficient *scale* to be efficient.

Furthermore, individual firms and industries tend to use a limited set of measurement methodologies, but the science and technology of measurement is highly interrelated and can be applied to the problems of many different industries. Thus, the measurement-related research of a particular firm or even an entire industry may have insufficient *scope* to be efficient.

In sum, the number or range of applications or the intensity of use of the research by a single firm may be insufficient to justify the minimum efficient scale or scope of investment in the needed measurement infratechnologies.

Management Practice

In addition to generic product and process technologies and the supporting infratechnologies, the competitive position of a technology-based industry is increasingly determined by the extent to which it adopts advanced *management practice.*

Manufacturing practice is the catalyst for using product and process technologies and infratechnologies effectively. Without good manufacturing practice, new products will not be developed with the required quality or the timing relative to foreign competition, nor will new processes be productive and integrate efficiently with product development. Such practices as "concurrent engineering" and "total quality management" include concepts and standardized methods and techniques for assuring quality and increasing productivity, for enabling product mix flexibility, and for integrating R&D, production, and market development to decrease time to market.[3]

In essence, these practices greatly increase overall economic efficiency and hence competitiveness by combining elements of an industry's technology with corporate organizational and marketing strategies. Such "disembodied" technologies and practices greatly leverage the productivity of technology embodied in process equipment and the product itself.

However, because of their multidisciplinary nature and broad, multi-industry scope of use, industry underinvests in the development and utilization of these generic manufacturing practices. Nations, such

---

[3] Many infratechnologies and much of what is defined here as management practice would be defined in the traditional economics literature as "disembodied technologies", meaning that they are techniques for using the technology embodied in physical equipment.

as Japan and Germany, that have emphasized the cooperative development, standardization, and wide dissemination of such practices have experienced significantly greater growth in shares of global markets. These nations have instituted a range of programs to capture the inherent "economies of scope", with subsequent economic benefits in terms of increased quality and productivity. Both research institutions and technology transfer centers have taken on this role.

Major examples of evolving manufacturing practice that are having particularly significant impact include

> **Concurrent Engineering (CE)** -- the simultaneous design of products and production processes optimizes both the quality of the final product and the efficiency (productivity) of the production process;

> **Total Quality Management (TQM)** -- a total-organization concept for quality assurance that has been embraced in all industrialized nations as a means for significantly improving the quality of manufactured products, the manufacturing process, and, in fact, the entire corporate organization.

In economies such as the United States that are characterized by non-integrated, multi-enterprise industry structures, firms must be encouraged to coordinate various elements of management practice to help achieve the same levels of standardization attained by Japanese firms through more rigid organizational (*Keiretsu*) integration. As the following chapters will show, this infrastructure role is slowly being taken on by several types of institutions, both public and private, ranging form consortia to government laboratories.

Implementing New Infrastructure Roles

Industrialized nations are in various stages of evolving and implementing strategies for providing technology infrastructure elements, in particular, generic technology and infratechnology. These competitive factors have led to the growing need for a model, such as the one summarized by Figure 3-2, as the conceptual basis for strategy formulation and new growth policies.

In this evolutionary process, several themes are becoming accepted:

o   although technology is the single most important determinant of long-term economic growth, it does not automatically move from laboratory to marketplace, nor does it readily become widely used within an economic sector;

o   because the typical civilian technology is a complex entity, consisting of a number of proprietary and nonproprietary elements, a variety of private and public institutions must make critical contributions at the right times; and,

o   for technology to make its required contribution to competitiveness and economic growth in general, private and public institutions that produce it must be integrated at several stages with business and economic institutions.

However, moving from these general themes to a specific national strategy with assigned functions and appropriate levels of resources requires a comprehensive policy structure. A number of nations in both Europe and Asia have over several decades developed their individual models of the functions for both public and private institutions that contribute to a technology-based economy. Moreover, these models specify relationships among institutions that perform strategic planning, fund or conduct research and development, transfer various elements of civilian technology, and facilitate rapid commercialization and market penetration.

Where models have been continually improved over time, implementation of superior infrastructure policies have occurred and those nations' domestic industries have gained competitive advantage. *It is not that an optimal model exists.* Rather, once a consensus on a reasonable one is achieved, a nation can energize itself and accelerate its rate of economic growth. In fact, beyond having a workable model to serve as the basis for strategic planning, the most important attribute of a nation's overall strategy is *adaptability*. Japan has become a superb example of adaptive planning, constantly altering long-term "visions" of future technology applications and the necessary technology investment and infrastructure support.

One example of the requirement to adapt the conceptual model is a trend in manufacturing technologies that blurs the distinction between the generic technology and the supporting infratechnology. A decade ago, the generic technology and infratechnology elements of the typical manufacturing technology were largely separate. Infratechnologies were important for R&D and post-production acceptance testing. However, over the intervening period, trends toward automation, concurrent engineering, and total quality management to achieve higher quality and productivity have resulted in the integration of infratechnologies and the generic technologies (and their applications).

A particularly important example of this trend is the integration of measurement functions into the production process in order to effect real-time process control. This approach enables higher yields and greater quality by correcting design and production errors as they occur, rather than waiting to the end of the production run to detect unacceptable product. To be effective, both corporate strategy and technology infrastructure policy must adapt to this integration by re-defining R&D objectives, manufacturing organization and practice, etc.

A major question is what do such trends in technology infrastructure mean for a nation's long-term ability to compete in global markets. Competitiveness is a multi-faceted concept, but in the final analysis it connotes an economy's ability to generate domestic growth and export earnings which add to a steadily increasing standard of living. This statement is not the same as the objective of attaining a positive trade balance. The latter can be attained through depreciation of the exchange rate -- along with a decline in the standard of living. In the modern world, steady increases in a nation's standard of living can only be achieved through the acquisition and effective use of technology.

In large, developed economies such as the United States, the appropriate economic growth strategy requires that a *portfolio* of a substantial number of emerging and strategic technologies be under development at any point in time to diversify risk and broaden the future industrial base. This is a very different concept from the hotly debated "targeted industry" strategy.

In the latter approach, a few technologies among many of equal rank are singled out as priorities and given intensive government support. Such a strategy may be the only feasible one for a smaller industrialized or developing economy -- although such strategies must be tied to a multinational infrastructure. However, a large, technology-based economy can and must continually nurture its comparative advantage -- a diversified technological base -- by simultaneously pursuing development of a large number of emerging technologies and their supporting infrastructure.

To implement such a concept requires (1) a comprehensive conceptual framework of technology-based competition and (2) an effective planning process. Without the first, inaccurate strategy and policy analysis result, and, without the second, poor use of analysis in designing and implementing strategies and policies occurs. Because of such dysfunctions, certain technologies will receive excessive attention, while others will be largely ignored.

An example of the latter, is microwave technology. It lacks a singular and organized private-sector constituency and thus does not even show up on critical technology lists. The only government entity in the United States to have an explicit program to support commercial applications is a small effort by the Electronics and Electrical Engineering Laboratory of NIST. Yet, microwave components and devices account for almost $40 billion in annual shipments in the United States, which constitute about one-seventh of the total value of shipments for electronics.

Such imbalances in attention to and hence infrastructure support for critical technologies will occur without a systematic analytical and planning effort by industry and government. The proliferation of emerging technologies along with more mature technologies with significant economic impact complicates already difficult technology infrastructure planning problems created by the shortening of technological life cycles.

Support for R&D. Many of the emerging technologies that will provide a competitive advantage in the 1990s need modest but critical infrastructure support. A significant portion of this support will be focused on early-phase or "pre-competitive" research. A few "enabling" or "leveraging" technologies have such broad downstream market impacts and create such large upstream demand on component markets that they may warrant special research support. Examples are advanced (engineered) materials and optoelectronics. Others, such as high-definition imaging systems (HDIS), biotechnology, and factory automation (specifically, flexible computer-integrated manufacturing or FCIM), also require substantial infrastructure support. A particularly important characteristic of several of these technologies, such as HDIS and FCIM, is their "systems" character. This characteristic has important implications for the type and magnitude of infrastructure support.

The first major effort in the United States to increase the supply of technology infrastructure was the 1984 National Cooperative Research Act. Two factors motivated this piece of legislation. First, other industrialized nations, particularly Japan, were increasingly promoting cooperative research with some apparent success. Second, the increasing pressures of foreign competition required adaptation of the traditional U.S. philosophy of competing. The conventional wisdom was that cooperation of any kind, including early-phase R&D was anti-competitive and U.S. antitrust laws so stipulated. The 1984 act relaxed these inhibitions for "pre-competitive research". In the six years following the promulgation of this Act, approximately 200 notices of intent to form a research consortium were filed with the Antitrust Division of the Department of Justice.

While this activity significantly expanded the scope as well as the depth of resources available for producing technology infrastructure, the specific rationales and hence roles for consortia have not been completely thought out. For example, SEMATECH has been labeled a "model" for cooperative research. It is, in fact, a quite unusual case compared to the other consortia formed since 1984.[4]

In a technology-based economic growth framework, research consortia are formed for several reasons: (1) economies of *scope* exist and are not captured by individual firms; that is, firms have less than comprehensive market strategies with respect to the potential applications of the technology and therefore will underinvest; (2) the research process is *complex*; that is, a wide range of complementary research skills and research facilities, not totally available in individual firms, are required to achieve efficiency at the targeted phase of the research process; and (3) economies of *scale* exist with respect to the research process, so that resource pooling is needed to make the risk-

---

[4] It does, however, have significant implications for future government-industry cooperation and will be discussed in detail in the next chapter.

adjusted rate of return on the research attractive to individual firms.[5]

For emerging technologies with high technical risk, capital-intensive R&D, and systems integration requirements, the scale and scope effects can reduce individual company investment to levels well below the minimum thresholds needed for market penetration and a competitive position in global markets. In the United States, these factors have been influential in significantly restraining investment in technologies such as optoelectronics and high-definition imaging systems.

Taken together, these three factors provide a strong argument for using consortia. The failure of individual firms to capture the economies of scope reduces their expected benefits from the technology. The complexity and scale factors further reduce the expected return. These market imperfections occur primarily at specific points in the life cycle of the technology. For example, one major problem area resulting in underinvestment occurs during early-phase (generic) technology research. In this case, the assessment that the above factors make the targeted research "pre-competitive" provides the basic rationale for industry and government cooperation. Such targeted early-phase technology research is indicated by the shaded area in Figure 3-3.

This philosophy, in effect, moves the "pre-competitive line", which divides *individual* private investment from cooperative private or combined public-private investment, upward to include early-phase R&D. The adjustment is a change from the traditional government role of supporting only basic research, and it is the same basic philosophy that has evolved in other industrialized nations over several decades. In special cases, such as the serious problems of the U.S. semiconductor industry in the area of memory circuits, this line has been moved upward all the way to the "pilot-plant" stage.

---

[5] For example, employees of several firms participating in SEMATECH observed that they had learned considerably more in the year or so of their association with this consortium, than they could have learned in their parent companies due to the cross fertilization of research cultures, perceptions, and simply technical exchanges. Similarly, member firms of several applications for funding to the new Advanced Technology Program at NIST pointed out that the application process served as a catalyst to initiate joint planning for cooperative research that had been tried unsuccessfully in the past.

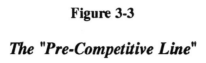

Figure 3-3

The "Pre-Competitive Line"

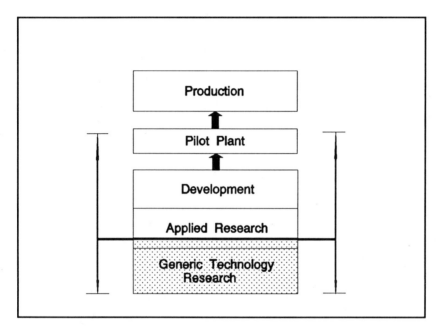

In contrast, when the market imperfection is more incremental and continuous in nature (for example, relatively small but sustained levels of underinvestment in applied R&D due to imperfections in risk preferences or capturability), then a technology infrastructure mechanism is not the appropriate strategy. Instead, financial incentives such as an R&D tax credit are a more efficient response, because the objective is to achieve *incremental* but sustained shifts in resource allocations by industry within a basically proprietary phase of R&D. In other cases, these more minor imperfections in later-phase R&D are handled by (usually two) firms combining complementary assets in a "joint venture".[6]

---

[6] It is important to note the differences between research consortia and joint ventures, because they are functionally different and therefore have different policy as well as strategic implications. R&D joint ventures combine complementary assets,

In the mid-1970s, Japan perceived the inefficiencies in the existing industry and research structures in the United States and Europe. They therefore turned to a new technology-based growth model, reflecting the externalities in early-phase technology research. An early and successful application of this model was semiconductor technology. In 1976, they launched their now-famous VLSI project. In four years, this cooperative research project between industry and government had caught up with and, to some degree, passed U.S. and European firms in semiconductor processing technology.

In a second, less-appreciated application of this model, Japan pursued the economies of scope inherent in the processing technology by establishing in 1979 a similar cooperative research project in the important area of optoelectronics. Optoelectronics is a critical technology for communications, data and image storage and retrieval, and possibly data processing (through optical computing). Through *cooperative* planning and subsequent cooperative research at the generic technology stage, the Japanese were able to accelerate the optoelectronics technology to the *applied* research stage. At this point, the Japanese Government basically removed itself from the technology development process (i.e., the pre-competitive line had been crossed). Individual Japanese companies, having the advantage of an early technological lead now greatly increased their *individual* investments in applied optoelectronics R&D. The result is Japanese dominance in this critical technology.[7]

---

which include actual proprietary technology assets as well as research skills to achieve economies of scale and scope or time compression. Thus, the joint venture announced in December 1990 between Motorola and Toshiba to develop chip sets for HDTV applications combines Motorola's microprocessor technology assets with Toshiba memory circuit capabilities to develop a proprietary chip set compatible with the so-called MUSE standard for direct satellite HDTV broadcasts. Texas Instruments and NHK have a joint venture with similar objectives.

[7] Many more examples can be offered of economies of scope and its importance in achieving long-term competitive position. Advanced components of emerging information technology systems offer good cases in point, including displays (miniature televisions, computer monitors, automotive map navigation), storage technology (digital audio tape, high-performance computer disk technology), and optical storage (consumer compact and laser discs, industrial applications such as training, archiving, etc.). See National Advisory Committee on Semiconductors [1991, vol. 2, p. 3-4].

Over the 1980s, the Japanese have applied this model in one emerging technology after another. They support a wide range of technologies through the research consortium mechanism. Support for early-phase technology research is given to emerging technologies that industry and government have *jointly* determined have significant economic potential. The Japanese Government is therefore neither focusing on a few "picked" technologies, nor is it making funding decisions unilaterally.

In addition, the Japanese have understood much better than others that the typical industrial technology is not an isolated entity. Thus, while most support programs are targeted at individual technologies, the Japanese view is that maximum economic gain is only realized when developed technologies are also "fused" to create yet another tier of market applications. The term *"gijutsu yugo"* or "technology fusion" first appeared in the MITI *Vision of 21st Century Industrial Society* in 1986, and has been evolving since that time.[8]

One implication of the stated objective of achieving more balanced growth is a *redirection* of technology-funding, although a more accurate prediction would probably be that the growth in funding will come in *new* areas through expansion rather than redirection. To some extent, the continuing diversification of Japan's R&D portfolio is already leading them in this direction, as stated in MITI's *International Trade and Industrial Policy in the 1990s.*[9]

This document continues to emphasize the Japanese focus on flexibility and a systems approach to the development and use of technology. The later is exemplified by a continuing high regard for

---

[8] For example, the Human Frontiers Science program for research in biometrics was predicated on the promise of technology fusion: study how the brain works and you can make a better computer; study how cells transfer energy and you can devise new energy conservation technologies. In one of the MITI projects, called "Ultra-Advanced Manufacturing Systems", the aim is to apply such technologies as ion beam implantation, CVD, and patterning with excimer lasers to the fabrication of physically large products, such as propellers, artificial organs, and pipes for use in clean rooms [source: Microelectronics and Computer Technology Corp.]. Individual firms can hardly be expected to include such apparently unrelated applications in their market strategies, nor would they have the necessary technical and market capabilities. MITI views the low likelihood of such cross-applications as a major "market failure".

[9] Japan MITI [1990].

manufacturing in the face of increased demand for services and by emphasis on the importance of infrastructure, including standardization. The Japanese strategy of continuous improvement (*Kaizen*) is fairly well known. Less known is their systems approach to creativity. The management technique is the "lotus blossom" method, better known in Japan as the MY method.[10]

The Japanese have always paid considerable attention to industry structure as an element of growth policy. MITI's policy seems to broaden the criteria beyond the previous focus on economies of scale and scope, plus cash flow flexibility, to now include consideration of management, labor, customer, final consumer, and international interests. Small and medium firms are seen as essential to providing new ideas, innovations, and general creativity to the economic system.

The European Community is pursuing at least portions of the same general strategy through its EUREKA and ESPRIT programs. Neither Japan nor Europe can be said to be "targeting" specific technologies with these programs. In fact, the opposite is the case. They are supporting the capture of externalities in early-phase technology research across a wide range (i.e., a portfolio) of emerging technologies. The ultimate objective is to provide their domestic industries with a broad and deep *technology base* from which private firms will then make decisions about which specific market applications to pursue through applied R&D, investment in production facilities, and marketing.

It should be noted that Germany has implemented more aggressive R&D-support policies than Japan in terms of where the pre-competitive line is drawn. Several substantial programs were initiated in the 1980s in which small firms received 40 percent of *development* costs and 20 percent of subsequent capital expenditures. Such a policy constitutes support that goes beyond the generic

---

[10] Tatsuno [1989, pp. 8-9]. The "lotus blossom" method, developed by Yasuo Matsummura of the Clover Research Center, involves placing a "seed" (generic) technology, such as HDIS, at the center of the conceptual lotus blossom. Researchers and users are then asked to identify potential direct applications, which become the core for the next round of applications. This process is repeated again and again until hundreds of applications are generated. In addition to stimulating creativity, another clear advantage of this systems approach is an unsurpassed capturing of the economies of scope inherent in the generic technology.

technology research stage to encompass all of R&D and into the production stage.

Small and medium firms in Germany have been successful in targeting niche markets on a global basis in order to capture economies of scale. The German Government has, in effect, promoted a more diversified industry structure by aggressively helping these firms. At the other end of the policy spectrum, European countries are collectively using programs such as JESSI (the European counterpart to SEMATECH) to not only advance generic technology research but also to promote integration of a European electronics industry which is viewed as too segmented.[11]

Support for Commercialization. Major dysfunctions have occurred in the ability of a number of industrialized economies to translate the results of R&D into commercially successful products and processes. Reasons include out-of-date industry structures (particularly insufficient vertical integration), poor intrafirm organization (particularly inadequate integration of R&D, production, and marketing), and high levels of unwillingness to assume the risks associated with new technologies. These problems interact with each other and collectively inhibit rates of investment in new technology. Because aggregate productivity growth is driven in the long run primarily by widespread acquisition and use of technology and associated management practices, the existing dysfunctions must be addressed.

Contrary to some elements of the economics literature, technical knowledge does not *transfer* or *diffuse* without cost. In fact, considerable effort is often required by individual firms to acquire and internalize generic technology so that it can be effectively used in subsequent internal applied R&D. Studies have shown that direct personal contact is the single most effective means of transferring technical knowledge. Thus, research consortia by providing direct

---

[11] JESSI stands for Joint European Silicon Semiconductor Initiative. It is an ambitious eight-year, $4 billion cooperative research program by 40 electronics firms and the EC Commission, Germany, Belgium, France, the United Kingdom, Italy and the Netherlands. The objectives include not only developing technology to produce memory and logic circuits using 0.3-micron feature size by 1996, but also developing equipment, materials, and design tools. Original projected funding levels were between $400 million and $500 million per year, to be funded 50 percent by the participants and 25 percent each by the EC and the national governments.

contact among a number of firms have a second potential advantage in addition to capturing externalities in early-phase research -- namely, efficient technology transfer.[12]

There are significant economies of scale in the facility/skill requirements for providing the transfer of technical knowledge, which create the rationale for government assistance in reducing state-of-the art technologies to levels which can be readily absorbed. These conditions were one factor in the creation of the Regional Centers for Manufacturing Technology (MTC) program (under NIST) to transfer manufacturing technologies to small and medium firms. Transfer of the actual manufacturing technology can be combined with transfer of associated manufacturing practices. The direct contact and personnel requirements for efficient transfer are being accomplished in cooperation with regional government and educational institutions.

However, the current five MTCs (funded at an annual rate of $16 billion) are just the beginning of what is required to upgrade the production technology of major elements of U.S. manufacturing. The Germans, for example, have a substantial network of technical institutes for achieving this type of technology transfer, and Japan, an economy two-thirds the size of the United States, has about 170 technology transfer centers funded at a level of $500 million annually.

Creating a viable technology base is one step, effectively and quickly utilizing it is another. U.S. industry is particularly bad at sharing generic, competitively neutral information in a timely manner. In fact, defining such information as competitively neutral has been a major barrier to getting as fast a start in follow-on R&D, as do the Japanese when a technological breakthrough occurs.

Support for Market Development. A number of successful industries in European and Asian nations have focused on *market share* as the primary strategy objective, believing that all other strategic objectives follow from this one. In today's global markets, market share is determined by the six critical competitive factors identified in Chapter 1: technological innovation, design and process flexibility, quality, productivity, timing (speed-to-market), and marketing/services.

---

[12] As will be discussed in Chapter 4, effective technology transfer from a research consortium requires considerable planning and organizational adjustment by both the consortium and the member firms.

Technology is the main driver of the first four and, surprising to some, is increasingly important for the last two. Other factors are also important (organizational strategies, human resources development, supplier relationships, etc.), but they are subservient to the six primary ones, which are, in turn, the drivers of market share.

The intrinsic complexity of new technologies creates externalities. When new technologically-advanced products enter the marketplace, a substantial level of uncertainty typically accompanies claims for enhanced performance. Buyers and sellers often disagree over methods for verifying this performance. Disputes can lead to protracted efforts involving considerable cost, as both buyer and seller allocate engineers and other resources to the task of resolving the disputes by trying to rationalize, say, different existing measurement infratechnologies. Independent efforts can even be undertaken to develop product acceptance algorithms, when none are available.

Without an agreed upon measurement infratechnology and other technical bases for promulgating a consensus standard on acceptance testing, transaction costs associated with performance verification will be high. Such costs not only add to the market price of the good but delay market penetration. Bilateral agreements (between two firms) on standards are very inefficient. Typically, the proliferation of competing acceptance test methods only adds to aggregate transaction costs. The cumulative effect is slow diffusion of the new technology.

Increasingly, even when such disputes are resolved in the domestic market, major foreign markets may have evolved different solutions, based on different infratechnologies and hence standards. Such situations result in barriers to the penetration of foreign markets by domestic firms. Moreover, foreign firms can sometimes penetrate the domestic market while domestic firms attempt to develop and agree on the technical basis for acceptance testing and other infrastructure for reducing transaction costs.

The Dynamics of Technology-Based Competition

The competitive elements of the typical technology-based industry as described so far are necessarily simplified in a number of ways, including representing them in a static mode. Obviously, the dynamics of technology-based economic activity is an extremely

Figure 3-4

The Technology/Product Life Cycle

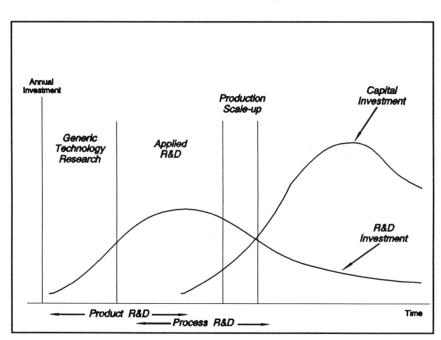

important aspect of overall competitive position analysis. The *time* variable exerts increasing influence on competitive position, as technology life cycles shorten through increased R&D worldwide, as production technology becomes increasingly flexible and hence responsive to changes in demand, and as market development strategies become more global and generally sophisticated.

Figure 3-4 provides a simplified representation of a typical expenditure pattern over major stages of a technology life cycle. The relative as well as the absolute time periods for each phase in the technology-based growth process will, of course, vary among technologies and global competitive structures. Moreover, it is well known that the research and development process is not totally linear, in that "feedback loops" occur through all phases. These feedback loops convey essential information for adjusting future R&D and production directions. They are therefore an essential management tool and their role will be discussed later.

The point to be made is that the R&D process does have an important linear dimension, namely that from one phase to the succeeding one the technology becomes more applied or market-oriented. The important variables are the general patterns of R&D and capital expenditures and how the composition of these expenditures changes over the technology and product life cycles. The expenditures on generic technology research are relatively low compared to later-phase applied R&D, especially development.[13] However, these expenditures are critical because of (1) their broad impacts and (2) the critical timing effect on later-phase R&D and ultimate commercialization decisions.

Pre-competitive generic technology research becomes a critical lever in accelerating all subsequent steps in the technology-based economic process. It is also true that the subsequent phases of R&D and the production and market development stages have their own efficiency requirements that can be met by other types of technology infrastructure or by solely proprietary activity by individual firms. Various types of standards, for example, greatly affect the timing as well as the composition of capital investment decisions, and hence the shape of the capital investment curve in Figure 3-4. Practices such as concurrent engineering (CE) and total quality management (TQM) are important determinants of the efficiency of applied R&D and production.

A major objective of technology-based strategies is to compress in time the expenditure curves in Figure 3-4, without significantly raising their height. The emphasis here is on *all* expenditure curves, i.e., the entire technology life cycle. While generic technology is essential as the "grist" for the rest of the cycle, the Japanese have proven over and over how this technology can be acquired and then efficiently applied and improved upon in succeeding R&D phases and into production. In other words, private investment by firms and the supporting infrastructure must seek not

---

[13] For example, in 1989, U.S. expenditures for development were approximately three times that for applied research, which, in turn, were about 50 percent greater than expenditures for basic research. U.S. National Science Board [1989].

only to decrease the time required per stage, but also increase the efficiency with which each stage is conducted.

Figure 3-5

Linkages with the Semiconductor Industry

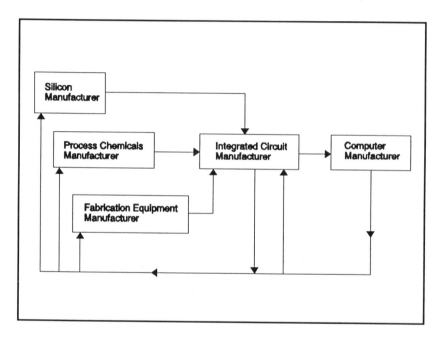

Up to this point, the focus has been on the "typical technology-based industry". However, much of the analysis in subsequent chapters will revolve around the dynamic interaction among industries. For example, the issue of vertical integration in the semiconductor industry has been analyzed with respect to long-run competitiveness.[14] In Japan, a significant separate semiconductor industry does not exist, as is the case in the United States. Instead, semiconductor production is part of a vertically-integrated *electronics* industry, which, in turn, is embodied within the even more broadly integrated *Keiretsu* structure.

---

[14] See Tassey [1990].

The interdependence of technology-based industries, using semiconductors as an example, is shown in Figure 3-5. Each industry has a life cycle similar to the one in Figure 3-4. The individual industry life cycles must be coordinated for aggregate (multi-industry or production-chain) efficiency to be achieved. Industry structure, as well as behavior, play important roles in achieving this coordination. Moreover, this group of industries is only one part of a much larger group of interdependent industries that ultimately serve final product and service demand in an advanced economy. In the previous chapter, Figure 2-1 showed this broad interdependence for information services. How industries organize themselves and interact have significant implications for the roles of technology infrastructure and the mechanisms by which it is provided.

Technology-Based Competition in the 1990s

Prior discussion of the conceptual model has focused on the typical technology and shown how firms add value in the economic system by drawing upon various elements of technology infrastructure and combining these and traditional inputs with application of their own competitive assets.

Underlying this presentation is the traditional *sequential* process of adding value. However, the linear aspect of this process is relentlessly being replaced by a much more *simultaneous* construct in which the several stages of technology-based economic activity overlap in time. This is an evolutionary step in the basic strategies for technology-based competition that goes beyond the current approach to improving overall efficiency and time compression by using a sequential process with feedback loops.

The simultaneity concept offers considerably greater competitive advantage. The Japanese, not surprisingly, are the current leaders in the conceptualization and implementation of this approach. They have recently begun to further compress the product life cycle by deciding in advance that they will abandon a new product within a given period of time. This strategy has the effect of increasing the degree of overlap of successive product life cycles and hence forcing R&D, production, and marketing to also interact concurrently to a greater degree. Figure 3-6 indicates the evolution of

technology-based competition towards a process whereby simultaneity
gains importance relative to linearity.[15]

Figure 3-6

Evolution of Technology-Based Competition

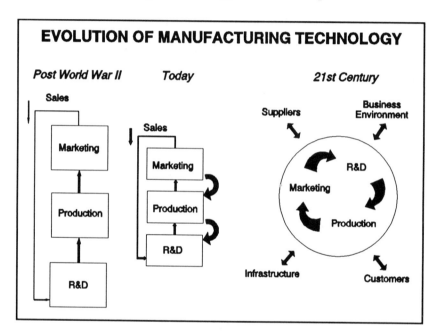

In the post-World War II environment, the typical technology
and related product life cycles were quite linear and stretched out in
time. Feedback loops existed in only a minor way, as indicated by the
left-hand diagram in Figure 3-6. In the last several decades, more
efficiency has been added to this process by strengthening feedback
loops between stages as well as by improving the technology and
general management practice within each stage. Steady advances in
computer-aided design (CAD) have greatly speeded up the R&D
process. Production automation has increased yields and improved

---

[15] Elaine Bunten-Mines, Rick Jackson, and John Simpson of NIST contributed
to this conceptualization.

quality. Information technology has benefitted those two stages and also the market development stage in which quick and accurate customer feedback has become an essential part of improving competitive position.

Still, the majority of improvement has occurred *within* individual stages. Now, new techniques such as *design for manufacturing* and *rapid prototyping*, and new management practices such as *total quality management* have begun to link the three basic stages. This increased linkage is represented by the stronger feedback loops in the middle diagram. Yet, the process retains a significantly linear character.

The right hand diagram shows how the future technology-based industry may be conceptualized. Here the feedback loops are replaced by more or less complete integration of the three basic stages. The circular flow representation indicates the high degree of simultaneity of decision making and response among the stages of economic activity. Flexibility in responding to increasingly differentiated customer demand in increasingly shorter periods of time will require rapid design change and virtually instantaneous manufacturing response. Management practices such *just-in-time (JIT)* delivery and *concurrent engineering (CE)* have begun the evolution toward a more integrated economic structure. That such an evolution is occurring can be seen in plants such as Motorola's "Bandit" plant in Florida, which can respond to customer orders for pagers within four hours (that is, actually manufacturing the product in four hours from the time they get an order).

Even more significant for this evolutionary trend is the increasing overlap of what heretofore have been separate product life cycles. The sophistication of strategy and management practice will have to undergo a major quantum leap forward in order to effectively manage simultaneous product and process change, not only within one technology but across several linked and overlapping ones.

However, significant change across an economy and over time will only be possible with major improvements in both hardware and software technology as well as substantial contributions from new technology infrastructure. In the 1960s and 1970s, automation occurred in individual manufacturing steps. Changes to the activity at a particular step had to be physically made. For example, a numerically controlled (NC) tool has to have a paper tape punched and manually inserted in the tool every time a design change is required. After additional manual adjustments by the NC tool's operator to account for the peculiarities of that particular tool, the part could then be produced in volume.

In the 1980s, *flexibility* began to be built into manufacturing systems so that design changes could be electronically communicated to the machine and its operation reconfigured automatically. However, such *flexible manufacturing systems (FMS)* were limited to groups of machine performing a few sequential steps. These "manufacturing cells" still were isolated in a functional sense from other steps in the R&D and manufacturing as well as marketing stages. Not only is the so-called "automated factory" not yet a reality, but major technical and infrastructure advances will have to occur before such a factory can be linked "seamlessly" with R&D and marketing to create the simultaneous economic system shown in Figure 3-6.

The implications of total integration, when achieved, are profound: *virtually instant response to demands for custom design with production volume as low as a single unit.* Many of the changes in industry strategy and structure that will be required for this goal to be reached are discussed in Chapters 4 through 7 in the context of needed changes in the supporting technology infrastructure. The point to be made here is that for a model of technology-based competition to evolve which is represented by the right hand diagram of Figure 3-6, the interfaces within and between the stages in the technology-based economic process will have to become invisible from a functional point of view.

Moreover, this discussion has focused on a so-called typical technology-based firm. Some of the more burdensome interfaces are the boundaries between two firms. The producer-user interface is a well-documented barrier to time compression and overall efficiency gains within a vertical production chain. A number of new mechanisms are coming into increasing use to reduce these interfirm barriers (JIT, corporate partnering, electronic data standards, etc.). A traditional way of removing these barriers is for firms to merge and thereby remove existing obstructions due to different organizational and strategic philosophies and protocols.

Such vertical and horizontal integration has been the hallmark of many Japanese industries. Where outright organizational integration has not occurred, the Japanese have used the *Keiretsu* structure in which firms are tightly interlocked through cross ownership, interlocking boards of directors, etc. Thus, the circle in Figure 3-6, which represents a highly integrated firm could be thought of as expanding in size as organizational merger and integration occur over time. Such an economy would evolve toward fewer but larger firms or groups of interlocked firms.

For economies like the United States that have achieved much economic progress from the existence of small and medium innovative firms, such a prospective evolution toward Keiretsu-like industry structures should be viewed with great concern. Many have predicted this path, such as Ferguson [1990]. However, the potential benefits of seamless integration among all stages in the technology-based economic process extend beyond the boundaries of the single firm to a network of vertically-*aligned* firms that can remain independent, realizing the consequent benefits of independent creativity and opportunity, while gaining at least the same level of efficiency as vertically-integrated firms.

For example, a promising development in microprocessor technology is RISC (Reduced Instruction Set Computing). The most successful RISC architectures are from relatively young and small companies -- Sun Microsystems, MIPS Computer Systems, and Cypress Semiconductor. The computer industry, which uses these chips, has undergone tremendous change in just one decade. Of the six largest (mainframe) computer manufacturers in 1980, only IBM remains a leader.[16] Through innovations in microcomputers, they have been replaced by startups such as Apple, Compaq, Dell, and Sun Microsystems.[17]

However, small, innovative companies have to be able to sell their limited product lines into the production chain. Thus, compatibility problems and other standards-related issues must be efficiently resolved. As Chapter 6 will demonstrate, the type of standards infrastructure that evolves along with a new technology can

---

[16] The other five, Burroughs, Univac, NCR, Control Data, and Honeywell have been virtually eliminated from the industry.

[17] The argument for the continued competitiveness of small semiconductor and computer firms is made eloquently by T. J. Rogers, Chairman of Cypress Semiconductor. See, for example, his testimony before the House of Representatives Committee on Science, Space and Technology's Subcommittee on Technology and Competitiveness, July 1991.

greatly alter opportunities for success for firms of all sizes. Under an industry structure facilitating innovative opportunity, Figure 3-6 would evolve into an industry model consisting of many circles, representing many independent firms whose activities are connected across their functional interfaces.

Multiple firms or enterprises will have to be "seamlessly" linked by a complex and effective infrastructure in order to achieve the same degree of simultaneity as portrayed for one firm by the circular flow of economic activity in Figure 3-6. The types of infrastructure necessary to achieve "*multi-enterprise*" integration include standards for electronic product data transfer, process models to improve, for example, manufacturing logistics, and demonstrations and test beds to help firms implement the new manufacturing systems concepts within the broader industry structure.

The Japanese, of course, see manufacturing evolving this way as well. They continue to invest huge amounts in manufacturing automation and associated manufacturing practice. Recognizing that they do not have all the research elements in place, they have proposed international research consortia, such as the Intelligent Manufacturing System (IMS) project, to collectively produce the needed infrastructure.

Application of The Model to HDTV

The product technologies relevant for applications such as "high-definition television" or HDTV are evolving under a fairly typical model of industrial competition in which externalities ("spillovers"), incorrect strategies, and mismatches between domestic industry structure and that of foreign competition combine to slow attainment of competitive position. Such problems are particularly severe during the early phases of a technology's development. For example, externalities retard efficient investment in generic technology research. By defining such technology as "pre-competitive", it is dubbed infrastructure and can then be produced through more efficient mechanisms. Joint industry-government programs are under way in Europe and Japan to accelerate the pre-competitive technologies that provide the basis for future applications of high-definition, multi-media digital communications.

However, in the United States, the abortive industry-government debate over HDTV in 1989 set back what evolutionary process existed for moving toward similar policies. This debate should have been over technology infrastructure for the broad range of applications of the underlying generic technology -- of which HDTV is but one application. Because HDTV is only one of a number of business and consumer applications, the target technology was correctly perceived by critics as too focused for government support. Moreover, because HDTV was viewed as a consumer good, the argument was again correctly made that such a downstream application would benefit only a relatively small market -- too small, it was argued to "pull" the upstream production chain (semiconductor components, displays, etc.).

The correct approach would have been to propose a program to provide technology infrastructure for the generic technology, *high-definition imaging systems* (HDIS), from which HDTV and a number of other applications will be derived. The irony of the current disorganized U.S. approach is that, as has often been the case in other areas of technology, U.S. firms have *individually* been very innovative at the component level.

The European and the Japanese have pursued organized strategies, but ones that are focused on less advanced (analog) technology. Of course, the Japanese have demonstrated in the past that initially pursuing a lower-level version of the technology is part of a conscious plan to gain production and marketing experience, while more advanced forms are evolving.

U.S. firms have targeted the more advanced (digital) technology. However, without a systems-level strategy, which requires much technology infrastructure to be in place, any U.S. technological advantage may be wasted once again. This case is an excellent example of how not understanding the process by which a major technology evolves and spawns many important applications in diverse market leads to paralysis and subsequent underinvestment.[18]

---

[18] A 1989 Congressional Budget Office study took just this approach, criticizing proposals for supporting HDTV that claimed significant upstream demand would be created for components such as semiconductors. The study did not propose an alternative technology focus that would justify a major government program. The Japanese and the European have no such conceptualization difficulties. The Europeans are collectively pouring $300 million into EUREKA Project No. 95

Simply using a more generic label for the core technology, such as HDIS, would at least have created a calmer environment in which to make more intelligent strategy and policy decisions. However, this step would not have been sufficient, because the basic policy processes were not in place for identifying an "enabling" technology and then rationalizing industry and government roles for providing the technology's elements and its supporting infrastructure.

HDIS actually encompasses a series of technologies, including displays, image processing and storage, and various electronic and optical components used in the production and transmission of information. The avowed policy targets therefore should have been such pre-competitive generic technologies as high-resolution displays, application-specific integrated circuits (ASICs), and supporting interface standards and other infratechnologies.[19]

Business applications of HDTV will precede consumer markets. High-quality imaging for information, advertising, promotion, training, etc., has great potential. In Japan, the long-term vision factor and the commitment to the required infrastructure has already promoted investment. For example, the Dentsu Advertising Agency has invested in software R&D for image creation that takes advantage of the extremely high resolution.

The enhanced definition of HDTV will even change the strategies of the support industries. HDTV provides such sharp detail that facial wrinkles of actors and actresses become conspicuous when conventional shooting methods are used. Consequently, the Shiseido Company has begun research on cosmetic methods to offset the

---

(HDTV prototype systems and standards). The Japanese have already invested huge sums in "generic HDTV" with estimates ranging from $750 million to $1.5 billion. They are pursuing the generic technology because they expect the broad applications in systems other than entertainment (including traffic control, plant monitoring, long distance diagnosis, and on-board navigation) to be "endless".

[19] The research programs of the National Institute of Standards and Technology (NIST) fit this latter model. They support generic technologies and infratechnologies that contribute to the broad digital imaging technology base. Specifically, NIST is pursuing five supporting technologies: high resolution vision, high resolution displays, real time signal processing, high data rate transmission, and high density information storage. Because these five areas support applications by a number industries, the resulting economies of scope cause the underinvestment phenomena that rationalizes the government support role.

clarity. A systems approach diffuses information on research needs and thereby promotes R&D in the right time frame.

Even more important in terms of rationalizing the right set of national strategies is the fact that the market applications of this set of technologies are diverse, including numerous electronics and computing industries, with both business and consumer uses. Applications range well beyond "TV sets" to include defense systems, computer displays, computer-aided design, and interactive video for training and marketing. Major components of these applications will be "interoperable" across these applications, hence yielding economies of scope to investment in the underlying generic technology.

Very large markets will develop for components such as displays and digital signal processing chips, not to mention versions of already widely used chips such as DRAMs. However, no company in any country is currently pursuing all of these markets. In fact, most are involved in one or, at most, two or three of them. Thus, economies of scope due to application diversity are not captured by individual firms and underinvestment results.

By not pursuing all elements of a technology and treating it as a system, initial competitiveness in single elements can be expected to erode. For example, computer-aided design (CAD), in which the United States is the current world leader, will become critically dependent on digital display capabilities. If the Japanese are allowed to dominate digital display processing, they will have gained a major advantage in challenging the lead of the U.S. CAD industry.

In support of the earlier discussion that pointed to the systems nature of many of the key emerging technologies, HDIS technologies will also create economies of scope by virtue of their use in integrated systems which merge the functions of several existing classes of products. For example, the "TV set" in the home is going to pack enough processing power and machine memory to serve as a stand-alone computer or as a node on a whole host of networks, which will provide services ranging from videotext to movie rentals to TV telephone systems.

The Japanese are also working to develop HDTV-standard displays and adapt them to personal computers. In keeping with their total systems approach to planning, they simultaneously are investing considerable resources in *multi-media database systems*, in which moving pictures, still pictures, voice and sound data, and text data from a variety of sources can all be accessed and processed on one machine, perhaps attached to a network. NEC and Mitsubishi Electric are particularly active in this area, which is destined to become the software brains of the TV/computer of the future.

The economies of scope can be even broader than the above discussion indicates. European and Japanese manufacturers are already planning to invest in a wide range of peripheral devices, such as printers, copying machines, cameras, and VTR players.[20] In fact, the Japanese have a label for this broader set of technologies: "multifunction, multi-media processing (MMP) technologies".

Japanese companies must view this technology as having important derived demand for semiconductors because several of them, including Sony and Matsushita, have established major new DRAM production facilities in anticipation of HDIS-related internal demand. Substantial demand for other classes of semiconductor components, such as SRAMs and processing chips, will arise as well. In fact, the Japanese already refer to VTRs as "IC hogs". Any system that processes image data is going to be memory-intensive. "Put any of these systems together and the memory requirements will expand exponentially.[21]

In 1991, two years after the abortive effort to establish a U.S. national program for this systems technology, a clearer view began to emerge of both the target set of technologies and the mechanisms to be used. No longer referred to as "HDTV", broader generic technology labels, such as "HDIS" were substituted. The multiple applications of the generic technology, which provided the rationale for industry-government cooperation were emphasized. Potential markets for such diverse products and services as education, teleconferencing, and financial services created increased support for providing not only the generic technology but other essential technology infrastructure, such as test beds and, in particular,

---

[20] VTR stands for *video transmission recorder*, which is a more appropriate name than *video cassette recorder* (VCR), given its role and configuration in future information systems.

[21] *Nihon Kogyo Shimbun* (Japan Industrial Daily), July 16, 1989. Mark Eaton , Director, International and Associated Programs for the Microelectronics and Computer Technology Corp. (MCC), provided this source as well as valuable insights into the HDTV issue.

standards that would allow the integrating character of the technology to be realized.

But, sufficient private investment will only be forthcoming for such a complex systems technology when institutional mechanisms and financial resources for providing these types of technology infrastructure are in place. So far, the process of providing it is just beginning. However, the needed infrastructure does not have to be totally available. The fact that an acceptable process is under way would be sufficient to elicit the desired private investment.

One particular area of the needed infrastructure for HDTV will be a set of technical network standards. The proposed North American version is Integrated Services Digital Network or ISDN. ISDN can be provided through both satellite and cable systems to offer so many new information service opportunities, in addition to a range of manufacturing roles, that established companies and entirely new ones will rush to make investments in this area -- once the nature of the infrastructure becomes apparent. This is already happening in Japan. Experimental broadcasting is underway to give manufacturers of high-definition vision receivers a "real-life" test bed for product engineering with respect to such important performance attributes as screen quality.

Strategy formulation will be helped greatly by realizing that HDTV is but one service that will be provided over ISDN. Small-scale ISDN services started in Japan in April 1988 as "INS-net 64" and the "INS-net 1500", with a higher capacity, started in August 1989. According to Japan's Ministry of Posts and Telecommunications (MPT), full deployment of ISDN in the Japanese economy would create an annual market just for terminals of over $100 billion.

Unfortunately, policy formulation can be stymied by apparently conflicting economic indicators. For example, existing and emerging major categories of equipment such as digital PBX (private branch exchange), the TV conference system, the TV telephone, and super high-speed facsimile can evolve up to a point without ISDN. Moreover, *image communications* -- the likely first major use of ISDN -- requires a large minimum potential market to generate investment. This is because ISDN is a public network and large numbers of subscribers are required to economically communicate with one another. Thus, demand for the services provided by ISDN much reach some threshold which is relatively high. This phenomenon is typical of complex technology-based infrastructure and must be addressed by public policy.

Such a situation creates a "chicken or egg" problem for both industry and government strategic planners. Without the infrastructure in place, demand growth is retarded; but without the expression of demand, investment in infrastructure is harder to rationalize.

In summary, the technology infrastructure underlying an emerging systems technology, such as HDTV, is not only complex but at least some of its elements have alternative forms until one form is chosen. Ignoring the importance of this infrastructure *and* the process by which it is put into place, can leave an entire national industry in a reduced competitive position, or no position at all.

Summary

Technology-based growth policies, now evolving around the world, are increasingly able to remove market imperfections in the three major stages of economic activity with the following results:

o   *The efficiency of early-phase R&D is increased so that technology life cycles are shortened without significantly raising costs.* This creates the critical competitive advantage of emerging technologies being available earlier which, in turn, enables the privately-funded applied R&D leading to commercialization to occur faster. Government programs in various nations, including laboratory research, government-industry research consortia, etc., have been able to advance generic technologies to the applied R&D phase for a range of economically important technologies such as ceramics, polymers, composites, biotechnology, computers, software, electronic components, superconductivity, optoelectronics, robotics, machine tools, etc. These more rapid advances give the domestic industry a running start in determining which applications of the generic technology to pursue, conducting the applied R&D, and reaching the marketplace ahead of foreign competitors;

o   *Commercialization is facilitated by more efficient technology transfer.* Government laboratories, research institutes, transfer centers and extension services, cooperative programs, trade associations, and other mechanisms have more rapidly diffused new technologies; wider use means higher percentages of a nation's economy will be introducing new products (innovations) at any point in time -- making a nation's economy as a whole more competitive; and

o *Market development is accelerated by productivity and quality programs, and by other infrastructure such as standards.* Market share is the single most important strategy variable for most industries; they therefore target faster productivity growth and quality improvement strategies to move quickly beyond initial commercialization to penetrate global markets and take market share away from lagging competitors in other nations.

The typical industrial technology used to be thought of as a "black box", i.e. a homogeneous entity that was created in a singular fashion and then used in one piece to drive economic activity. Today, industries and governments realize that global competitiveness in manufacturing requires several distinct elements: (1) *product* technologies, (2) *process* technologies, (3) supporting *infratechnologies*, and (4) a set of complex and sophisticated manufacturing *practices* to enable these technologies to be used effectively. Even these four basic categories are now viewed as having several distinct components.

Emerging product and process technologies, along with U.S. competitive positions relative to other nations have been identified and analyzed in numerous government and industry reports. The third category of technology elements, infratechnologies, which consists largely of measurement methods and science and engineering data, is so ubiquitous and the economic impacts so disguised that its importance has been overlooked until recently in the United States. The fourth category, manufacturing practices, has just begun to receive needed analysis. Such practices enable the product and process technologies as well as the infratechnologies to be efficiently developed and productively used by providing the overall organizational and market strategy frameworks in which the other three major technology elements must function.

The conceptual model presented here is intended to provide a more realistic view of the typical technology-based industry and the elements of technology infrastructure that support it. In the following chapters, various elements of this model will be expanded upon.

The most important points to be made here are (1) not only is technology-based competition more complex than many realize, but the elements of the typical industrial technology come from a range of diverse private and public sources that must coordinate their activities; (2) the major trend toward increased product variety is leading not only to demands for greater flexibility at the R&D and manufacturing stages, but is requiring enormous increases in the complexity of information and the speed with which it moves within and among firms, and (3) both the major technology elements and other supporting infrastructure (including information) must also be produced rapidly from diverse sources and disseminated quickly to an even more diverse industrial structure.

Appendix

Definitions of Terms

orismology: defined by Webster's New Collegiate
Dictionary as "the science of defining technical terms"

applied research: the conversion of generic technology into specific
prototype products and processes with fairly well-defined performance
parameters, that can be used to make market-specific development
decisions. The technology has now been embodied in a configuration
which performs the generic function in specific ways (certain
applications or markets are the ultimate objective). Some attention
has been given to production and cost considerations in order to
estimate market penetration potential. The research output is a
commercial prototype in the sense that "proof of commercial concept"
has been achieved. (This endpoint contrasts with the endpoint of
generic technology research which is a *laboratory* prototype providing
"proof of technical concept"). "Proof of commercial concept" allows

the substantially greater resources typically required in the development stage to be committed.

> **Example:** the conversion of a *laboratory* prototype for a new integrated circuit into a *product* prototype which has specific performance parameters (say a 16-megabyte random access memory (RAM) chip with certain storage and access times and a specific circuit density); the achievement of this commercial prototype allows reasonable estimates of the manufacturing costs and interfaces with other electronic components before commitment to the development phase.

basic research: search for knowledge of scientific principles. Discovery of these principles does not lead nor is it intended to lead to an application (a new product or process). Thus, it is almost totally nonproprietary in character and, as a result, exhibits pervasive and systematic underinvestment by industry.

> **Example:** the discovery of certain principles of solid state physics which allow scientists to explain and predict semiconductor properties in certain classes of materials.

Note: To the Japanese, "basic" research has a different meaning. The Japanese use "basic" in the sense of "fundamental" or "undergirding", rather than theoretical. Thus, a portion of what they call basic research includes what is defined here as generic technology research.

competitiveness: the ability to systematically increase the performance, productivity and quality of products and services, so that the economy grows fast enough to increase the standard of living at desirable rates within the context of global markets.

In a more operational sense, *competitiveness at the industry level* means increasing the performance, productivity and quality of the economy's product and service mix in order to maintain substantial global market shares, without relying on currency depreciation. Market share is necessary to generate the cash flow which funds subsequent technology and product life cycles. *Competitiveness at the national level* means attaining and maintaining global market shares in enough industries to achieve a balanced and diversified growth pattern for the economy as a whole, so that the national standard of living increases at acceptable rates over time.

concurrent engineering: the simultaneous design of products and production processes so that, on the one hand, the production process is optimized with respect to the manufacturing requirements of the product (derived from its market performance requirements), and, on the other hand, the product is designed to facilitate efficient manufacture. Concurrent engineering enables, for example, quality-enhancing attributes to be designed into the product, while the production process is configured to ensure maximum yield, thereby increasing productivity. More broadly, concurrent engineering is the integration of product design, manufacturing approach, and servicing design.

demonstration: the temporary operation of a new technology for the purpose of either (1) confirming the commercial potential of the technology (in which case, it is a demonstration of a commercial prototype, i.e., the end of applied research, or (2) confirming the ability to manufacture the new product (i.e., confirming that development has been successfully completed and manufacturing scale-up can begin), or (3) revealing the infrastructure, such as product interfaces required for successful introduction into a market environment (i.e., the technology has been proven, but confirmation is needed of the ability of the new product to function in the larger system of technologies that constitute the marketplace configuration).

development: the honing of the commercial prototype into a form which can be produced in quantity at a cost that will achieve the desired market penetration. This stage involves the precise determination of product parameters, including packaging and interface specifications when appropriate, and an emphasis on manufacturing requirements.

> **Example:** the evolving of a commercial prototype integrated circuit into a configuration with specific geometries, materials, interfaces, and performance parameters, which can be produced at a unit cost

sufficient to penetrate the market for the existing
generation of memory circuits.

domestic firm: a firm in which the majority of total value added
results from operations within the domestic economy. According to
the Bureau of Economic Analysis, which is charged by Congress with
monitoring the activities of foreign firms in the United States, a
foreign *affiliate* is a firm operating in the United States that is 10
percent or more owned by foreigners. This definition is different from
a foreign-*controlled* firm, where presumably 51 percent or more of the
firm is owned by foreigners. Thus, a pure domestic firm would have
to be more than 90 percent or more owned by U.S. citizens.

dual-use technology: technologies that have both military and
commercial applications, where the applications, at a minimum, derive
from the same generic technology. Thus, parallel R&D efforts are
not required until possibly the final stages of development.

enabling technology: technologies which provide essential building
blocks for a number of applications. This term is often mistakenly
used interchangeably with *generic technology*. But, while the latter
refers to a *phase* in the R&D of a particular technology, the term
"enabling" refers to the wide *range of uses* that some technologies
permit in terms of downstream applications or markets.

> **Example**: semiconductors are a critical component in many
> products, ranging from televisions and VCRs to
> communications equipment to medical devices, and thus
> "enable" a wide range of applications.

generic technology research: the first phase in *technology* research;
the objective is to show that the *concept* for an eventual market
application "works" in a *laboratory* environment and thus reduce the
typically large *technical* risks before moving on to the more applied
phases of R&D.

More specifically, generic technology research is a major step
in the sequential evolution of a typical industrial technology. It is the
organization of scientific principles into a *functional technical concept*.
The term "functional" means that an ultimate market application is
the objective. This application objective distinguishes *technology*

research from *scientific* research. Use of the word "technical" implies that technical performance is the target at this phase of R&D rather than economic or market viability. Moreover, use of the word "concept" implies that individual performance parameters, which collectively comprise the targeted market objective, are not well defined at this early point in the R&D process.

Consequently, a research objective to pin down specific market performance attributes would not be a rational one, given the high levels of risk and uncertainty with respect to overall performance of the technology that exist at that point. Rather, the research objective is to show that the technological concept "works" in a laboratory environment. Narrowing individual performance parameters for specific market applications is accomplished in later phases of the R&D process, once the initial high levels of technical risk have been reduced during this phase.

> **Example:** the use of principles of solid state physics (the basic science) to demonstrate in the laboratory the technical *concept* of an integrated circuit which performs memory functions; that is, the research results demonstrate the potential to perform the function of data storage and retrieval faster and in greater volume using more equivalent transistors per square centimeter of silicon substrate (i.e., the chip). Success of this phase means that the technical risk has been reduced to the point that investments in specific applications can be rationalized.

horizontal integration: diversification on investment in product lines at the same level in the production chain (for example, several different types of integrated circuits).

infratechnology: practices and techniques, basic data, measurement methods, test methods, and measurement-related concepts which increase the productivity or efficiency of each phase of the R&D, production, and the market development stages of economic activity.

Infratechnologies are by nature widely used and thus have large nonproprietary elements from the point of view of individual firms. These infratechnologies include (1) evaluated scientific data used in the conduct of R&D, (2) measurement and test methods used in R&D, production control, and (buyer) acceptance testing for market transactions, and (3) highly accurate technical methods and procedures such as those used in calibrations of equipment.

Infratechnologies are not "embodied" in a product technology in the same way as the core technology (i.e., the generic technology). Instead, infratechnologies leverage and, in some cases, make possible the organization of core technology elements into efficiently functioning systems by, for example, providing algorithms for combining these elements with human factors to achieve corporate objectives such as total quality.

Infratechnologies also facilitate the development, manufacture, and marketing of applications of the core technology. For example, highly precise measurements and organized and evaluated scientific and engineering data are necessary for understanding, characterizing, and interpreting relevant research findings. Measurement and testing concepts and techniques also enable the process control necessary for higher quality and greater reliability at lower cost in production. Finally, infratechnologies provide buyers and sellers with mutually acceptable, low-cost methods of assuring that specified performance levels are met when technologically sophisticated products enter the marketplace.

> **Example**: each new generation of integrated circuits has a greater "packing density" (number of conducting lines per square inch of silicon chip) than the current generation; this performance-enhancing achievement requires narrowing channels (the conducting lines), but assurance of this achievement at the **research** stage requires an ability to measure the width of the "thinner" and more closely packed lines as well as to test the circuit's performance.
>
> Furthermore, the master copy of the circuit or "mask" must be aligned during **production** of the new chip, requiring additional measurement-related methods. Other measurement and test methods are needed for areas such as quality control and reliability testing. These methods collectively constitute the infratechnology for the efficient manufacture and sale of semiconductor devices. When the new integrated circuit is **marketed**, the customer will want assurance that all performance specifications have been met. This assurance requires test methods which are non-

destructive and mutually acceptable to both buyer and seller.

These and other infratechnologies are generally *competitively neutral*, in large part because of their typical widespread and uniform use. Specifically, they are often separate or "disembodied" (but not always) from the proprietary technology developed by industry. This fact is often reflective of the substantial breadth of applications (economies of scope) that exist. In addition, the required agreement among competitors and among buyers and sellers as to what specific method to adopt makes infratechnologies nonproprietary in character. The combination of these facts means that much of their development needs to be accomplished by R&D cooperatives and government laboratories, and then disseminated as standards by industry groups.

innovation: the *first* commercialization or market introduction of a technology. In the case of a new product technology, an innovation is the first market introduction. In the case of a process technology, an innovation is the first use to produce products for sale.

Innovation is a very important event, but its importance has been overstated because of misuse of the term. In particular, it has been used to describe aggregate market penetration by the technology. Thus, its definition has been broadened to cover the entire technology life cycle, including not just the first market use but the stream of improvements that typically follow. Statements such as "innovation determines productivity growth" are misleading. One firm innovates and may earn substantial profits as a result, but until competing firms imitate and the user (i.e., demand) side of the market widely adopts the new product, aggregate productivity growth will not be significantly advanced. Moreover, many other factors affect productivity growth. Such misuse of the term can confuse both economic and policy analysis.

manufacturing practices and techniques: Concepts, practices, and methods of combining elements of an industry's technology with corporate organizational and marketing strategies. These "disembodied" technologies greatly leverage the productivity of technology embodied in process equipment and the product itself. Examples include not only the organization-wide practices such as total quality management and concurrent engineering, but also techniques such as expert systems and risk assessment models that greatly increased the quality of information that drives much of the manufacturing technology management and investment decision making.

pilot plant: a low-volume operation of a new system of process equipment or an entire production sequence. The objective is to gain operational experience that enables adjustments to equipment, process control techniques, etc., and thus permit scale-up to high-volume production.

pre-competitive technology research: R&D involving some degree of cooperation among firms who are potential competitors, sometimes with government participation. The research objective is typically early-phase (generic) technology, although in some cases (e.g., SEMATECH) later phase R&D and even pilot plant stages are undertaken. The ultimate objective is to collectively remove sufficient technical risk to enable *individual* firms to then make applied R&D and subsequent commercialization decisions in a *timely* manner relative to the investment strategies of foreign competitors.

More specifically, the level of knowledge in early-phase technology research is relatively low and both the technical and commercial risks are relatively high. At this point in the typical technology's evolution, long-run competitiveness is enhanced by cooperation among firms and between industry and government, rather than through competition among firms. The pre-competitive "line" is crossed (i.e., firm-to-firm competition becomes the efficient mechanism) when technical risks are sufficiently reduced to allow timely corporate strategic decisions with respect to particular market applications. Enabling such decisions in the proper competitive time frame should bring forth the required private investment to advance the technology to the point of commercialization.

This term does not refer to a fundamental phase in the evolution of an industrial technology. Rather, it represents that technology research taking place before the "dividing line" is reached between cooperative advancement of the technology and the point at which firms begin individually pursuing proprietary applications of the technology. Its "position" in an industry's technology life cycle is significantly affected by the competitive dynamics of the domestic and global markets for the technology.

production chain: the sequence of economic activities by which raw materials are converted into components, components are combined into devices, devices are combined into systems, and systems are used in providing services. In economic terminology, the chain ends with "final demand" -- the market transaction after which no more value is added. In an input-output model of an economy the sum of the cells in the matrix comprising final demand constitutes the Gross National Product (GNP). From an economic growth policy point of view, the main concern is the *efficiency* with which this chain is organized and what policy changes can improve the level of efficiency.

proprietary technology research: technology research, the results of which can be "captured" or "owned" by the originator (funder/conductor) of the research. The degree to which the results of R&D become proprietary is only partially correlated with the various phases of the R&D process. Early-phase generic technology research tends to be less proprietary on average than later-phase applied R&D, but the pattern with which this progression towards more proprietary character occurs is influenced by factors such as the industry structure (average firm size, size distribution, etc.), the nature of the technology (complexity, capital intensity, etc.), and foreign competition.

public good: a public (as opposed to a private) good is one which is widely and jointly consumed by a large number of individuals, and the consumption of this good by one individual does not diminish the ability of another to consume it. Moreover, the nature of a public good is such that the owner has considerable difficulty in preventing others from consuming it. This last characteristic is what economists call the "free rider problem". The greater the degree to which these characteristics apply, the greater the "public" content in the good.

An example of a "pure" public good is national defense. Anyone who invests in a submarine to patrol a coastline for personal protection is also simultaneously protecting millions of others (the "free riders") at no cost to them. Thus, no individual would invest in a submarine because nothing approaching an adequate return on the investment could be captured, so the public sector provides such goods.

A less pure public good would be something like a bus line. In this case, at least some of the return required to bring forth private

investment can be captured, but if public objectives other than
transportation, such as labor mobility for lower income workers,
reduced pollution, etc., are included, the level of private investment
could still be insufficient. In other words, a spectrum of goods exists
which exhibit varying degrees of public content and hence varying
degrees of underinvestment by the private sector. Conversely, this
spectrum of goods requires varying degrees of support by government.
    Both generic technologies and infratechnologies are
infrastructure to the extent that they exhibit varying degrees of public
content. For example, in the case of infratechnologies, some basic
measurement methods and standards such as those for electricity are
used by many industries, so that the portion of the benefits realized by
any one industry is small. In other cases, methods (for example, those
which measure attenuation and backscatter in optical fibers) are
industry specific. For the latter, some degree of industry support may
be justified. That is, because one industry captures a significant
portion of the benefits from the infratechnology, that industry can
rationalize financing a portion of the research, even though that
research is still most efficiently accomplished at a government
laboratory.

R&D joint venture: a strategic partnership, usually between two
firms, that combines pre-existing technology assets with
complementary research skills to seek advances in *proprietary*
technology (i.e., applied R&D). The arrangement may, or may not,
include the establishment of a new organizational entity.

research consortium: a multi-firm (or, more generally, a multi-
organization) arrangement that usually pursues early-phase (generic)
technology research. The relatively wide access to the research results
(in contrast to a joint venture) qualifies the research output as
technology infrastructure. Such arrangements may, or may not,
include a new organizational entity. Companies, universities,
government agencies, and non-profit organizations may take part in a
research consortium, though membership may be restricted to less
than the total population of potential beneficiaries.

standard: A formal agreement to achieve reduction in variety or
uncertainty, which, in turn, realizes efficiency in (1) production
through the realization of economies of scale, (2) certain desired

attributes in products, such as quality, (3) the physical and functional interfaces between pieces of equipment making up an economic system, and (4) the transfer and use of information with economic value (such as product definition data), and (5) market transactions through designated methods of acceptance testing.

As defined, these "industry" standards (voluntarily set by industry) are different from "mandatory" standards or *regulations*, promulgated by government.

technology: physical, chemical, and other organized functional information relevant to the design, production, and marketing of products and services. Technology may be embodied in the physical or chemical composition of products as well as their functional design, or it may be "disembodied" in the form of practice or technique by which embodied technology is used.

technology infrastructure: a range or group of technology-related elements that have a common-use or "public" character to them and therefore are not fully provided by individual firms. Like more familiar economic infrastructure (roads, bridges, airports, waterways, etc.), technology infrastructure is widely used and reused by buyers and sellers. The common role of the various elements of the technology infrastructure is to *facilitate* proprietary technology development and use. Examples include generic technology, infratechnology, standards, and technical information relevant for market research and planning.

technology diffusion/transfer: the dissemination of technical information and the subsequent adoption of new technology by potential users. Assimilating a new technology into the strategy and organizational structure of a firm is seldom a simple process. Engineering, management, and production skills may not be adequate for efficient integration. As a result, technologies are often adopted (i.e., "diffuse") at very slow rates. Numerically controlled machine tools are an example. In such cases, the productivity benefits to the national economy accrue slowly. Technology diffusion/transfer can be accomplished through written documents and specifications or through personal contacts. Technology also diffuses through debatable practices such as "reverse engineering".

test bed: A laboratory facility where new products can be tested to determine compatibility with the performance and interface requirements of the larger product system in which they will have to function in the marketplace.

total quality management: the integration of all aspects of the firm's activity, including R&D, production and marketing, for the purposes of (1) generating and exchanging information of quality-related attributes of both the firm's products and services, and (2) designing and implementing firm-wide strategies. Quality objectives and strategies are viewed not only as a total-firm activity but also include relationships with suppliers and customers.

vertical integration: the combination of economic activity at several stages in a production chain, either through organization merger or through formal agreements between separate organizations from the several stages. Note: this term is sometimes applied to firms that produce at one level in a production chain *and* also produce the manufacturing equipment needed at that level. Manufacturing equipment is not part of the actual chain by which value is successively added (it is a "factor" of production). Therefore, it is better to refer to such a firm by a different label, say, "diagonally integrated".

4

Research Consortia

"We must all hang together or surely we will all hang separately"

Benjamin Franklin

The development and use of generic technology is one of the emerging major battlefields in global technology-based competition. The nature of generic technology is such that if its supply is left to individual firms, underinvestment will occur. This underinvestment can be substantial enough that the affected industries lose any chance of being competitive in global markets early in the technology's life cycle.

Successful industries, on the other hand, are found in nations that have recognized that at least major portions of the typical generic technology should be regarded as infrastructure. They have therefore proceeded to establish appropriate mechanisms for funding, conducting, and diffusing generic technology research.

In this chapter, these mechanisms will be described and assessed with comparisons made among Japan, Europe, and the United States. Efficiency criteria will be derived and the relationships with other competitiveness factors identified, although these other factors are discussed in later chapters.

Globalization and the Demand for Research Consortia

Little disagreement remains over the course of technology-based competition. The central and relentless trend is toward total globalization. The adjective *total* means that firms conduct all stages of economic activity -- R&D, manufacturing, and marketing -- on a multinational basis. This trend has been brought about by several factors. The most important ones being closeness to market, labor cost advantages, trade barriers, and, more recently, access to sources of technology in the foreign market.

As previously argued, the central theme of a nation's economic growth strategy in the face of the globalization of markets should be to provide an economic infrastructure and general environment that is conducive to attracting *global* investment into the domestic economy. Moreover, investment should be distributed across the all stages of economic activity. Investment in marketing operations or even production and marketing will have the long-term effect of relegating an economy to relatively low rates of economic growth. Thus, investment must also occur at the R&D stage, including early-phase research upon which an entire generation of proprietary applications depends.

However, because of the externalities inherent in early-phase technology research, substantial underinvestment occurs. Such underinvestment has been accentuated by the increasingly intense and diverse nature of global competition. A major reaction to this increased competition, particularly in Japan and Europe, has been to focus on the "public" character of *generic* technology and its appropriate designation as technology infrastructure. Having labeled it as such, appropriate infrastructure policies can be formulated.

The "public good" character of generic technology has led to a variety of cooperative mechanisms for funding and conducting the research and then disseminating the research results. Because in many nations much generic technology research is funded in whole or in part by public funds, a number of issues are constantly raised concerning the net benefits to the domestic economy.[1]

Figure 4-1

Research Targets of Consortia

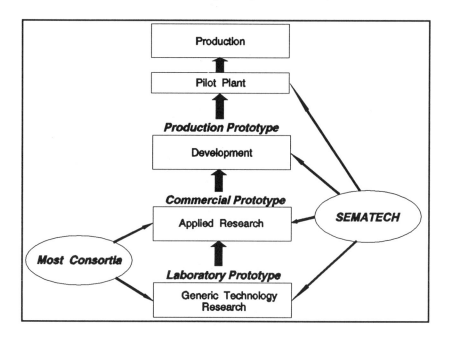

In fact, most research consortia will focus on the early-phases of the R&D stage, where economies of scope and the opportunities for combining complementary technology research assets of different firms and government laboratories are high. As shown in Figure 4-1, most consortia will target generic technology research and, to a lesser extent, applied research.

---

[1]   A recent study stated that "most industry participants [in the study] expressed skepticism about the results of generic research contributing to competitive advantage, and thus they are not willing to support it to a large extent. Many stated the belief that it is the role of the Federal government to pay for the major share of this type of research". See Government-University-Industry Research Roundtable and Industrial Research Institute [1991, p. 8].

The competitive rationale for firms combining research assets at the generic technology phase of R&D is simply that the maximum level of competition is not the optimal level. Under a maximum competition philosophy, individual firms in the domestic industry compete against each other drawing upon the science base to launch into individual technology research programs in a "winner take all" approach. The underinvestment and duplication of effort problems inherent in early-phase technology research are largely ignored in favor of the so-called "free market" approach.

In the "modified competition" approach, the adopted philosophy is that having several domestic competitors in return for being competitive *as an industry* in the emerging world market for the new technology is a preferred growth strategy; that is, from the individual firm's perspective, it is deemed better to be one of a number of players than not a player at all.

While most research consortia target early-phase technology research, some also target applied R&D and provide other infrastructure services such as test beds for "finished" products that must now integrate into larger product systems. They also have elaborate technology transfer mechanisms and even promote vertical and horizontal linkages or integration among member firms. The one U.S. consortium that displays all of these roles is SEMATECH.

SEMATECH: Outlier or Model for the Future?

For the United States, SEMATECH represents the first major commitment of public funds to the objective of enhancing a *commercial* technology through the research consortium mechanism.[2]

---

2   SEMATECH is a consortium of 14 U.S. semiconductor manufacturers and the Department of Defense. It began operations in 1987 with the stated objective of achieving parity with Japan by 1991 and global leadership in chip making technology by 1993. Its private members are Advanced Micro Devices, AT&T, Digital Equipment, Harris, Hewlett-Packard, Intel, IBM, LSI Logic, Micron, Motorola, National Semiconductor, NCR, Rockwell International, and Texas Instruments. The consortium's three-phased strategic plan calls for the development and demonstration of manufacturing technology for semiconductor devices with circuit dimensions of 0.8, 0.5, and 0.35 microns in 1989, 1991, and 1993, respectively. (A micron is one millionth of a meter.) Congress appropriated $100 million annually for fiscal years 1988 through 1992. These funds and any provided by state and local governments

Because of SEMATECH's size, visibility, and the commitment of public funds, the usual issues concerning the viability of the cooperative research mechanism have been magnified.

A report to Congress by the Department of Commerce for the Advisory Council on Federal Participation in SEMATECH refers to the benefits from SEMATECH as *indirect*, namely, the "economic and national security benefits that result from limiting the potential for cartels in world markets". These markets include memory chips, semiconductor manufacturing equipment, and materials.

Direct benefits are viewed as less certain because of potential "capturability" problems. For example, most SEMATECH members have joint ventures with foreign (mainly Japanese) companies. The policy issue is, therefore, to what degree will the benefits of the public investment in SEMATECH end up being captured by the American economy? This question has been raised in analyses of the consortium's progress and prospects for success:

> "Because many SEMATECH members make and sell
> semiconductors in major market areas outside North America, and
> can be expected to use technology developed by the consortium in
> their overseas operations, the *direct* economic benefits of public
> investment in SEMATECH (e.g., jobs, tax revenues) cannot be
> confined to the United States [domestic economy]."[3]

However, the transfer of technical knowledge *between* firms, through copying (reverse engineering), licensing, or other means, which the economics literature focuses on as paths for technology diffusion, should not be a major deterrent to the use of the research consortium mechanism. In R&D-intensive industries, the relatively short technology and related product life cycles mean that the results need only be kept secret long enough to give the owners of the intellectual property a relatively short lead in time. Thus, the Microelectronics and Computer Technology Corp. (MCC), which conducts computer and related research, delays licensing results to nonmembers for three years. The 22-member consortium believes

---

must be at least matched by industry contributions.

[3]   Mayer [1990, p. ES-3].

that this is sufficient time to give members the required head start on proprietary product development.[4]

However, the concern raised by the Advisory Council's report is that joint ventures between SEMATECH members and non-U.S. firms may negate the consortium's positive impact on the U.S. economy, not only by permitting the premature release of SEMATECH's developed technology to foreign rivals but, in the long term, by inviting the exploitation and absorption of the financially and technologically-weaker partners. In the opinion of the report, however, SEMATECH's members are well-schooled in the protection of information they consider proprietary. The report also argues that in their various joint ventures with foreign firms, "they [U.S. firms] are not obviously or necessarily the weaker partners".

Nevertheless, part of the context in which one should analyze SEMATECH is the existence of the numerous joint ventures between U.S. and Japanese firms. A joint venture is a mechanism by which two firms combine complementary technology assets to accelerate and generally make more efficient the conduct of *applied* R&D or achieve economies of scale in production or both. Indicators of the relative strength of a domestic industry can be derived from examining the composition of joint ventures, as well as to what degree domestic firms benefit from them over time.

In the 1960s and 1970s, U.S. firms had a clear technological lead in most aspects of semiconductor technology as well as a dominant market share position. They licensed technology to the Japanese for ridiculously low prices on the grounds that Japanese firms were not serious competitors and that the Japanese market was too small to be a target for penetration.

The experience of the 1980s radically changed this lackadaisical view towards pricing technology assets and hence bargaining behavior when negotiating joint ventures. In a particularly well-publicized example, U.S. firms not only lost market-share leadership but technological leadership in the critical area of memory circuits. For a time in the middle 1980s, it seemed as if U.S. firms were too technologically inferior in the memory area to offer complementary assets sufficient to induce joint ventures with firms to whom they had once virtually handed technology free of charge. In

---

[4]   See Merton Peck [1986].

fact, at one point only two U.S. firms were still producing DRAM (dynamic random access memory) chips.

The situation improved after 1988, in part due to increasing pressure by the U.S. Government on Japan, but also due to the prospects for substantial technology infrastructure support from SEMATECH. Such support will be critical to reviving long-term R&D investment in the domestic industry. Production joint ventures with at least some of the production located domestically may result from the need of the foreign partner to get around trade barriers and gain entry into the domestic market or to access lower-cost capital. However, the location of an R&D joint venture may signify an attractive "local" technology infrastructure as well as relative R&D strength on the part of the domestic partner. Over time, SEMATECH should have a positive "infrastructure effect".

SEMATECH may have one of the most comprehensive sets of objectives of any single consortium in the world. Its highest priority is *developing advanced semiconductor chip manufacturing processes.* Pursuit of this objective (with the largest share of its funds) includes research projects ranging from generic technology through development and then low-volume production runs (pilot plant phase).

Its second highest priority is projects that improve *cycle phasing* of semiconductor product development. That is, the objective is to accelerate technology development in cases where earlier access to advanced equipment, materials, or process technology will result in accelerated time-to-market and thereby enable a significant competitive advantage to be attained. The third priority is the set of projects that are high-risk but also have high potential economic benefits -- i.e., the externality rationale that is resulting in increasing support for generic technology research generally.[5]

Table 4-1 compares SEMATECH's objectives with those of consortia in the general area of electronics. JESSI is the European counterpart to SEMATECH in semiconductor research. ESPRIT in

---

[5] Most observers tend to regard this last role as the primary one for research consortia.

Europe and MCC in the United States are pursuing downstream technologies in electronics and information technology.[6]

The first objective of advancing manufacturing R&D is being implemented by conducting research at SEMATECH's Austin facility and also by funding external R&D projects. Partly because start-up costs at the Austin facility are declining and partly as a result of a conscious strategy shift toward more external funding of R&D projects, a pronounced change has occurred in the mix of internal and external funding. In 1990, its third year of operation, SEMATECH increased external funding to 53 percent in 1990, up from 30 percent in 1989 and 20 percent in 1988.[7]

One of the ways to improve the phasing of life cycles for new generations of products, manufacturing processes, and process equipment is to actively promote technology diffusion into the marketplace. SEMATECH is doing this by purchasing equipment from equipment suppliers and giving the equipment to member semiconductor manufacturers to use for several purposes: test in their own production lines, compare to foreign alternatives, improve upon, and share the resulting technical knowledge. The equipment vendors benefit both from equipment sales and technical feedback that enhances product improvement efforts -- both events occurring earlier in the product life cycle than would have been the case in the absence of the SEMATECH role.

Such roles are radical for the U. S. economy, which has embraced *laissez-faire* approaches to market activity, emphasizing arms-length competition. The Japanese industrial structure, on the other hand, readily provides this type of integration. The interaction between producer and supplier in Japan occurs not only through the organizational linkages of the *Keiretsu*, but also through the cultural bias towards cooperation.[8]

---

[6] ESPRIT stands for European Strategic Programme for Research and Development in Information Technology and JESSI is the Joint European Submicron Silicon project.

[7] Mayer [1990, p. ES-4].

[8] The Japanese applied this approach more than a decade earlier in semiconductor production equipment. Nikon caught up with the U.S. supplier GCA through close cooperation with Japanese semiconductor manufacturers participating in

Table 4-1

Objectives of Electronics Research Consortia

Consortium	Generic Technology Research	Applied Technology Research	Infratechnology/ Open Systems Research	Promote Vertical Integration	Improve Cycle Phasing
SEMATECH	yes	yes	yes	yes	yes
JESSI	yes	no	no	yes	yes
ESPRIT	yes	no	yes	no	no
MCC	yes	yes	yes	yes	yes

the famed VLSI project in the 1976-1980 period. The emphasis of the VLSI project was on the manufacturing process, with one-third to one-half of the budget going for purchase of equipment (including a GCA wafer stepper). The project managers selected Nikon to develop a made-in-Japan stepper. Through close collaboration, a stepper was developed that gained a reputation as being more reliable than GCA's. (See U.S. Congress, Office of Technology Assessment [1990]).

Earlier technical feedback is but one example of how a consortium can facilitate *information* infrastructure. In particular, such information generation and transfer improves the *integration* of separate but interdependent industries. If the information flows are both comprehensive and timely, separate industries (in this case, semiconductor chip manufacturers and semiconductor equipment suppliers can compete without actual organizational integration (i.e., merger or acquisition). SEMATECH facilitates information flows through other mechanisms, including workshops, advisory boards, and symposia, which not only convey generic technical and market planning information but culture a taste for cooperation.

Such mechanisms can integrate an industry vertically, without organizational merger. The importance of life cycle phasing is especially great where timing is critical to competitive position. In the case of semiconductor equipment, poor coordination between equipment suppliers and semiconductor manufacturers has been especially disastrous for the small firms that typify that industry. Annual worldwide sales of semiconductor equipment are only about $10 billion, but having quality equipment is obviously critical to the production efficiency of the much larger semiconductor device industry. Moreover, given the exceedingly short semiconductor product life cycles, the timely availability of this equipment for each new generation of semiconductor device can make a substantial difference in the ultimate global market shares of semiconductor device manufacturers.[9]

The range of functions performed by large research consortia, such as SEMATECH and JESSI are summarized in Table 4-2. The mechanisms chosen by a consortium to execute each of these functions not only vary across consortia but change during the evolution of any one consortium, as evidenced by SEMATECH's shifts in strategy.

As large as SEMATECH is, neither it nor any R&D consortium can be viewed as a "cure" for competitive problems in an industry. Yet, both JESSI and SEMATECH are regularly chastised

---

[9]   According to VLSI Research [1990], Japan's share of the world semiconductor equipment market rose from 23.5% in 1985 to 42.2% in 1989, while the U.S. market share fell from 61.4% to 47.8%.

Table 4-2

Functions of Electronics Research Consortia

Consortium	Conducts Research at Dedicated Facility	Funds Research at Member Firms	Formal Technology Transfer	Provides Pilot Plant Conformance Testing	Develops Standards
SEMATECH	**yes:** $63 million in 1990	**yes:** $137 million in 1990, $100 million in 1991 (out of a total budget of $200 million)	**yes:** frequent on-site meetings and regular communication with home companies	**yes**	**yes:** for both equipment suppliers and chip manufacturers
JESSI	**no** (but participating EC nations are building supporting R&D facilities)	**yes:** must average $800 million/year to meet total budget by 1996	**no**	**no**	**no**
ESPRIT	**no**	**yes:** $400 million in 1990	**yes**	**no**	**yes**
MCC	**yes:** $60 million	**no** (but research is coordinated with member R&D projects)	**yes:** similar to SEMATECH	**no**	**yes**

and threatened with funding cutbacks for failing to have quickly "saved" the European and U.S. semiconductor industries, respectively. At a maximum, R&D consortia can supply several elements of technology infrastructure. It is the degree of effective use of this infrastructure, along with other factors, that ultimately determines competitive position. Even with all infrastructure in place, satisfactory competitive position will not be achieved if the structure of the industry itself is misaligned with the demands of the global marketplace. The report to Congress by the Advisory Council on Federal Participation in SEMATECH makes the point that

> "even at their most successful, SEMATECH and similar measures are palliatives -- selective and temporary efforts to compensate for general conditions in the U.S. economy that have contributed to competitive weakness in a range domestic industries."[10]

In 1989, one year after SEMATECH became operational, several of the consortium's members took steps to reenter or expand their presence in world DRAM markets. Texas Instruments began construction of DRAM manufacturing facilities in Italy and Taiwan. TI is also involved in a joint venture with Hitachi to share the expense and the risk of developing 16 Megabyte DRAM product technology. Motorola, with technology licensed from Toshiba, achieved high-volume production of 1Mb DRAMs at plants in Scotland and Mesa, Arizona, and began construction of 4Mb facilities in Sandai, Japan and Oak Hill, Texas. Micron Technology made plans to manufacture 4Mb DRAMs at its new fabrication facility in Boise, Idaho, using product and process technology licensed from fellow member IBM. Finally, Advanced Micro Devices continued the construction of a submicron research and production center "to apply the manufacturing technology advances expected from SEMATECH."[11]

Some of these strategic actions may be solely the result of the desire on the part of U.S. companies to re-diversify horizontally, but

---

[10] Mayer [1990, p. 3].

[11] See Mayer [1990, pp. 5-6]. Texas Instruments is representative of the problem of a consortium member creating value added outside the domestic economy. All of TI's recent investment in chip production capability has been outside the United States.

discussions with SEMATECH and industry officials also make clear the fact that the existence of a consortium with capabilities to significantly leverage both technology development by individual semiconductor manufacturers and the equipment supply industry positively influenced these decisions. From a national growth policy point of view, the fact that some of the new manufacturing capacity will be in the United States is an important development with respect to the goal of regenerating large and diversified value added in the domestic economy.

From a bleak situation in 1985-86 when most U.S. merchant firms abandoned DRAM R&D and production, a significant resurgence is occurring. This phenomenon has been helped, and likely made possible, by the existence of SEMATECH. Although these developments assure a continued U.S. presence in world memory markets, a larger presence cannot be predicted. When one is behind, one has to run *faster* than the leaders to catch up. The Japanese semiconductor manufacturers have exceeded expenditures by U.S. merchant producers on new plant and equipment by 15 percent or more in every year since 1982. This margin jumped to about 60 percent ($1.5-2 billion per year) in the 1988-89 period, with about half of these expenditures dedicated to memory circuit production.[12]

At its inception, SEMATECH was viewed as a largely self-contained operation consisting of on-site R&D plus the design, construction and operation of three "demonstration" fabrication lines. Under this arrangement, while SEMATECH would not produce for market, it would function in other respects like a world-class manufacturing company.[13]

However, this extreme version of a consortium was discarded in June 1989. SEMATECH was re-organized to significantly increase off-site R&D projects. SEMATECH's Austin fabrication facility is now used mainly at the end of a project to demonstrate the deliverable in conditions that simulate the pressures and complexities of high-volume semiconductor production. This organizational arrangement was motivated at least in part by a desire on the part of

---

[12] Estimates provided by Dataquest.

[13] Mayer [1990, p. 15].

members to address somewhat more applied and hence shorter-term R&D projects, while still providing at least some of the expensive and technically-demanding "pilot plant" environment for obtaining production scale-up data. To provide a fully-integrated production line might not have been a reasonable objective for the consortium in any event. To do this, SEMATECH would have to receive final products from member firms, thereby possibly exposing proprietary designs.

No matter how successful SEMATECH turns out to be in achieving its several goals, it cannot "save" the U.S. semiconductor industry by itself, nor should it be expected to. The detractors of SEMATECH and other research consortia, who make unreasonable demands on this one infrastructure mechanism, simply do not understand the complexity of technology-based competition.

The U.S. semiconductor industry will have to solve a number of other important issues, such as whether or not actual (organizational) vertical integration is needed to provide cash flow flexibility (as the Japanese argue). Or, alternatively, whether or not "multi-enterprise" integration, achieved through advanced technology infrastructure, can provide the functional interfaces that allow independent firms in the vertical production chain to attain synergies similar to what SEMATECH is now instituting between semiconductor manufactures and equipment suppliers.

MCC: A Multi-Dimensional Consortium

The example of SEMATECH indicates that the performance of research alone is too narrow a view of so-called "research" consortia. Clearly, to be effective a research consortium must emphasize activities besides research. Just as individual firms that keep their basic stages of economic activity separate will perform poorly, so will consortia not succeed that remain functionally isolated from their members.

One of the best examples of the evolution of a research consortium from a relatively isolated institution with modest payoffs into an effective multi-dimensional source of technology infrastructure is the Microelectronics and Computer Technology Corporation (MCC). MCC is actually a "consortium of consortia". It has about 35 multi-firm project areas and each one is slightly different in structure and approach. Under the direction of Craig Fields, MCC has increased the strength of its relationships with its members in several critical areas: planning, technology acquisition, and technology transfer.

Effective planning is not just a matter of identifying and agreeing upon the right objectives and implementing appropriate research projects. Timing is also essential and not only with respect to the initiation of the research. Projects must be planned to be completed in a period of time that fits within the planning horizons of member firms. MCC found that its original project planning horizons had to be shortened to meet members' targets.

Another element of a research consortium's operations that is receiving increased attention is technology transfer. For a number of years, mention was made of the so-called "shadow R&D" operations of member firms in Japanese consortia, but the importance of this strategic element is just now beginning to be appreciated in other countries. Most consortia members have well-established R&D operations with long-range plans and interfaces with other parts of their firms, and it is these operations that must absorb and utilize a consortium's output. Thus, not only must a research consortium's planning be integrated with that of its members, but the technology transfer linkages must be set up *in the beginning* of the project to ensure timely and substantive transfer. Technology transfer does not happen automatically.

Under Craig Fields, MCC has allocated considerable effort to increasing staff exchanges in both directions. Joint planning has been upgraded by allocating more of the time of senior staff to this activity. MCC has also recognized that the results of a research project will have to be integrated into the broader technology bases of member firms. Thus, effort is now allocated to infrastructure issues such as "standards, platforms, languages, and frameworks."

The consortium has pressured members to allocate the resources necessary to internalize the research results. That is, member firms are now setting up the equivalent of the Japanese "shadow R&D" mechanism. The importance of this step derives not only from its central role in the technology transfer process, but because it increases the ability of member companies to make decisions to commit the typically larger resources required by later-phase R&D. Thus, not only the timing of such decisions but the actual decision itself is facilitated by having internal project teams formed and geared to pick up the technology.

Originally, MCC consortia were horizontal in structure. In 1991, however, it formed a vertically-oriented consortium to develop "multi-chip modules".[14] In addition to simply forming the consortium of potential users of this new electronic device technology, MCC provided an "open-systems" format that is directing the research toward a result that will provide a standardized means of integration of the new technology from multiple suppliers into the members products. Thus, MCC is supplying a sophisticated "hybrid" technology infrastructure; i.e., the technology itself and the complementary infratechnology (standardized interfaces).

MCC has also initiated a "CAD Framework Laboratory Consortium" to promote "standardization of the interfaces between CAD tools and the software that supports their use". The standards will comply with those adopted by the industry's CAD Framework Initiative Inc. The CAD Framework Lab is to fulfill one of the CAD Program's founding objectives -- to serve as an industry leader and conduit between CAD users and suppliers.

MCC's Carnot project is developing a complex set of software tools that will allow access to -- and maintain consistency of -- data in distributed heterogeneous environments. The project will also provide "bridges" between older, closed computing environments and present and future open systems.

Members of the consortium are electronic system suppliers, semiconductor manufacturers, both broad-line and niche CAD tool vendors, and computer workstation manufacturers. The anticipated benefits are to electronic system and semiconductor component designers who will gain more rapid access to new CAD technology

---

[14] Multi-chip modules will be the next generation of electronic devices. At the "device" level, a number of semiconductor components must be functionally as well as physically combined. The current technology is the "printed circuit board", but this physical configuration will not allow the coming high-speed microprocessors to function. New "packaging technology" will be needed. The technology of the interfaces among the various semiconductors devices (microprocessors, memory circuits, etc.) is very complex. MCC's Open Systems Program has attracted companies that are not vertically-integrated and do not have the resources to develop the technology individually. The objective is to develop the technology with standard interfaces, so that upstream suppliers will both have the technology when the members need it and will constitute a multiple-firm source of supply.

from *multiple* vendors. This benefit was difficult to attain in the past because lack of standardization leads to problems interfacing new technology from multiple vendors.

The Consortium/Member Interface

MCC also is beginning to spin off companies. These new firms would be tied to consortium members through either royalty obligations or through agreements to provide their products to members at a 50 percent discount. This mechanism is attractive from an industry structure point of view because it provides a second investment option to direct transfer to member firms, who may not deem the technology within their strategic sphere.

Whatever the technical success of a research consortium, the ultimate measure of success is the *extent* and *rapidity* of use by consortium members. Japanese companies make substantial commitments to internal R&D that in total dwarf the investment in the consortium. When this approach is not taken, competitive failure results. The U.K.'s Alvey program, a five-year $360 million cooperative research effort in advanced computer technology was labeled a failure for this reason in a report commissioned by the U.K.'s Department of Trade and Industry and the Science and Engineering Council.[15]

The fact is that most of the rest of the world has yet to understand why and how the Japan uses research consortia. The Japanese correctly regard the generic technology research phase as a step in an overall systems approach to technology-based competition. Japanese firms therefore automatically set up internal "shadow" R&D programs. They are similarly both willing and able to send their best scientists and engineers, given that these people are only away from their firms for the duration of specific projects, rather than for an extended period of time.

Moreover, the Japanese concept of the dynamics of competition allows them to rationalize cooperating at an early phase of a technology's development. They realize that they are individually

---

[15] Bird [1991].

better off to collectively accelerate the technology to the applied R&D phase *ahead* of competitors in other nations.

The Alvey program appeared to "fail" not because it did not advance information technology, but rather because the effort was not tied to the strategies of participating firms. Instead, these firms tried to make participation part of a separate strategic focus and thus chose, for the most part, to collaborate separately with potential suppliers and customers. The participating British companies did not regard participation as an extension of their internal R&D strategy. 70% of the companies formed vertical relationships, rather than working with potential horizontal competitors at the generic technology research phase. The report concluded that firms do not like to collaborate with competitors. While this conclusion seems to accurately represent British strategic concepts, it is definitely not the Japanese model.

The important point in terms of organizational strategy is that R&D consortia should focus primarily on, but not be constrained too closely by, projects within member firms that have more applied R&D objectives. Many corporate central research laboratories (CRLs) have been tied too closely to the R&D operations of the company's business units and have suffered a loss of role efficiency as a result. Often a company's central research laboratory allocates resources to projects on the basis of sales, which ties resource allocation to existing, mature technologies rather than to future breakthroughs that have the potential to radically change an industry's basis for competing. General Electric's allocation of resources shows the proper approach. In 1987, GE's core manufacturing business accounted for 30 percent of total sales but only 17 percent of CRL expenditures. In contrast, its high-technology businesses, which represented 41 percent of sales, had a claim on 78 percent of CRL dollars.[16]

Similarly, research consortia have to resist the temptation to become extensions of members' R&D operations, pursuing relatively short-term projects to "keep members happy". It appears that many corporate central research labs target at least a 30 percent improvement in performance from projects undertaken. Consortia should target at least that much, and in most cases more.

---

[16]   Lewis and Linden [1990, p. 34].

Finally, not even a large consortium such as MCC can capture all of the economies of scale and scope that exist in the early-phase R&D desired by its members. Thus, MCC has begun to license technology that complements its internal research programs. Such "imported" technology is assessed, benchmarked and transferred to the consortium's member companies. This "brokering" role might turn out in some technical areas to be as important as a consortium's research programs.

Industry-Government Consortia

In Japan, industry-government consortia are virtually an automatic part of early-phase R&D. When high-temperature superconductivity was demonstrated in 1986 for the first major advance in superconductivity research in 23 years, a worldwide explosion in research was stimulated. One the first steps taken by the Japanese was to establish a research consortium. The MITI-sponsored Superconductivity Technology Centre (ISTEC) includes 80 Japanese companies and is a major element in MITI's approximately $37 million-per-year research program. In Europe as well, through EC-sponsored programs as well as EUREKA, the number of research collaborations has virtually exploded.

In the United States, the Defense Advanced Research Projects Agency (DARPA) in the Department of Defense provided the U.S Government's financial contribution to SEMATECH and therefore has been cited as an example of an effective government agent for funding cooperative research. However, most of DARPA's funds in the past have gone to individual firms.

Nevertheless, it has an excellent track record in helping to advance the early phases of technology research for a number of critical technologies. For example, it has been credited with stimulating many of the major advances in computers.[17] DARPA has contributed to varying degrees to areas such as time sharing, interactive computer graphics, computer networking, artificial intelligence, computer security, and parallel processing.

---

[17] See Flamm [1988].

Craig Fields, a former director of DARPA, credits the agency with creating the field of materials science through investment in a dozen interdisciplinary research laboratories.[18] DARPA's contributions in the materials areas include research into the materials themselves and the processes for manufacturing them (such as rapid solidification).

Fields characterizes DARPA's "main mode of operation" as funding early-phase research projects that take from two to ten years to complete. The projects end with a "concept demonstration" or a "prototype" or a "technology demonstration". Fields believes that "this focus mirrors exactly the place where there's been the greatest deficit in investment...There's a lot of private-sector investment in one-to-two year activities, and a lot of public-sector investment in basic research. But there's a real depression in two-to-ten-year research". His characterization of DARPA's research focus and his rationales for its overall strategy coincide with the rationales for government support of *generic* technology research presented in Chapter 3.

From a broader policy point of view, Fields also supports the "portfolio" concept described in the previous chapter. He states that "the issue is to be as good as you can be in as many critical areas as you possibly can...A nation that is at the forefront of a whole range of high-technology areas and can put that knowledge to use is going to be in better shape than a country that may have one specialization it can lose".

DARPA is now beginning to fund additional consortia. A DARPA-supported consortium in superconductivity has been formed, and additional consortia (through a $50 million appropriation) are planned for advanced composites, optoelectronics, and flat panel displays.

However, much debate has ensued over the ability of DARPA to simultaneously pursue DoD's mission-oriented research agenda and the distinctly different needs of the civilian economy. For example, DARPA-funded generic technology research in flat panel displays, which have many military applications, also have civilian applications in areas such as high definition television (HDTV). DARPA is not likely to fund the generic technology research in other elements of

---

[18]   See "The Government's Guiding Hand: An Interview with Ex-DARPA Director Craig Fields", *Technology Review*, February/March 1991.

high-definition imaging systems (HDIS) or to be sufficiently concerned with technology infrastructure issues such as industry standards.

The decreasing overlap between defense and civilian technology needs led the U.S. Congress to establish a civilian counterpart to DARPA at NIST. The Advanced Technology Program (ATP) is currently a small but growing effort, which allocates part of its funds to research consortia; it made its first research awards in February 1991.

The excellent record of DARPA has instilled hope that it can perform the dual-technology role. However, the growing gaps between military and civilian technology requirements make this objective increasingly unlikely; therefore, an increasing responsibility for funding pre-competitive generic technologies will likely fall to ATP.

Government-funded generic technology research is a somewhat broader policy issue into which the consortium mechanism falls. The Advanced Technology Program can fund either consortia or individual firms. The arguments for consortia, as already stated, include efficiency in the funding and conduct of generic technology research, possibly later-phase research under special conditions, improved cycle phasing, vertical integration, and efficiency in technology diffusion. These advantages have led to questions about the rationale for ATP funding individual firms.

However, when this issue is viewed from a "production chain" point of view, a good rationale can be developed. Funding research at a large downstream user of certain technologies with the capabilities to both manage the research and then transfer the research results to suppliers can be more efficient than the alternative, which is for the government to try itself to identify and fund the research at a number of the suppliers. Especially if the suppliers are small firms, determining which suppliers, if any, are capable of conducting specific parts of the research and then synthesizing and disseminating the research results can be difficult management problems.

For example, one of the recipients in the first year of ATP awards was AT&T Bell Laboratories. The grant was for "fabrication and testing of precision optics for soft X-ray projection lithography". AT&T does not manufacture semiconductor processing equipment, but some of the Bell Labs' staff felt strongly that this technology had great potential and that AT&T would need this equipment in the future. These staff could not sell the needed research internally, nor could the small equipment suppliers that AT&T depends on afford to undertake such risky and expensive research.

The ATP funds, which will amount to approximately one-third of the projected cost of the five-year research project, provided sufficient leverage to induce AT&T management to commit to the remaining two-thirds. The resulting technology will be transferred to the small equipment suppliers. In effect, AT&T is imitating the successful practice of its Japanese rival, Nippon Telegraph & Telephone (NTT), which for years has funded research and then transferred the resulting semiconductor manufacturing technology to its domestic suppliers.

As documented by Howell *et al* [1988], seven major microelectronics-related cooperative research programs entailing approximately $750 million in government funds have been undertaken in the past 15 years. Counting all cooperative projects over a more broadly defined electronics industry, a study by the U.S. Department of Commerce documents 30 projects in the past 25 years. European nations have started 13 in the past 10 years.[19]

Assessing the Economic Impacts

Although early-phase research typically requires a number of years to achieve major milestones in terms of technical advance, sponsoring government officials and private-sector CEOs often become impatient. Moreover, lack of a focus on the role and expected output of collaborative, pre-competitive research leads to unreasonable evaluation criteria and thus unfair criticism. European government officials, for example, seemed to fault JESSI for the financial and management crisis at Philips and the persistent weak performance of other European electronic companies, as if JESSI were supposed to single-handedly effect major changes in an overly-segmented industry structure and an inferior technology base. ESPRIT has been similarly criticized. While acknowledging that ESPRIT has improved technical information flows between

---

[19] U.S. Department of Commerce, International Trade Administration [1990, pp. 34-35].

companies, it is also criticized for having produced little commercially useful technology and therefore "needs redirection".[20]

Thus, the problems in the United States with efficiently producing and utilizing technology infrastructure have also appeared in Europe. After achieving significant implementation of cooperative research programs such as ESPRIT and JESSI, both in terms of scope of research topics and depth of investment, impatience began to take over. Senior European Commission officials began expressing concern with EC policies for electronics industries, saying that they were not making the industry more competitive and needed to be rethought. The EC budgeted approximately $2.4 billion in 1990, with much of it targeted for multi-company collaboration schemes such as ESPRIT and JESSI. The validity of these budgetary allocations is now being challenged.

In time, properly conceived and managed consortia will produce the generic technical advances that should be expected of them. The problem is that unless policy makers correctly understand both the nature of the research objectives of collaborative research and the typical time frames in which such objectives can be accomplished, the utility of this mechanism will be reduced and so will be the resulting technology infrastructure.

A major solution to this problem is to design and implement *early in the life* of a collaborative project an evaluation process that not only measures ultimate economic impacts, but which also yields intermediate measures of impact. The latter set is particularly important for elements of technology infrastructure such as generic technology which take a long time to develop, to transfer, and finally to be utilized by individual corporations in the development and commercialization of products and processes. Doing this establishes clear goals and the measures of success/failure against these goals. Table 4-3 provides a sample list of impact measures that cover the general life cycle of a cooperative research project and its subsequent impacts.

Extensive use of the consortium mechanism is too recent and the typical time to payoff is sufficiently long so that few empirical studies of the benefits to overall competitiveness have been completed. However, a study by Link and Bauer [1989] for the U.S.

---

20   *New Technology Week*, November 5, 1990, p. 2.

Table 4-3

Impact Indicators for Research Consortia

TARGET OF IMPACT	NATURE OF IMPACT	TIME PERIOD
Investment Behavior	Acceleration of R&D investment decisions	short
	Larger investment ("pooling-of-risk" and "demonstration" effects)	short
	More pre-competitive generic technology research	medium
	Establishment of new or larger internal R&D programs ("shadow R&D" effect)	medium
Industry structure	Number of firms making investment commitments	short
	Increased vertical or horizontal integration	long
Return on investment	Significance research results in terms of technological breakthroughs	medium
	Number of participating firms committing to follow-on R&D	medium
	Number of products and processes commercialized	long
	Shortened time-to-market	long
	Productivity gains	long
	Quality gains	long
	Size of resulting markets and market shares	long

National Science Foundation suggests that firms engaged in cooperative research (1) invest more in R&D than they would have in the absence of the stimulative effects on strategic planning from the information sharing that accompanies the actual cooperative research and (2) realize an increase in efficiency of their *internal* R&D due to the transferability of basic technical knowledge and related research skills.[21]

In summary, many analysts and policy makers tend to downgrade the importance of research consortia and the roles that they perform for several reasons: (1) generic technology, the focus of most research consortia, is just becoming widely recognized as not only the first but also a critical step in technology development; (2) because the amount of resources allocated to each successive phase of R&D typically increases significantly as the technology evolves, funds for early-phase generic technology research are relatively small compared to development, and this early-phase research is therefore deemed less important; (3) because consortia have been ineffectively structured and managed in the past, their potential has been assessed to be relatively limited; and (4) the traditional view that significant economic activity stops at the boundary of the firm leads to a bias against any interfirm activity.

Trends in the Use of Research Consortia

In a study for Dataquest [1991] by the Wharton School, propensities to form different types of alliances during the 1980s by semiconductor companies in the four major regions of the world (United States, Japan, Europe, and Asia/Pacific-ROW) were analyzed. Of the types of alliances studied (acquisitions and mergers, joint ventures, equity investments, licensing, second sourcing, cooperative agreements, and technology transfer), more than 60 percent of the alliances formed in Japan are cooperative agreements, compared with 50 percent in the United States (almost the world average). However, acquisition is used 13 percent of the time in U.S. agreements, compared with 2 percent in Japan.

---

[21] Link and Rees [1990] provide evidence that these benefits are also realized by firms that engage in cooperative research projects with universities.

The Japanese tendency toward greater use of cooperative agreements reflects their more refined model of technology development, especially early-phase research, while the U.S. emphasis on acquisition probably reflects both the availability of small, capital-starved firms and the need of larger firms to vertically integrate.

Emerging technology-based economies are technology followers and thus would be expected to rely on licensing and technology transfers as major alliance strategies. For example, these two strategies make up 35 percent and 15 percent, respectively, of Taiwan's total alliances. This compares with approximately 8 percent and 10 percent for the United States and 7 percent and 10 percent for Japan (which once used these two forms to a much greater extent).

These trends mean that understanding the roles that research consortia can play (and cannot play), given the existing economic conditions, is an essential element of strategic planning for technology infrastructure. Knowing how to design a consortium in terms of the phase or phases to be targeted, the timing of the research, and the number and scope of participants are critical elements in the planning process and greatly affect the estimated benefits to be derived from participation. In economies where research consortia have been used for some time, such as in Japan, the criteria for their creation and scope of participation are well established. Various institutions, public and private, are geared to contribute to the planning process as well as the formation of a consortium and the subsequent conduct of the research agenda.

In the United States, this level of infrastructure expertise has yet to be reached. To date, SEMATECH is the first and only major R&D consortium to which major government funds have been committed. The advent of NIST's Advanced Technology Program (ATP) will create an experience base, but some longer period of time will be required to develop criteria for more sophisticated options such as vertically-integrated versus horizontally-integrated consortia or the choice of particular phases in the R&D stage to target.

With respect to potential participants, another problem facing the United States is the fact that most of its national laboratory system is charged with pursuing specific missions that are not market driven -- whether these objectives are defense or civilian (energy independence, for example). In one recent study, "industrial officials noted that the primary issue that gets in the way of industry-federal laboratory collaboration is that the laboratories do not have a clear mission related to the development of [commercial] technology or an understanding of industry as a customer".[22]

A number of efficiency issues must be addressed by research consortia. "Start-up" or fixed costs are typically incurred, which can be a deterrent to participation if these costs are significant. Such costs are typically large when the strategy of the consortium is to construct a dedicated research facility (MCC, SEMATECH). A large number of participants obviously reduces these costs for individual firms. However, a larger number of participants introduces increased management problems, such as difficulty in setting research agendas and in general communication. Some consortia, such as MCC, address the problem of different research agendas by allowing members to participate on a project basis and pay only for the research only on those projects.

The composition of membership in a research consortium in terms of industry structure is another major issue. Specifically, consortia can be organized horizontally or vertically. The motivations for forming these two basic types of consortia are distinctly different. Horizontal consortia consist of potential future competitors and target technologies at a specific level in the production chain. Motivations usually include the capture of economies of *scale* and *scope*.

Vertical consortia may also target a single level, where that level is viewed as a "weak link" in the vertical production chain. However, here the motivation is more strongly influenced by the needs of firms operating at levels above and below the target level. To these firms, the success of the consortium's R&D means an efficient source of supply or a viable market, depending on whether they are below or above that level, respectively. Because such firms often do not even have R&D operations at the target level, they are likely to have strong economies-of-*scale* as well as general risk-pooling motivations.

The MITI/NTT VLSI projects of the late 1970s are credited with "enabling Japanese firms to commercialize the 64K DRAM six to twelve months ahead of schedule -- a tremendous competitive

---

[22] Government-University-Industry Research Roundtable and Industrial Research Institute [1991, p. 19].

advantage in an industry characterized by short product life cycles".[23]
The VLSI projects effectively ended dependence on foreign sources of
semiconductor process equipment, as well as introducing many
Japanese firms to microelectronic manufacturing and applications.
The first optoelectronics consortium (1979-1984) helped start an
entire industry in Japan, which now dominates the world market for
that technology. Certainly, a demonstration effect was at work here
as well as a research benefit. In any case, the economic benefit --
world leadership -- constitutes an enormous return on the collective
investment.

As discussed here, research consortia can be seen to play
several important roles, not just in research but in technology transfer,
investment decision making, and modifying industry structure. Lack of
understanding of the roles of consortia and other agents of technology
infrastructure arise from insufficient analysis of the technology-based
economic system. For example, the denigrating of consortia because
relatively small amounts are spent on early-phase technology research
compared to applied R&D ignores, among other things, the
importance of technical risk reduction at this point in a technology's
life cycle and the need to overcome mismatches between existing
industry strategies and the potential applications of the new
technology being pursued.

Whatever, the objective of a consortium, being organizationally
separate from (external to) the member firms means that it will only
be as effective as its ability to transfer research results to the members
in a timely manner. Efficient technology transfer depends on several
factors: (1) the extent to which member companies embrace the
cooperative R&D as an integral part of their respective strategies, (2)
the degree to which members establish parallel internal or "shadow"
R&D projects that are complementary to the consortium's project, (3)
the degree to which they send top-quality staff to the on-site portion
(if any) of the consortium's operations, (4) how member firms position
returning assignees; and, (5) for consortia such as SEMATECH that
actually develop equipment, the degree and the speed of adoption of
this equipment in internal manufacturing processes.

Once again, the Japanese have demonstrated that they have
evolved a more sophisticated model. The dynamics of competition

---

[23]   Howell *et al* [1988, p. 66]

results in individual firms being reluctant to commit highly-valued technology assets (labor and capital, as well as technology itself) to a centralized cooperative research facility. Even though the Japanese have been very successful with such facilities (optoelectronics, for example), MITI has adapted its funding policies to the competitive dynamics by funding more research within the individual firms, while setting up transfer mechanisms to ensure that the research results are shared.[24]

Another criticism of large consortia, such as SEMATECH, is that they "centralize" the research agenda and thereby reduce the range of R&D. This can happen as documented by a Congressional Budget Office study:

> "Small semiconductor manufacturing equipment producers reported that semiconductor firms are less likely to fund R&D independently of SEMATECH and that SEMATECH has an elaborate decision making process that results in only certain firms being funded."[25]

Semiconductor firms were also reported to be relying on SEMATECH to conduct most, though not all, of their long-term R&D.

However, SEMATECH is certainly an atypical consortium in an atypical industry situation. The U.S. semiconductor industry had fallen way behind its Japanese competitors in manufacturing technology. Upon its inception, SEMATECH instantly became virtually the sole source for long-term R&D by virtue of the fact that no other U.S. sources of technology infrastructure existed. The vast U.S. Federal laboratory system, except for NIST, was oriented largely toward non-market objectives. DoD's VHSIC program, for example, was not an important source of the type of generic technology needed by U.S. semiconductor firms. Perhaps even more significant is the fact that the seriousness of the competitiveness deficit forced SEMATECH to be much more vertically integrated (well beyond generic technology research) than the vast majority of consortia.

Still, from a long-term efficiency perspective, picking some firms over others (and hence greatly influencing which firms succeed)

---

[24]   An excellent analysis of Japanese R&D funding practices is provided by Fransman [1991].

[25]   See U.S. Congress, Congressional Budget Office [1990, pp. 32-34].

is not a desirable practice. In economic terminology, it can be a "second-best" solution at most. Technologies may be passed over that, in a more pluralistic infrastructure environment, would have received the investment required to have their commercial viability demonstrated.

The only situation where such a step might be rationalized is when a strong conviction exists that the industry in question is too fragmented and is thus in need of consolidation (as is argued to be true for the U.S. semiconductor equipment industry). Just such an argument has been made in Europe for its semiconductor industry and, therefore, one of the objectives (unstated) of JESSI is to promote consolidation.

Summary

The essential requirement for understanding the roles of research consortia and developing effective strategies for their use is to emphasize not only the underinvestment phenomena that originally rationalized cooperative research, but also its interactions with the dynamics of technology-based competition. Competitive forces greatly influence what can be called "market failure". The ability to assume risk (of both the technological and scale-of-effort kinds), to allocate enough time to see early-phase research through to completion, and to capture economies of scope in subsequent market applications are all affected by the degree and nature of global competition faced by a domestic industry. Thus, the relative importance attached to the basic rationales for using the research consortium mechanism -- risk pooling, time reduction, and achieving economies of scale and scope -- will vary significantly across technologies.

Arguments that research consortia are not important because they "only demonstrate the economic potential of a technology" or because "relatively small amounts of funds are allocated to them" ignore the dynamics of the overall technology-based competitive process.[26] Economic efficiency is as important in the early phases of R&D as it is in the later development phases and in the subsequent production and marketing stages of the economic process. The

---

[26]   Porter [1990b, pp. 634-635].

critical sources of market failure -- high risk, significant economies of scale and scope, and short-term planning -- found in early phases of the R&D stage of the typical technology life cycle provide a strong rationale for cooperative research mechanisms.

By defining the output of early-phase research as "pre-competitive" and therefore as technology infrastructure, a much more efficient process can be invoked to advance the technology to the later phases of the R&D process, where individuals firms can efficiently take over. As with any other aspect of technology-based competition, however, the efficiency with which the appropriate strategies are executed can vary greatly, as has been seen in the varied strategies and experiences of the United States, Europe, and Japan.

Negative opinions of the utility of research consortia result primarily from the failure to consider a model such as the one presented in Chapter 3 and expanded upon here. Without the perspective of such a framework, too much tends to be expected of single infrastructure mechanisms. No matter how successful SEMATECH is within the limits of its objectives and capabilities, the U.S. semiconductor industry cannot succeed on its contribution alone. As proven by the Alvey Program in the United Kingdom, if other elements of competitive position are not in place, research consortia can not turn an industry around.

5 Industry Structure and Investment in Technology Infrastructure

"The trouble with the world isn't ignorance -- it's people knowing all them things that ain't so"

Mark Twain

One area of technology-based competition which has been particularly slow to receive constructive attention is the relationships between industry structure and other strategic variables. Structural factors such as size distribution, product composition, and relationships with infrastructure have always evolved over the life cycles of technologies underlying individual industries. During the past several decades, however, the rate of change in industry structure has increased in response to faster technological change and the globalization of markets.

Moreover, differences in these structural changes among industrialized nations have become pronounced in a number of critical industries, such as semiconductors and machine tools, contributing to the differences in competitive position. In particular, differences in vertical and horizontal integration have emerged as important distinguishing characteristics among competing domestic industries. To a large extent, these different industry structures have resulted from indigenous factors, but an external factor -- foreign direct investment -- is having increasingly important structural impacts.

Because the United States was by far the largest single industrialized economy for most of the post-war period and because it was also the dominant source of industrial technology during this period, great reliance was placed on *internal* domestic market efficiency. A strong *laissez-faire* approach has been taken by the U.S. Government, relying almost totally on the internal dynamics of the marketplace to make investment decisions with respect to technology beyond basic research. Industry structure evolved largely in response to the internal competitive dynamics.

A second major element of this philosophy was the belief that more competition was always better than less, with respect to maximizing domestic market efficiency. Antitrust laws were written so that almost any kind of cooperation beyond simple joint ventures was illegal. Foreign direct investment has been considered simply a part of the competitive dynamics of the domestic market. Conversely, little attention has been given to the roles this investment might be playing in both bringing technology into the domestic market and taking technology out. Such movements of technology can have pronounced effects on the demand for and the impacts of technology infrastructure.

With such emphasis on domestic competition, alternative industry structures were seldom considered in growth policy debates. When the "competitiveness problem" became part of the U.S. policy agenda in the 1980s, industry structure began to be considered in limited ways, but it certainly has not been regarded as a major element of industrial growth policy. In this chapter, the current evolution of industry structure will be analyzed relative to trends in global investment behavior, emphasizing interactions with technology infrastructure.

Foreign Direct Investment

In recent years, one of the more emotional issues connected with the economic growth objectives of industrialized nations has been foreign direct investment (FDI) -- defined as foreign ownership of a domestic economic asset (i.e., a business) as opposed to ownership of a financial asset (stocks, bonds, etc.).

The issue is an increasingly important one. Between 1973 and 1987, the volume of world foreign direct investment experienced a five-fold increase. This growth rate is much higher than the growth in world trade, which is, in turn, higher than the growth in world output.[1] Such a high growth rate, by itself, underscores the significance of this type of investment for current national growth strategies.

It is a particularly important issue for nations such as the United States which are experiencing high rates of inward FDI. During this 15-year period of intense growth in FDI, the U.S. share of total inward FDI grew from 9.9 to 25.2 percent. Since 1988, recorded inflows of foreign direct investment into the Untied States have exceeded U.S. direct investment outflows, in spite of an increase in U.S. investment abroad, especially in Europe. If the inflows were to continue at the current rate, the book value of foreign direct investment would double in relation to GNP by the end of the decade.

The official U.S. position on FDI during the 1980s was that the free flow of ownership of assets across national borders is beneficial. In identifying bilateral obstacles to trade, the Bush Administration has expressed its attachment to the principle of expanding a rules-based system for opening markets rather than the pursuit of "managed trade". Policy initiatives have been designed to ensure that domestic and foreign firms have equal opportunities to compete and that markets, not governments, determine the outcomes.[2] This *laissez-faire* approach towards FDI is not copied by most other industrialized nations, although a few such as Germany and the Netherlands come close.[3]

A study by Graham and Krugman [1989] for the Institute for International Economics (IIE) indicated that between 1977 and 1987, the stock of FDI in U.S. manufacturing grew from 5 percent to more

---

[1] See Lee and Reid [1991, p. 25].

[2] *Economic Report of the President*, February 1990, p. 247.

[3] Spencer [1989].

than 12 percent of total U.S. manufacturing assets. The IIE study also estimated that foreign-owned firms operating in the United States account for nearly one quarter of U.S. exports and one-third of U.S. imports.

Most foreign FDI in the United States takes the form of acquisitions rather than "green-field" (from scratch) investment; in 1988, the ratio was $60 billion to $5 billion.[4] Concern over the rate of increase in FDI falls into three categories: (1) a domestic industry is being bought up cheaply; (2) foreign firms may be acquiring undesirable concentration of market power; and, (3) "screwdriver" plants are being set up to import components for assembly. The first two categories of concern are supported by the high ratio of acquisitions to "greenfield" investments.

Analysts who are more concerned with technology-based growth policies, as opposed to investment in general, have more focused concerns. For example, Dorothy Robyn [1989] wrote that "outside acquisition of high-tech startups in biotechnology and microelectronics deny this country the large economic 'rents' from emerging technologies. And when the fruits of research are thus appropriated, subsequent development and manufacturing may well be done outside of the United States."

Even recent research that dismisses concerns of erosion of the U.S. technology base still find specific problems. For example, Glickman and Woodward [1989] cite evidence that foreign ownership denies U.S. workers certain high-skilled positions. Their survey of foreign firms in the automobile, semiconductor, and computer industries indicates that there are fewer U.S. employees doing R&D there (3.1 percent) than in comparable American-owned companies (6.6 percent). However, they also cite a study showing that Japanese plants in the United States invest four times as much in training new workers, and twice as much in retraining existing workers, as do comparable U.S.-owned plants.[5]

Much of the early debate on this topic focused on the establishment of foreign-owned *manufacturing* facilities in industries such as motor vehicles, because of the effects on employment. In the

---

[4]   OECD [1990a, pp. 59-61].

[5]   Robyn, [1989, p. 89].

1970s and early 1980s, investment by U.S. firms in foreign production was counteracted to some extent by increased foreign direct investment in the domestic U.S. economy, especially by the Japanese.

However, concern has been expressed that with their propensity for vertical integration, the Japanese will take over entire U.S. production chains ranging from the high-tech, such as electronics, to the more traditional industries, such as automobiles. Moreover, several studies have pointed out that foreign-owned affiliates, especially the Japanese, import higher percentages of their inputs than do U.S.-owned firms.[6] Although the foreign direct investment position of Japanese firms is actually only about one-quarter of the total European position and less than individual European nations such as the United Kingdom and the Netherlands, the tendency of Japanese firms to import more from their parent companies has raised concerns about long-term employment impacts.[7]

Conversely, the Japanese inclination toward vertical integration, has caused alarm because it raises the specter of foreign control of entire domestic production chains. This latter trend has been especially evident with respect to the automobile and the other industries in its production chain. Not only have Japanese motor vehicle companies greatly expanded U.S. domestic production capacity while U.S.-owned firms have cut back, but virtually all new investment in U.S. steel production is Japanese. The Japanese have made large investments in rubber and tire production capacity.[8]

Analysts continue to praise this trend as "saving the rust belt", and state governments have provided large subsidies to induce foreign investment in their states. What policy recommendations that have been made focus on upgrading U.S. suppliers to these foreign-owned or "transplant complexes".

A potential problem with these patterns of FDI is that they can reduce the long-run growth potential within the domestic economy. Even when "transplant complexes" arise, so that some

---

6   See Graham and Krugman [1989] and Lee and Reid, editors [1991].

7   Country-by-country data on foreign direct investment can be found in the U.S. Department of Commerce, *Survey of Current Business*, August 1990, p. 41.

8   See, for example, Kenney and Florida [1991].

vertical integration occurs domestically, maximum domestic value added is not achieved. For one thing, even with substantial re-investment of profits, foreign ownership claims do result in some export of capital. But this can hardly be cause for complaint, given that U.S. firms do the same thing in reverse. Global markets will have increasingly greater international capital flows.

This FDI can have a positive long-run effect by rekindling the competitive motivations of a currently moribund domestic industry and eventually result in a competitive resurgence, although the presence of imported goods in the domestic market should have the same effect. The real problem is that these "transplant complexes" cannot be said at this point in time to be complete vertical production chains. In particular, anecdotal evidence suggests that major portions of the first stage in the production chain, R&D, is reserved for the home country -- especially in the case of the Japanese.[9]

Because the globalization of markets means that capital must and will flow into and out of domestic economies, the growth policy issues should revolve around how to maximize the contributions of this "international" capital to long-term domestic economic growth.

The Technology Impact of FDI

Acquisitions of domestic companies and joint ventures between domestic and foreign firms in which technology is a major factor in the arrangement are proliferating. Yet, both the scope as well as the magnitude of these investments are not well known. A survey by Ernst and Young found that firms in the biotechnology industry currently average three "strategic alliances", with the largest companies averaging nine. Over a third of these partnerships are with foreign firms. Only a portion involve equity investments by the foreign partner, but this number is growing and affecting even the largest firms, as evidenced by the sale of a majority interest in industry

---

[9]   As Peter Drucker [1991] puts it, "new Japanese strategies call for...firm control of...'brain capital'".

leader Genentech to Swiss pharmaceutical giant Hoffmann-La Roche.[10] Of course, these alliances can be a mechanism for acquiring new technology as well as for exchanging it.

Occasionally, a particular investment elicits strong reactions from a domestic government. The U.S. Department of Justice in early 1991 rejected the attempted purchase of Semi-Gas, the world's largest supplier of gas cabinets and purification equipment for semiconductor device manufacturing, by a Japanese company (Nippon Sanso). The DoJ decided that the sale to Nippon Sanso, which is the largest supplier in Japan and number two in the world, would dampen competition in an industry that is already quite concentrated. This decision also may have been influenced by arguments that the sale would cede complete control of the technology to foreign sources. SEMATECH, which purchases equipment from Semi-Gas, raised one of the strongest objections to potentially another loss of U.S. control over an important technology in a critical production chain.

Such actions further raise the issue of whether the free flow of foreign direct investment is good for an economy. More specifically, the economic growth issue is whether potential systematic differences in strategies exist between foreign and domestic investors, and hence in the composition of these investments.

As with most elements of technology-based competition, observed behavior is not homogeneous. For example, consider the following two statements made at 1990 Congressional hearings and quoted in *New Technology Week*:

> "What is best for America is to take advantage of the best technology available, no matter what the source. Where a technology is born is not really as important as where it is put to use."
>
> Neil Vander Dussen,
> President and CEO,
> Sony Corporation of America

> "A company should be defined as American by its commitment to U.S.-based research, development and manufacturing, and its

---

[10]   Ernst and Young [1990]. Fast growing industries such as biotechnology become important to domestic economies quickly. In the 1990, this "infant" industry had approximately $4 billion in worldwide sales.

investment in providing Americans with the skills and knowledge
necessary to compete in a global economy".

Mark Rochkind
President, Philips Laboratories
(subsidiary of N.V. Philips, Ltd.
of the Netherlands)

These two statements imply decidedly different philosophies with respect to the breadth of participation in the U.S. domestic economy.

In the end, it is an empirical question to what extent R&D is shifted or maintained outside the domestic economy, or to what extent the scope of domestic R&D investment in a particular technology is limited as a result of FDI -- i.e., how many foreign investors follow the Japanese company Sony's philosophy and how many follow the Dutch company Philips' philosophy.

In summary, concern has been expressed that foreign acquisitions result in the reduction or even the termination of R&D by the domestic subsidiary, with the knowledge production (R&D) occurring in the foreign company's home country. To the extent that R&D is shifted to the purchaser's home country, FDI would contribute to a significant reduction in the potential value added in the domestic market. That is, over time, value added would become constrained to manufacturing and marketing.

In a worst case scenario, a number of industries' potential growth rates would be significantly reduced over time and the domestic economy would be constrained to the status of "off-shore" producer for countries with the knowledge base. In fact, one can envision a scenario in which a foreign company decides to move a production facility out of the host country, perhaps because it is too isolated from the knowledge base. The host country would then be relegated to begging the foreign company to keep the plant within the domestic economy, with its moderate-skilled (and moderate-wage) jobs.

Moreover, to the extent that research is conducted in foreign firms' home countries, there is little reason for universities to maintain curricula in the particular field or for domestic graduate students to choose those technical areas, nor for government labs to conduct relevant research. Consequently, the domestic technology infrastructure erodes, and, once dissipated, reestablishing it is not easy.

Krugman and Graham [1989] attempted to support the argument that FDI does not affect domestic R&D investment by comparing R&D per worker for all foreign investment with the comparable ratio for the U.S. economy as a whole. They make a similar comparison for the manufacturing sector, as that is where most R&D expenditures occur.

However, in 1988, the major manufacturing industry groups -- chemicals, electrical and non-electrical machinery, instruments, and transportation equipment -- accounted for 87.5% of R&D expenditures in the U.S. manufacturing sector. Department of Commerce data show that 85.4% of foreign direct investment in R&D occurred in these industry groups in that year.[11] Thus, relating R&D intensity of FDI in the United States to all U.S. manufacturing gives an inaccurate comparison. Clearly, at a minimum, one needs to examine these R&D-intensive industry groups.

Thus, in Table 5-1, R&D investment as a percentage of sales is calculated for both foreign affiliates and U.S. firms in the comparable major industry group. Note that the technology base in each of these major industry groups is still quite diversified. The ratios show slightly higher intensity of R&D investment for foreign affiliates in chemical-related industries (largely European firms), which accounts for approximately 60 percent of all foreign affiliates' R&D investment. The foreign affiliates in the other four major industry groups, generally regarded as among the most technologically advanced, all display lower ratios of R&D to sales than do their U.S. counterparts. It now becomes clear that the patterns of FDI are not as simple as appears to be the case when examining highly aggregated economic data (i.e., for all manufacturing).

To get closer to comparisons of industries based on single generic technologies (and therefore comparable industry and government R&D objectives), R&D/sales ratios are calculated in Table 5-2 for several critical technology-based industry groups that makeup the major industry groups in Table 5-1. Except for electronic

---

[11]   Some careful attention to definitions is in order here. The Bureau of Economic Analysis, whose data are used in the following tables, defines a foreign *affiliate* as a firm operating in the domestic United States whose ownership is at least 10% foreign. This is significantly different from a foreign-*controlled* firm, which is difficult to define but usually would require at least 51% foreign ownership.

Table 5-1

R&D Intensity of U.S. Affiliates of Foreign Firms
Compared to U.S. Industry for Major Industry Groups

Major Industry Group (SIC)	R&D Expenditures as a Percent of Sales				
	1987		1988		
	Foreign Affiliates	All U.S. Firms	Foreign Affiliates	All U.S. Firms	
Manufacturing (D.)	2.51	2.31	2.38	2.27	
Chemicals (28)	4.53	4.22	4.81	4.07	
Machinery (35)	3.77	4.97	2.76	4.99	
Electrical Equipment (36)	4.31	6.19	4.12	5.99	
Transportation (37)	0.90	4.08	0.82	3.96	
Instruments (38)	4.00	4.65	3.37	4.67	

Source: data for FDI in R&D and sales by foreign affiliates in the United States are from U.S.
Department of Commerce, Bureau of Economic Analysis [1990a]; data for R&D by domestic U.S.
firms abroad are from the U.S. National Science Foundation [1990]; data for sales by U.S. firms are
from U.S. Department of Commerce, Bureau of the Census [1989, 1990].

Table 5-2

R&D Intensity of U.S. Affiliates of Foreign Firms Compared to U.S. Industry for High-Technology Industry Groups

| Major Industry Group (SIC) | R&D Expenditures as a Percent of Sales | | | |
| | 1987 | | 1988 | |
	Foreign Affiliates	All U.S. Firms	Foreign Affiliates	All U.S. Firms
Pharmaceuticals (283)	9.73	10.54	10.07	10.76
Computers & Office Equipment (357)	9.17	13.62	8.97	13.91
Audio, Video & Communications Equipment (365, 366)	4.28	13.57	5.13	13.29
Electronic Components (367)	10.47	7.33	7.04	7.23

Source: same as Table 5-1.

components in 1987, U.S. firms are investing in R&D at higher rates than the subgroup of affiliates of foreign firms.

These data indicate that foreign parents of domestic affiliates in a significant number of critical technology-based industries are depending upon knowledge bases developed in their home countries. As indicated above, firms from different nations seem to have significantly different strategies, and anecdotes can always be found that go against the general pattern. But, it is aggregate or average trends that have the ultimate influence domestic economic growth.

Of all nations with significant investment positions in the United States, the Japanese are the most controversial. This is in part because they seem to keep much R&D at home. Of course, Japan is the most R&D-intensive economy, so it has more domestic R&D capability and therefore has more incentive to invest in domestic production of technical knowledge.

But what has raised even more concern is the fact that the Japanese are aggressive worldwide searchers for new technology. From discussions with analysts that have closely followed Japanese investment practices in the United States, it is estimated that between 1985 and 1990 Japanese firms made direct investments in approximately 300 small, high-technology firms. Small firms of this type represent a major source of innovative technology. If this technology is basically appropriated by a foreign production chain with reduced follow-on investment in these firms, the domestic production chain declines.[12]

Finally, the above discussion has focused on direct foreign investment in the United States. U.S. direct investment in other countries must also be analyzed to help understand the differences in the incentives for investment in general in the domestic industry and in same industry in other nations. As indicated in Table 5-3, foreign affiliates of U.S. companies have approximately doubled their annual R&D expenditures over the decade of the 1980s.

---

[12]   Ongoing U.S. Government studies indicate that in 1990, the Japanese also had approximately 1200 guest researchers working in Federal laboratories throughout the Untied States and had about $35 million in contract research with these labs. Many more Japanese scientists, engineers, and business executives visit U.S. corporations and government laboratories each year. All these activities are part of a worldwide technology accumulation strategy.

Annual R&D investment by U.S. affiliates of foreign-owned companies increased by almost a factor of five. In absolute terms, foreign affiliates now collectively conduct more R&D in the United States than U.S. firms' affiliates are conducting elsewhere. This situation can be attributed to the still considerable U.S. technology base, including superior institutions (universities, government laboratories, etc.) that contribute technology infrastructure.

However, the *intensity* of this investment is a more accurate indicator of strategy and potential impacts on domestic economic growth. As shown in Table 5-2, many foreign-owned affiliates in the United States have not been making these investments at the same level of intensity in a number of technologically-advanced industries as U.S. domestic firms in the same industry.

Table 5-3

R&D Expenditures by Foreign Affiliates of U.S.-Owned Firms and by U.S. Affiliates of Foreign-Owned Firms
(Billions of $U.S.)

R&D Expenditures	1980	1985	1987	1988	1989
Foreign affiliates in the United States	1.9	5.2	6.2	7.4	9.3
U.S. affiliates abroad	3.2	3.7	5.2	6.3	6.5

Source: data for FDI in R&D and sales by foreign affiliates in the United States are from U.S. Department of Commerce, Bureau of Economic Analysis [1990a]; data for R&D by domestic U.S. firms abroad are from the U.S. National Science Foundation [1990].

The reverse is even more the case for U.S. firms. Their foreign subsidiaries conduct proportionately less R&D abroad relative to sales, as shown in Table 5-4. These data are supported by a National Science Foundation study [1991] of R&D investment in Japan by U.S. firms. The study found that the extent of this R&D is much less than the level of sales by the U.S. subsidiaries would predict. Moreover, a large majority of the R&D that these firms do conduct is applied research which supports product development specifically for the Japanese market. "Japanese R&D facilities created solely to conduct research remain rare and tend to occur primarily within the chemical or pharmaceutical industries."[13]

Table 5-4

R&D Intensity of U.S. Subsidiaries in Foreign Countries Compared to U.S. Domestic Firms

Industry	R&D as a Percent of Sales -- 1988		
	U.S. Domestic Firms	*Majority-Owned U.S. Foreign Subsidiaries*	*All U.S. Foreign Subsidiaries*
Pharmaceuticals (283)	10.66	3.14	2.99
Computers & Office Equipment (357)	13.86	2.25	1.94
Electronic Components (367)	7.53	1.08	0.93

Source: sales data from the U.S. Department of Commerce, Bureau of Economic Analysis [1990b]; R&D data from the U.S. National Science Foundation [1990].

However, options available to U.S. firms investing in R&D in Japan are much more limited than is the case for Japanese firms investing in the United States. Japanese companies can give grants to or contract with U.S. universities or other U.S. research institutions. They can participate in providing technology-based venture capital or

---

[13]   Some Japanese have recently argued that U.S. semiconductor firms need *more* product support and test facilities in Japan in order to expand market share.

take over existing U.S. companies. These mechanisms are basically closed to U.S. firms operating in Japan.

Nevertheless, the NSF study indicates that U.S. companies can establish productive R&D facilities in Japan. U.S. firms, while still experiencing great difficulty in exporting technology to the parent company in the United States, have found that Japanese R&D management practices have contributed "significantly to higher R&D productivity". Factors cited were systematic planning, program continuity, and senior management support for R&D as keys to future corporate viability. Also, respondents to the NSF study's survey indicated that they can participate in government-sponsored research projects and have better access to information from such projects.

However, after all the influences -- both positive and negative are analyzed -- the aggregate data indicate that both the U.S. and the average of nations with whom it competes invest considerably less in R&D relative to sales outside their home countries. The implication is that domestic growth policies should be concerned with developing incentives to foreign affiliates to expand the scope as well as the scale of R&D investment.

Strategy Implications

The importance of maintaining high rates of early-phase R&D by private firms within the domestic economy cannot be overemphasized. Michael Porter, for example, found in his comprehensive study [1990b] of successful industries in 10 industrialized nations that proximity to innovative suppliers and specialized (technology-based) infrastructure were critical factors in determining competitive position.

If foreign direct investment is the result of some trade barrier (such as "voluntary" export quotas), the foreign company may not make a broad or long-term commitment to either knowledge production or improving the productivity or quality of the domestic suppliers with whom it may be forced to do business. Conversely, a growth strategy that promotes a competitive domestic industry structure and a healthy supporting technology infrastructure will presumably attract FDI that is targeted across all stages of economic activity from R&D to marketing. Such investment can contribute to a competitive advantage for the domestic economy.

As an example of an implementation of the latter philosophy, the U.S. Congress' Conference Report on the 1991 appropriation for NIST allows participation in the Advanced Technology Program by foreign-owned companies that have made this broad multi-stage commitment to the U.S. domestic economy and whose home countries allow participation of U.S.-owned companies in similar research programs.

The European Community has a less effective definition of a domestic firm for purposes of participating in government programs within the EC common market. Article 58 of the Treaty of Rome (the EC's Constitution) defines an EC firm as one "formed in accordance with the law of a member state and having [its] registered offices, central administration, or principle place of business in the Community". Accordingly, subsidiaries, but not branches, of foreign-owned firms are considered EC firms. Under this type of definition, foreign-owned firms can presumably participate in programs such as cooperative research, even if their domestic activities are limited to manufacturing, assembly, and marketing, or even just assembly and marketing.

Alternatively, one can simply argue that the strategic objective should be simply to gain access to needed complementary technology assets from wherever the source. The decision of where to find these assets could be left to the consortium, with no further restrictions imposed. The most important point is that instead of being so concerned about foreign participation in domestic research consortia, a nation should be glad that consortia are located in the domestic economy where more domestic firms can participate and the technology transfer to those firms is likely to be more rapid. Foreign participation in government-sponsored research programs should be allowed if those firms "bring to the table" their share of the required research assets. Allowing participation by a foreign firm thus becomes a *management* problem, not an arbitrary legal one. If the foreign firm then invests in domestic production facilities, so much the better.

Moreover, if a domestic industry is substantially behind its foreign competitors, direct investment by these competitors can be a significant factor in providing the necessary investment in both domestic private-sector technology capability and public-sector technology infrastructure. More generally, the timing of investment can be critical. Thus, participation of foreign affiliates in a consortium may increase the efficiency of the research, including reducing the time required to carry it out.

U.S. firms have been made painfully aware of the tactic of numerous vertically-integrated foreign firms by which they withhold new technical developments until other divisions of their own firm (or, even other firms in that nation) have achieved a head start in incorporating the technology into downstream products. Joint ventures often solve this problem, but the domestic firm has to have an existing technology asset of value to bargain with.

There is even a tendency on the part of some firms in countries such a Japan to discriminate in the open market in favor of other domestic firms; that is, they delay or refuse to export certain critical technologies. This situation has been alleged to occur in semiconductor manufacturing equipment, for example. The existence of foreign affiliates of those firms would presumably reduce these tendencies. That is, FDI should thus help create a domestic supply that is presumably available in a timely fashion.

The long-term strategic problem for growth policy is to ensure a total value-added domestic economic structure. The most important stage of this strategy is knowledge production -- i.e., the location of R&D. The Japanese realize this better than most and, as a result, are particularly determined to keep knowledge production at home. Thus, when in early 1991 the U.S. Commerce Department ruled that several major Japanese computer display manufacturers were "dumping" those products in the U.S. market, allegedly to drive the infant U.S. industry out of existence, the largest Japanese exporter, Sharp Corp., quickly announced plans to *assemble* displays for laptop computers in the United States. the Japanese dominate this technology and, in the adversarial mode that ensued, only wanted to do the minimum necessary to gain access to the U.S. computer market.

The announcement by Sharp was greeted as a positive step by the American Electronics Association.[14] However, Sharp's U.S. plant only makes 50 percent of the value of each screen, with the most advanced work being done in Japan. This situation may be acceptable to U.S. computer manufactures, who were concerned about continued

---

[14] See Schlesinger [1991].

access to the displays from Japan and sided with their Japanese suppliers in the dispute.[15]

The major policy issue is that, with the Japanese penchant for vertical integration strategies, continuing to ignore the long-term consequences of the "hollowing out" of the domestic production chain in too many areas will most certainly aggravate current competitive problems.

The concern is, in fact, that this scenario is being repeated over and over. In 1987, Toshiba Corp. established a U.S. plant to make personal computers after the United States imposed duties on this and other products using Japanese chips that were alleged to have been dumped. And, of course, all major Japanese automobile manufacturers have set up major manufacturing facilities in the United States. These "forced" solutions have not brought with them the R&D needed by a domestic economy.

As shown in Table 5-1, foreign-owned auto manufacturers conduct very little R&D in the United States, thereby keeping the knowledge production at home. Many of the supporters of FDI cite anecdotes, such as Honda's automotive R&D center in Marysville, Ohio, as "evidence" of changing R&D investment patterns by foreign companies, particularly the Japanese. If such investments constitute the beginning of a trend toward "full-phase" R&D, then investment patterns are moving in the right direction. However, the aggregate data presented here clearly show that not enough "anecdotes" exist at this point in time to begin to allow a positive conclusion to be drawn with respect to patterns of FDI in R&D.

The major objective here is to articulate the policy issue. Control of knowledge production is control of the technology and product life cycles. Having the portion of the value added at the manufacturing stage located domestically may be better than nothing, but it is of limited benefit from a long-term growth strategy point of view. The main point is that domestic growth policy must find a way to expand the scope as well as the scale of R&D investment by foreign affiliates. Forcing such investment does not seem feasible. Instead, the domestically-owned firms and the institutions supplying

---

[15]   Alternatively, U.S. computer manufacturers can shift personal computer production to foreign sites (which several have threatened to do), in order to get around the cost penalties imposed on imported displays.

technology infrastructure must upgrade their R&D, not only for the direct benefit of domestic firms, but so that sufficient investment incentives are presented to foreign affiliates with technology assets to contribute to the industrial base.

As noted above, many analysts do not seem to see this problems in the "transition" to a true global investment environment. Robert Reich [1991a] argues that corporate strategies are becoming so global as to render obsolete the significance of national origin (including the location of a corporation's headquarters) for increasing numbers of multinational companies. His "*global web*" concept of corporate strategy dictates investment wherever the higher value added can be generated. In this model, no presumed hierarchy exists in which the "home" operations are at the pinnacle of the corporate management structure. Management is much more distributed geographically. Even "Japanese companies that have traditionally done most of their highest value-added work in Japan now must reconsider the economic and political advisability of this strategy." Reich also points out that "global investment is supplanting merchandise trade as the major engine of world economic integration -- and the key to a nation's wealth and well-being".

However, although Reich cites a number of specific examples of these trends, including companies that fall into the industries in the above tables, the aggregate industry data suggest that this process is far from complete. The significant differences in R&D intensity between U.S.-owned and foreign-affiliated companies (the latter including companies with as little as 10% foreign ownership) argue that significant value added at the all-important R&D stage is still systematically reserved for the home country.

A detailed analysis of the expanded influence of multinational corporations by Cantwell [1989] concludes that foreign direct investment is motivated by a strategy of "technology accumulation" which is implemented through an "international network" of investments at centers of innovation around the world. Treating technology as a homogeneous entity, Cantwell argues that production typically follows, resulting in a decline in exports from the home base. He regards this phenomenon as "an important element in the recent development of technological competition".

Furthermore, he states that "the growth of 'intra-industry' production may be associated with the decentralization of R&D activities within the [multinational corporations] concerned, even though strategic control of new technological developments may remain at corporate headquarters". Again, the available data presented here do not support the existence of this "trend" to any significant degree.

As Cantwell argues, companies do seem to be coming to regard the area of foreign research support as one element of a systematic strategy for accessing *external* sources of S&T information. Evan Herbert [1989] describes clearly the multi-faceted and integrated nature of Japanese strategies for acquiring and transferring technology from sources external to their companies and hence to their internal R&D programs. The efficiency difference between U.S. and Japanese firms seems to be the degree to which the importance and systems character of such activities are recognized.

Finally, the role of FDI should be kept in perspective. A database compiled by the Department of Commerce's Technology Administration shows that in the 1989-90 period only 23.0 percent of United States-Japan corporate linkages were in the form of foreign direct investment in the area of computers and peripherals, 4.3 percent in Aerospace, 12.1 percent in semiconductors, 26.4 percent in semiconductor manufacturing equipment, 11.4 in biotechnology, and 8.6 percent in computer software.[16] In other words, technology can flow into a domestic economy (as well as out) by a number of mechanisms.

However, the amount and composition of FDI should be regarded as an indicator of the health of a nation's long-term growth strategy. In this context, one can conclude that foreign direct investment is bad when (1) it restricts the competitiveness of the domestic economy at a particular stage in the economic process (such as R&D), or (2) when it disrupts the efficiency gains from vertical integration of domestic industries. In contrast, it is good when it leverages a broad, technology-based national growth strategy that seeks to expand value added at all stages of the economic process, including R&D. The policy objective therefore should be to influence the composition as well as the scale of foreign direct investment, specifically by providing incentives for major commitments by foreign firms to domestic technology investment.

---

[16]   See Guenther and Dalton [1990]. These FDI percentages include "mergers and acquisitions", which they treated as a separate class of linkages.

Scientific & Technical Information

As a major infrastructure role, the Japanese Government has helped remove barriers to efficient transfer of technical information through efforts such as reduction of language barriers via such tools as a Kanji version of the C programming language (enabling acquisition of designs and processes using software) and refinement of automatic English-Japanese language translation. As Herbert [1989] points out, "the Government of Japan is always in the background, largely through [MITI], studying, initiating, and coordinating strategic efforts".

Much overseas information gets back to Japan via databases. This technology infrastructure is produced by major information organizations in Japan. Supported by government funds and user fees, they maintain some of the more important of these databases. MITI also publishes a *Database Directory*.

The Japan Information Center of Science and Technology (JICST) is the central organization for information activities in the S&T area. In addition to collecting S&T literature, JICST is constructing a machine language translation system and dictionary. Japan's information industry has created the Database Promotion Center, which supports such projects as a survey of foreign dictionary databases to be used in machine translation systems and a database of dictionaries of English/Japanese technical terms as a translation support tool.

Herbert cites numerous examples of how Japanese firms have systematically set up and improved technology acquisition and transfer mechanisms. He concludes by stating that "given equal access to the same data, the Japanese tend to collect every scrap, and subsequently seem more thorough in extracting not only useful information but software with the power to instantly transfer processes. (For example, when Lawrence Livermore National Lab's supercomputer code for simulations entered the public domain not long ago, it was acquired by a Sumitomo Bank subsidiary, which then sold the code to major companies in Japan.)"

One of the more noteworthy information management devices used by Japanese companies is a forcing function to ensure "fusion" of technologies from previously separate application areas (i.e., industries). For example, Toshiba has a Division of Technical Planning and Coordination which works across all technologies to bring together the resources needed by the line-of-business units. This concept was promoted heavily by MITI, as a major player in supplying this type of technology infrastructure.

The effects of greater Japanese efforts to cultivate and utilize external sources of technology are evidenced by Edwin Mansfield's research [1988b] in which he finds that the Japanese are generally quicker and more cost-effective only when moving *externally*-developed technology through subsequent stages of the innovation process. Mansfield's study shows that innovation time and cost differentials vary from industry to industry but overall less of a gap exists when the technology is developed within an innovating firm. However, some Japanese researchers complain that the intensity of the search for foreign technology diverts resources from original research.[17] Moreover, Japan's acknowledged inadequacies in basic science truncates the basis for much original technology development.

Sheridan Tatsuno [1989a] has pointed out that in spite of the rigidities in Japanese industry structure, new ideas do generate and disseminate surprisingly rapidly through informal mechanisms, while in the United States labor mobility is being partially replaced by similar informal interactions over increasingly pervasive communications networks. Tatsuno also observes that the types of information requested by Japanese and American firms differ significantly, and, thus, so will the nature of information infrastructures that evolve in the two economies.

The Japanese are driven by the Buddhist way of thinking -- everything is cyclical in nature, which explains their obsession with improving the same product again and again. Products, like human beings are viewed as unfinished and always have to be improved.[18] The Japanese tend to think much more broadly with respect to the potential applications of a generic technology, so their search for relevant technical and market information is equally broad and

---

[17]   See Leonard Lynn [1985, p. 257].

[18]   Tatsuno [1989a, p. 6] cites Toshiba's experience with the laptop PC, that went through a 15-year "cycle" during which several intermediate products were developed but failed in the marketplace. Each time the product was recycled through R&D, with new technology and performance attributes resulting. Eventually, market success was achieved. In most economics, defeat would have been declared long before that success was realized.

general compared to other industrialized nations. Thus, concepts such as "fusion" technologies and their early embracing of research consortia are indicative of an above-average appreciation for a broad and widely diffused information infrastructure. Western nations have followed this general philosophy in *science* infrastructure (basic research), but are only beginning to experiment with similar attitudes toward technology infrastructure.

Organizational Integration

In spite of major changes over the past decade, many U.S. firms still suffer in the global marketplace from inappropriate organizational structures. Many companies are in industries where the product structures of foreign competition are vertically integrated. Moreover, the internal organizations of many foreign firms, particularly Japanese, are highly integrated in that R&D, production, and marketing work together as one unit.

A major structural issue is the optimal degree of vertical integration of the production chain. With technology and subsequent product life cycles shortening, reaction to changes in market demand is critical. Within the corporation, much attention has been given to "flexibility" in production technology, but product development must be equally adaptive. Communication between R&D and manufacturing is essential, not only in designing the product for manufacturing (concurrent engineering) but in timing the delivery of the product for use in "downstream" products or systems. The vertically-integrated company can greatly increase the efficiency of the required coordination.

As argued in previous chapters, economies of scope and hence horizontal integration is a much more important strategy for technology-based competition than has been the case in the past. Once again, Japan has been the leader in developing and implementing this strategy. The frequently cited Keiretsu is predominantly a horizontally-integrated organizational structure. A descendent of the pre-World War II *Zaibatsu* megaconglomerates, the *horizontal (or financial) Keiretsu* are centered on a bank, trading company, or major manufacturing firm. They have interlocking stock ownership which produces stable demand for goods, thus helping the member firms to take a longer-term strategic focus (for example, trading off current profits for more R&D).

However, the Japanese economy also has a number of prominent *vertical (or production) Keiretsu*, in which the major firm (e.g., automobiles) is primarily an assembler. According to MITI documents, such firms produce on average only about 30% of the parts they assemble into the final product, compared to approximately 80% for U.S. firms. Thus, the dominant firm must maintain stock ownership in order to exercise sufficient control over suppliers. Such structures are beginning to evolve in the United States in industries such as computers. The conventional wisdom in the United States is that the large company in such relationships controls the direction of the technology and even "trickles up" technology to its smaller suppliers.

These relationships seem also to be in place in Japan. However, a number of translated articles in the Japanese press, referring to a 1988 MITI study, indicate that large Japanese firms are increasingly relying on their smaller suppliers for product innovations, given these smaller firms' greater organizational and strategic flexibility and hence lower-cost R&D performance. An indicator of this trend is a greater frequency of joint R&D projects.

Such trends should be carefully considered, because they indicate that no optimal degree of vertical integration exists. Industries in the electronics area, where capital intensity is relatively low, experience many small firms continually entering, technological life cycles that are short, and technological advances at one level in the production chain greatly affecting the competitiveness of levels above and below it. These factors cause cash flow volatility at individual levels and thus provide an argument for relatively more vertical integration than in industries such as automobiles and aerospace with more stable industry structures and relatively longer technology life cycles.[19]

Some have argued that consortia are a surrogate for vertical integration, but such claims must be carefully qualified. Consortia can be a substitute at a particular phase of R&D (usually pre-competitive research). However, this mechanism in general cannot provide the

---

[19]   See Tassey [1990] and U.S. Congress, Office of Technology Assessment [1990, pp. 142-143].

benefits of all the "feedback loops" at the three major stages of the production chain.

An example of the negative impacts from the lack of vertical integration is the U.S. semiconductor industry. Structural weakness in this industry has allowed foreign competitors to exercise sufficient market power to control technology and price. Compelling examples include the DRAM shortage in the mid 1980s, the inability of U.S. supercomputer companies to purchase the fastest chips (Japanese developed and manufactured), and the difficulty for most U.S. chip producers in gaining timely access to the most advanced foreign semiconductor manufacturing equipment and materials.[20]

The danger here is that competitors of domestic companies will be in a position to dictate both the quality of the technology to which the domestic companies have access, and the timing with which these companies can bring new products incorporating that technology to market. Because technology and time-to-market advantages are increasingly critical in international competition, this situation would permit foreign industries to determine the competitive fate of the domestic industry.

Vertical integration through some mechanism is essential to maintain timely technology flows from one level in the production chain to the next. Semiconductors, for example, are the enabling level in the electronics production chain. As a U.S. Government report put it, "In the end, the vast set of downstream industries, their revenue, and their jobs will be the prize for the nation that ultimately dominates semiconductor manufacturing."[21]

There are several instances in which Japanese firms have been accused of refusing to make their most advanced technology available to their U.S. customers. Examples include Hitachi and Fujitsu which both refused to sell their most advanced chips to U.S. systems firms, supplying them only their low-speed ones, while keeping their fastest types for internal use in such products as supercomputers. MELCO (Mitsubishi Electronics) also refused to make available its more advanced GaAs (gallium arsenide) chips.

---

[20]   Ian Ross [1989, p. 14].

[21]   David [1987, p. 5].

Dependency per se (say, silicon wafers) is not necessarily bad, if the domestic industry is dominant at one level and foreign competitors at another; that is, if the dependency is bi-directional between firms and nations. Within an industry group, dependent on a particular generic technology, a domestic industry must have a presence in the "technology driver"; or, if more than one driver exists, the domestic industry must be a leader in one of them in order to develop a "lever" to create mutual dependency.

In the absence of vertical integration, more elaborate information infrastructure is needed. Of an estimated 500 U.S.- and foreign-owned semiconductor equipment manufacturers operating in the United States, only a small percentage of this number are multi-product-line firms with annual sales above $50 million. A large number are one-product companies, and most have annual sales below $10 million.[22] In a GAO survey of semiconductor equipment manufacturers, company executives rated as "ineffective" working relationships between semiconductor manufacturers and their suppliers. This ranking followed closely behind the cost of capital as the most significant factor contributing to the declining competitiveness of U.S. suppliers.[23] In particular, the survey found that

o   25 of 31 suppliers stated that semiconductor chip manufacturers provide little financial support to their suppliers;

o   23 of these suppliers said that manufacturers do not involve their suppliers in their planning;

o   21 suppliers mentioned that relationships are based purely on short-term considerations; and,

---

[22]   Based on data from VLSI Research, Inc.

[23]   The General Accounting Office [1990, pp. 21-24] report on SEMATECH presented results from a survey of executives of 31 U.S.-owned semiconductor equipment suppliers.

o   21 suppliers noted that manufacturers do not
         share technical data on the performance of
         equipment with suppliers.

In response to the problems facing the semiconductor
equipment industry, an off-shoot of SEMATECH called
SEMI/SEMATECH was formed in 1988. SEMATECH's members
agreed in June 1990 to participate in a new "Partnering for Total
Quality Program" with SEMI/SEMATECH firms. Under the
agreement, SEMATECH members stated their intention to work
more closely with their key U.S. suppliers by sharing (1) strategic
goals and plans, (2) information about the technical performance of
the suppliers's equipment, (3) competitive analysis information, and
(4) some of the costs of suppliers's product development work.
     The process was made operational by creating operational
categories that could be worked on by the manufacturer/supplier
partnerships. For example, to enhance the technical performance as
well as the timing of supply of production equipment, information is
now being exchanged on topics such as manufacturing systems
support, clean room manufacturing assistance, and long-term process
development.
     Over time, an information infrastructure, such as that
developed by the Partnering for Total Quality Program, can have at
least two significant economic impacts. First, the categories of
information provided through this process can lead to more efficient
behavior within the individual organizations by virtue of more effective
external relationships. In the case of the semiconductor industry, the
overall intent of the information infrastructure provided by this
program is to enable closer working relationships between chip
manufacturers and equipment and material suppliers. In some cases,
these interactions lead to relationships other than just information-
sharing, such as cost-sharing of equipment development. In other
words, *virtual* integration is achieved.[24]
     Second, these improved relationships along with the
information infrastructure itself can lead to *organizational* integration

---

[24]   Cost-sharing is a particularly important element of cooperation
because it can provide some of the cash-flow flexibility normally only available
through organizational integration.

(i.e., mergers and acquisitions), if that is the most efficient long-run solution. Strategic decisions on vertical integration (material suppliers and chip manufacturers) or "diagonal" integration with equipment suppliers will be more efficient in the presence of this information infrastructure, which has been virtually non-existent among U.S. industries.

A final infrastructure role affecting industry structure is the provision of standards. As will be discussed in Chapter 6, standards can affect industry structure by greatly increasing the efficiency of interfaces between products that must work together as part of a larger technological system. SEMATECH and MCC are both working to develop equipment compatibility standards to provide a technical basis for increased vendor cooperation.

A general prescription, derived from the above analysis, is to argue that the correct complement of infrastructure can preserve the past structural advantage of many U.S. industries, under which small and medium firms were created, prospered through superior innovative behavior, and in many instances grew to be very large firms. Such dynamic evolution of industry structure resulted in either replacing older firms that had become "calcified" and lost their innovative capacity or pressuring these older firms into revitalizing themselves.

Summary

A tendency among analysts and policy makers is to deduce from the ever increasing technological and associated economic complexity that the scale of technology research and production of resulting products can only increase. Moreover, it is argued by the Japanese and an increasing number of western analysts that competitive pressures in core technology-based industries such as electronics will require vertical integration in the conventional intra-organizational sense, with future industry structures possibly resembling the *Keiretsu* of Japan.

However, this "capitulation" to the more rigid Japanese industrial structure strategy does not only not have to take place. In fact, such a development could strip western economies of two real strengths -- innovativeness and adaptability of industry structure. As many technologies evolve, the capital intensity of their production processes does not always increase, as often assumed. This is why, for example, so many small U.S. semiconductor and computer companies have appeared and prospered during the 1980s, even while their larger predecessors have struggled. Their contribution to overall industrial innovation must be preserved.

In addition, the increasing diversity of market applications creates new niche markets, even as older ones turn into larger commodity markets. These niche markets are more efficiently supplied by small and medium firms and the appropriate supporting infrastructure, as best demonstrated by the German economy.

Good arguments can be made for vertical integration of some type -- actual or virtual, although it seems clear that the optimal degree of such integration varies significantly across industries. In particular, the shorter the technology life cycle the greater the probability of a cash flow squeeze. Without the cushion of cash flow from products at other levels above and below that product level in the production chain, funds will frequently not be available to finance succeeding generations of the technology. Thus, a relatively greater degree of vertical integration is required in such industries.

In niche or low capital-intensive markets and in industries where high rates of product innovation are possible, small firms that are not vertically-integrated can enter and prosper. The critical strategy issue is whether a *multi-enterprise* industry structure can be evolved in which the creativity of many competing firms of all sizes can be preserved, while at the same time attaining the cooperation and diversification advantages of vertical integration.

A major potential influence on the evolution of industry structure is foreign direct investment. FDI has been perceived as a threat to a *multi-enterprise* industry structure, specifically by acquiring small innovative firms and maintaining significant R&D in the home country. Such trends will likely cause erosion of the technology infrastructure as well. However, if the economic environment, including technology infrastructure, is correctly conceived and provided (i.e., a total value-added strategy is implemented), the desired multi-stage investment flows can be induced from foreign as well as domestic market participants.

A modern technology infrastructure increasingly has the potential to not only integrate the internal operations of a single firm but to closely integrate multiple firms in the production chain and to make possible successful participation at single levels in this chain.

Moreover, this infrastructure can "pull" in the "right kind" of foreign direct investment and actually reinforce a multi-enterprise total value-added industrial growth strategy.

A major requirement for success is the *matching of industry structure with the supporting infrastructure.* Because different and relatively equally effective combinations seem to be possible, the key is the identification and establishment of complementary relationships.

6 Strategy and Standards

*"Why have one standard when two will
serve vendors twice as nicely and buyers
half as well?"*

PC Week

Critical emerging technologies with impacts on large numbers of industries have both a complexity and a "systems" character which raise the economic role of standards to a new, higher level of importance. This fact has not been lost on government policy makers around the world. In fact, more and more rescurces are being devoted to ensuring that standards are promulgated to leverage a domestic industry's "enabling" technologies and to provide the interfaces for these technologies with other elements of technology-based systems. The substance of these standards and the timing of their implementation are having significant impacts on industry behavior and structure -- trends which will have lasting effects on the competitiveness of the world's industrialized economies.[1] The analysis of these roles in terms of their interaction with corporate strategy and global economic trends is somewhat involved and thus may frustrate the more casual reader. Complex technologies, complex market structures, and alternative business strategies that include alternative strategies toward standards all combine to make this a complicated element of technology-based competition. Ignoring this complexity guarantees poor strategy formulation, including poor infrastructure support for standards.

The Evolving Role of Standards

One very general definition of a standard is "the result of a reasoned, collective choice and designed to serve as a basis of agreement for the solution of recurrent problems." Looked upon in this way, a standard is viewed as "striking a balance between the requirements of users and [producers], the technological possibilities of producers, the economic and social constraints on all concerned, and the general interest which is the responsibility of government."[2]

In terms of today's economic realities, economic text books give a narrow and over-simplified analysis of standardization and its economic roles. Standardization is largely limited to the single role of variety reduction for the purpose of achieving economies of scale in production. The reason is that from the industrial revolution until the present time, the economic efficiency of the majority of technologies

---

[1]   All industrialized nations are increasingly conscious of the impacts of standards on technology-based markets. For example, Japan is into its Seventh Industrial Standardization Long-Range Plan. In a position paper providing recommendations for this plan, the Japanese Industrial Standards Committee [1990, p. 29] stated that "it is important to maintain contact with research and development activities in order to standardize measurement, testing and evaluation methods and to ensure compatibility of products by forward-looking standardization. Thus, standardization can proceed in parallel with research and development. In doing so, standardization itself can become the object of R&D, especially in testing and evaluation methods".

[2]   Germon [1986].

depended on *generalized* machinery organized in a *rigid* system for high-volume production. Thus, scale economies dominated production strategies and were an important objective of standardization.

In the 1980s, rapid technological advances and the proliferation of market niches or segments have combined to shift the emphasis of production technology from economies of scale to economies of scope. That is, economic efficiency is increasingly being measured in terms of ability to service related but differentiated market segments with the same production technology.

Thus, the exact opposite of the traditional production structure is evolving -- *specialized* machines are being organized into *flexible* systems. This trend will place a premium on innovation in product design and flexibility in production, while maintaining the high levels of quality demanded by increasingly sophisticated users.

Moreover, the intrinsic character of today's dominant and emerging technologies is significantly different than in the past. Fewer product technologies are used in isolation. Instead, the newer technologies increasingly have a *systems* character. Data processing, communications, and factory automation are major examples. Increased emphasis on quality and productivity has driven *process* technologies towards integrated systems as well.

The technical and organizational concepts underlying this new set of economic strategies are radically different from the past and their diffusion into the U.S. economic system is therefore encountering significant barriers. One of these barriers to the adoption of many emerging technologies is the lack of appropriate standards at critical points in the technology's evolution. These standards perform different functions, only one of which is variety reduction.

In summary, these trends mean that any given technology exists less and less in isolation of other technologies. Consequently, the potential user's evaluation of that technology is increasingly affected by its "connectability"; that is, the ability to interface the technology with other technologies to create a system which (1) optimizes performance, (2) minimizes cost of initial purchase and life-cycle maintenance, and (3) minimizes long-run costs of component replacement due to obsolescence. The variety reduction and compatibility functions of standards are required for these three objectives to be achieved. Moreover, strategic objectives such as quality can no longer be defined solely with respect to the product in

isolation, but rather relative to its performance requirements within
the system of which it is a part.

The Economic Functions of Standards

Variety reduction allows economies of scale to be achieved in
the supply of each component of a system. Because of its importance
during the industrial revolution, variety reduction is associated with
the production of physical product. Today, however, it is also
associated with software. For example, computer software such as an
"operating system" must acquire a sufficiently large installed base
before many third-party applications software developers will invest in
the development and marketing typically required to launch a
proprietary product for a particular operating system.

For volume production of one component to lead to volume
production of others in the same system, compatibility between
components is required. Such *interface* standardization provides
incentives for the market entry of producers with comparative
advantages in the production of interfacing components. For
example, the introduction of automated manufacturing equipment in
the semiconductor industry and, in fact, the establishment of a
separate semiconductor equipment industry resulted in large part from
the standardization of interfaces between individual types and brands
of equipment.

A good example of the economic importance of standards to a
critical emerging technology is the evolution of automated discrete-
part manufacturing. Beginning in the 1950s, a slowly growing demand
for *precision engineering* and custom design created a demand for
flexible production techniques which could execute smaller production
runs or "batches" of related products without significant increase in
unit cost.

In the current decade, this concept has been escalated, not
only to complex systems of machines, but is now in the process of
being applied to the entire factory *and* to systems of factories. This
final evolutionary step -- "multi-enterprise integration" -- has profound
implications for overall national manufacturing strategies in the
decade ahead. In particular, such a concept provides a distinct
alternative to the Japanese *Keiretsu* model.

Numerically controlled (NC) machine tools were the first implementation of this trend in production strategy toward computer-integrated flexible manufacturing. Such machines were later integrated into groups performing related sequential functions ("machining centers"). Now, the total manufacturing process is becoming controlled electronically by a hierarchy of computer-based control systems.

Such integrated technology systems, based on the use of computers at all levels of operation within the manufacturing plant, require a broad array of standards for *cost-effective* and *timely* implementation by adopters. Within such systems, standards perform four important categories of functions:

Performance: standards are developed to ensure an acceptable level of product performance along one or more dimensions such as quality, efficiency, safety, and environmental impact;

Information: standards provide evaluated scientific and engineering information in the form of publications, electronic data bases, terminology, and test and measurement methods for evaluating and quantifying product attributes;

Compatibility: standards specify properties that a product must have in order to work (physically or functionally) with a complementary product or other components within a "system"; and,

Variety Reduction: standards limit a product to a certain range or number of characteristics such as size or quality levels.

Many of these standards, such as *interface* standards, do not affect the design of individual components (such as NC tools, or the components of NC tools) which make up advanced manufacturing

systems.[3] In fact, such standards allow multiple proprietary
component designs to coexist -- that is, they are *competitively neutral*.
An extremely important economic impact is a substantial increase in
competition at the component level, and therefore in design variety
and price advantage for the user. In effect, competitors can innovate
on "either side" of the interface, while the consumer of the product
system can select the particular components that fit that user's system
integration needs.

Interface standards greatly increase the efficiency of systems
integration by substantially reducing the cost of physically and
functionally joining components from different manufacturers to form
an optimal system for a particular user, and by allowing efficient
substitution of more advanced components as they become available
over time, thereby greatly reducing the risk of obsolescence of the
entire system. Widespread factory automation as it is evolving in
advanced economies would likely not occur without these standards.

In summary, corporations, especially large ones which are
more likely to use several different classes or brands of a particular
product, have substantial concerns about interfaces. The ability to
integrate equipment and software from different vendors (or even to
integrate different classes of equipment from a single multiproduct
vendor) has several effects: (1) system costs can be reduced and
performance optimized, and productivity thereby increased, (2)
competition among vendors for each element of the system lowers
prices, (3) addressing technological or functional obsolescence is
facilitated by the ability to replace individual components at relatively
low cost.

Evolving Corporate Strategies

Attitudes and hence corporate strategies towards standards are
quite different on the supply and demand sides of a market. This is
true both for product-specific standards and for standards providing
the interfaces between products. From the user's point of view, both

---

[3]   See Link and Tassey [1987a, Chapter 4 and 1987b] for a case study of
the varied roles of standards in the market for numerically-controlled (NC) machine
tools .

product architecture and interfaces among products affect not only system performance but also cost, including the cost of not having ready access to multiple suppliers when standards are not in place.

In the absence of interface standards, for example, investment in integration activity is required to achieve two objectives--actual systems optimization and overcoming the lack of multiple suppliers. The impacts on system cost are substantial. Similarly, the purchase of a particular product architecture can result in increased costs if few other suppliers support that architecture by making products that interface with it. The result is less than optimal system configurations at increased costs. Users (the demand side) therefore will always want standards for central product attributes as well as for product interfaces in order to allow system optimization and to benefit from supplier competition.

Figures 6-1 and 6-2 show some of the effects of standards on technology-based economic activity. In Figure 6-1, two firms in each of two industries, say computers and word processing software, choose strategies in which their entire product consists of proprietary elements. With respect to the two computer manufacturers (firms A and B), an important element of their product is the operating system because its structure determines the requirements for software firms (C and D) that write applications programs (in this case, word processors). Each software firm must write a different version of its word processor for each operating system market it wants to sell to.

This situation is more expensive for these suppliers, thereby raising average prices. It also presents the user side of the market with a choice of two undesirable alternative strategies: (1) purchase only one brand of computer and hope software will be developed now and in the future for that brand plus give up procurement flexibility by becoming tied to a single vendor; or, (2) reduce supply risks by purchasing computers from several vendors, but then be forced to invest in expensive translating strategies, so that users of different brands within the company can pass computerized information among themselves. These potential costs of non-standardization usually make users the aggressor in demanding industry standards.

However, suppliers also face risks from non-standardization strategies. A manufacturer must choose one of two strategic options with respect to standardization relatively early in the technology life cycle: (1) make its products compatible with an existing protocol or standard and thus obtain some security in exchange for sharing the

Figure 6-1

Technology-Based Economic Activity Without Standards

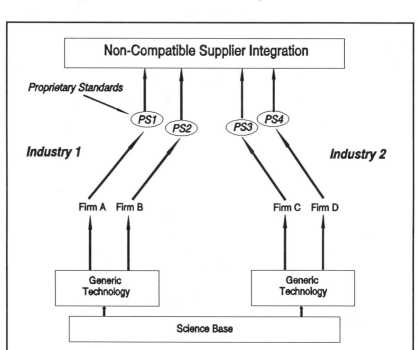

market, or (2) try to dominate the market and thereby force a defacto standard. The latter strategy frequently turns out to be an "all-or-nothing" option.

Somewhat ironically, many firms find themselves on both sides of the standards strategy fence. For example, a computer with a particular operating "architecture" must have all software, ranging from the operating system to applications programs custom-designed for it. Unless the manufacturer is completely integrated (supplying both hardware and software) -- something no company has totally achieved -- that firm is dependent on other manufacturers to supply compatible products. It will certainly want multiple suppliers to choose from, and thus will issue specifications to which it hopes several vendors will respond with viable products. In effect, these specifications are firm-specific standards in response to which a number of suppliers can design products.

Figure 6-2

Technology-Based Economic Activity With Standards

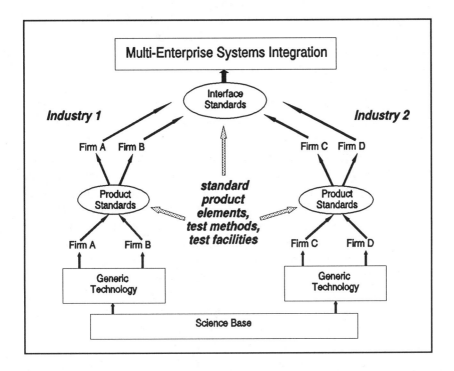

For example, Apple Computer Inc. made a brilliant move when it forced third party software developers to adopt a standard "graphical user interface", so that all programs running on Apple's computers presented the user with the same screen format and command structure.[4] However, Apple kept its hardware operating

---

[4] The term "graphical user interface" refers to the use of "menus" of images instead of characters to indicate instruction options for the computer user. Apple had pioneered this much-preferred format and had also made this approach even more attractive to users by sticking to a generic format for all application programs.

system proprietary (i.e., it did not adopt an "open systems" architecture strategy), which meant that Apple would prosper and fail entirely on its own ability to maintain sufficient market share.

In contrast, Sun Microsystems, Inc. "opened" its microprocessor architecture for its workstations in order to obtain "help" in maintaining market share. It was willing to share its markets in return for the increased probability that its architecture would become a standard.[5] These strategies toward standardization in the computer industry will be examined in some detail in the following sections.

Figure 6-2 shows how these costs of non-standardization can be reduced over the technology life cycle. The computer manufacturers could, for example, agree on a standard operating system, thereby facilitating software development. The software firms could agree on a standard graphical user interface (rather than wait for one or more computer hardware manufacturers to force such a standard). The result is that users of computer systems greatly benefit from reduced integration costs and still benefit from product variety.

Standardization is not an all-or-nothing proposition. In a complicated systems technology such as communications or factory automation, standardization typically proceeds in an evolutionary manner, with the pattern of evolution being determined by (1) the pace of technological change in each component category; (2) the disembodied technology development, which determines the overall system architecture and organization; and (3) the market structure (and, with it, the incentives and ability to force the standardization process).

The degree, as well as the timing, of standardization is important for the effective market penetration of a technology. In the case of NC machine tools, total standardization of data formats would have severely compromised the range of performance attributes desired by different users in the machine tools they purchased. Thus, a "degree" of standardization has been optimal, at least up to this point in the technology's evolution. In other words, "complete" standardization too early in the technology life cycle can constrain innovation.

---

[5]   There is some debate concerning the degree to which Sun actually has "opened" its architecture.

In summary, systems technologies are becoming an extremely important factor in determining the competitive position of a modern economy. Distributed data processing, communications, and factory automation are pervasive technologies and all are systems in that a range of equipment and multiple units of the same equipment are linked physically and functionally, sometimes over considerable distances. These technologies are important "drivers" or "enablers" of long-term productivity growth across much of the technology-based economy. The more complex the system's structure, the more important the strategic and economic impact of standards.

Over the past decade, the infrastructure role of standards has increased in importance because (1) the systems nature of critically important technologies means that competition is greatly affected by the degree of standardization at the interfaces between components, and (2) the shortening of the average technology life cycle has pushed the optimal timing for decisions with respect to standards to earlier points in these cycles. As the following sections demonstrate, the pattern of standardization and industry behavior and structure have a recursive relationship. Therefore, opportunities exist over much of the typical technology life cycle to adjust the standardization process to enhance an industry's competitive position.

Standards and Competition in Information Technology

Information technology provides a pervasive systems infrastructure that is driving much of the radical change not only in technology investment but in organizational structure as well. Standards are playing a multi-faceted and extremely important set of roles in the evolution of this technology.[6]

In the early years of the computer industry, standardization focused on physical interfaces and later on the functional interfaces between operating systems and applications programs. However, as the number of computer users grew and, especially as the large computer users accumulated many computers of each of several

---

[6] A Japanese Industrial Standards Committee report [1990, p. 35] states that "approximately half of the currently published ISO (International Standards Organization) standards (by page count) are related to information technology.

different types (platforms), the demand for "interoperability" -- the ability of computers made by different vendors to communicate -- increased rapidly.[7]

Users could invest in integrating different vendors' products themselves, but not only was this strategy expensive and time-consuming, it led to rigid configurations that became obsolete -- either technologically or with respect to new corporate market strategies. At such a point, companies frequently could not bear to scrap their investment and simply accepted the inefficiency of an out-or-date information system for some time.[8]

The technological solution now evolving is the concept of "open systems".[9] This computing paradigm in concept allows users to combine different vendors' products across several platforms, if necessary, without investing in custom integration. In the ultimate application of this concept, heretofore largely separate worlds of R&D, manufacturing, and management ("the office") can "interoperate" as one system with "seamless" connections among its many components.

In practice, achieving truly open computer systems has been extremely difficult. Compatibility has been partial at best. Vendors often claim to conform to open systems' requirements, but in reality

---

[7]   In computer terminology, a "platform" refers to a distinct class of processing power among computer systems. Thus, personal computers, workstations, minicomputers, etc., are platforms.

[8]   Automation of information collection, storage, processing, and distribution has evolved through three basic eras. In the first era, an organization's *information system* (IS) was the province of a dedicated computer unit in which computer specialists operated a single mainframe computer and provided batch-mode services. The second era was characterized by the emergence of stand-alone personal computers (Pcs) with distribution or communication functions handled in an off-line mode or through rather inefficient connections to separate communication systems. The third and current era is based on increasingly sophisticated network technology. In fact, the network *is* the system, with computers hanging on it as nodes. The mainframe computer still has a role in such a system, but as a "manager" of the information flows rather than the singular functional unit.

[9]   For an excellent review of the open systems issue, see Sheridan and Teresko [1991].

they conform only to a portion of the set of standards to which compliance is necessary. Moreover, even when true open systems compatibility is offered, users often find that "mobility" from their current proprietary system to the open system does not exist, even when the same vendor provides both. That is, transition products are not made available, leaving the user still with a severe obsolescence problem. Some companies, such as Digital Equipment Corp., are providing "migration" products. IBM, as a very large vendor, has provided internal connectivity among platforms that it sells through its System Applications Architecture (SAA).[10]

Product Standards. Successfully developing and marketing a new component frequently requires standardization as part of the overall strategy. However, when a technology is in a high state of flux, so will be the associated standards. Technology-based industries are characterized by change and the standardization process interacts with this change with varying degrees of responsiveness.

At times, lack of synchronization between standards and technological change can greatly retard market growth. 1988 was such a period in the evolution of personal computers. When one firm is dominant, as IBM was when it introduced its first PC in 1981, it can force standardization of hardware components and the more generic software such as the operating system. In particular, IBM chose Intel's microprocessor and Microsoft's operating system (DOS).[11] These selections for "standards" brought both companies to leadership positions. IBM also chose an available "bus" (the component of a PC which moves data from one part of the computer to another) .

But, by 1988, the market for PCs had grown faster than IBM's share, so that IBM's ability to set standards had declined. In 1988, PC

---

[10]   As an example of the complexity of the open systems concept, the Institute of Electrical and Electronics Engineers (IEEE) definition includes POSIX (Portable Operating System Interface for computer environments), the XPG3 portability standard, the International Standards Organization (ISO) communications standards, and American National Standards Institute (ANSI) compliance.

[11]   DOS stands for Disk Operating System. Its function is to provide an instruction interface between the hardware and the software (the applications programs which enable the specific computing functions to take place). Several versions of DOS existed at that point in time, in addition to Microsoft's.

users were faced with purchasing decisions such as whether to buy "clones" of the previous generation of IBM PCs (the so-called "AT compatibles") or IBM's newly introduced PS/2 generation. Decisions also had to be made concerning operating systems (the code that allows various applications software to tell the computer what to do). The AT compatibles had used DOS, but when IBM announced OS/2 as the future operating system for its PS/2 line, some clone manufacturers began adapting their machines for OS/2 as well as DOS.

The higher-end models of the PS/2 line had a new type of "bus" called the "Micro Channel". Independent of the performance enhancements of this new bus, owners of IBM ATs or AT compatibles who had purchased additional circuit boards found to their dismay that IBM's attempt to convert the PC market to a new standard bus would also obsolete their add-on boards. Finally, because the technology in the new PS/2 line was considerably more proprietary than that in the previous generation (which was built basically with off-the-shelf parts), IBM charged substantial royalties to clone manufacturers who wanted to develop PCs based on the new architecture.

This led IBM's major competitors to form a consortium (the so-called "Gang of Nine") to develop an alternative standard bus -- the Extended Industry Standard Architecture (EISA), which would offer a licensee-free alternative to Micro Channel.[12] The strategy had to be taken seriously by IBM because the nine firms collectively had a larger share of the IBM-compatible market than IBM.[13]

Although the technical success of EISA was far from assured and it would lag IBM's attempt to set a new standard by several years, this constituted the first serious threat from within the PC industry to IBM's dominance. EISA was instigated by Compaq. Compaq's competitive strategy was technological leadership and the company had been very successful in its implementation. However, few companies that are third in market share -- as was Compaq -- have

---

[12]   The Gang of Nine consisted of Compaq Computer Corp., AST Research Inc., Epson America Inc., Hewlett-Packard Co., NEC America Inc., Olivetti U.S.A., Tandy Corp., Wyse Technology, and Zenith Data Systems Corp.

[13]   In 1988, according to International Data Corp., the "Gang of Nine" accounted for 29 percent of this market, while IBM had 27 percent.

achieved the influence over standards that was Compaq's objective with EISA.

IBM was using two strategic advantages to increase market share in advance of any market entry by EISA. First, IBM, by virtue of its vertical integration, could control the supply of semiconductor components and thus not be subject to the marked swings in price and component availability that characterize the merchant semiconductor market. Second, IBM was therefore able to discount its PS/2 line to gain market share in advance of any product offerings by its competitors. IBM did just this beginning in late 1988. It followed with list price reductions and then discounts to its dealers in early 1989.

An interesting strategic element of this effort was the fear of participants that success of the consortium would convey too many benefits on Compaq. Members feared that Compaq's technical prowess and relatively large market share would result in its domination of the technical basis of the forthcoming standard, thereby allowing it to become "another IBM" and dictate future market directions.

Compatibility among EISA computers was to be measured by a software test suite being developed by members. However, no formal testing policy existed in the first half of 1989 as the bus specification, chips, and prototype computers were being developed. Potential users therefore had no prospect of satisfactorily determining the level of compatibility among EISA products. This was a classic example of the difficulty of determining and implementing the correct *degree* of standardization. Members recognized the problem, but their inability to satisfactorily address it created considerable discomfort among current users of the member firms' computers.

Some of the larger competitors, who also had been marketing their own proprietary designs, resisted this attempt to set a standard. They countered with announcements of provisions for compatibility of their respective hardware architectures and operating systems with available communications software from third parties. This approach ostensibly makes the interfaces between the equipment of different vendors "seamless"; that is, data can be passed without translation (reconfiguration).

In summary, the example of PC standards in the 1980s provides some good evidence of how different strategies combined with different industry structures can affect the infrastructure role of standards and hence competitive dynamics and ultimately industry growth.

Non-Product Standards. The above discussion focuses on the stand-alone personal computer (PC) and the effects of the evolution of standards on the structure of this product. Strategies taken by individual companies with respect to standardization can greatly affect their long-term market shares. However, the most important trend in personal computing in the early 1990s is the linking of computers together, not only of one class or "platform" of computers but several platforms. Here, a different type of standardization becomes important.

"Distributed data processing" using personal computers (PCs) and workstations actually began a strong growth trend in the mid 1980s. The steadily increasing performance/cost ratios for PCs and workstations coupled with the availability of "connectivity" products have enabled small and medium firms as well as large ones to purchase distributed computer systems. In fact, this trend has led to a halt in the growth of the data processing service industry, which leased time on mainframe computers to corporate users. Computer users have found the purchase of distributed computer systems more attractive for several reasons, but perhaps the most significant is the fact that these systems are flexible and therefore can be optimized for particular computing needs. The ultimate objective of information systems management is an open system platform bringing together all the disparate hardware and software that a network administrator might want to purchase for optimal system performance.

To put together a distributed computer system requires a number of components:

       o   work stations
       o   computer integration
             --   hardware systems (personal computers, minicomputers, mainframes)
             --   operating systems (DOS, OS/2, Macintosh, UNIX)
             --   front ends for data bases
       o   application development tools for software
       o   network hardware
       o   network management software

-- architectures
-- data-communication technologies
-- network control

Major users of computer systems have increasingly chaffed at the cost, uncertainty, and general inefficiency that they must bear as computer manufacturers squabble over Micro Channel vs. EISA or OSF vs. Unix International. Such battles are symptoms of deeper problems such as strategies targeted at "complete" control over markets in the uniquely American belief that innovative technology by itself can win market domination. The "all-or-nothing" philosophy has lead to poor long-term planning by industry and government and the lack of a process to identify the common systems and data needs of different industries.

As an operating system, the emergence of Unix offers an excellent case study in the evolution of a non-product standard. Unix offers important potential technical advantages over DOS. First and foremost, Unix offers a cost-effective alternative to DOS-based local area networks or LANs. Add to this the very important advantage that Unix offers the promise of interoperability -- it runs on every hardware platform (PCs, minicomputers, mainframes).

To date, Unix growth has been largely in the market for workstations. The advent of $5,000 workstation greatly expanded the entry point in the computer hardware market for Unix. At this price, Unix can challenge the most powerful PCs (based on Intel's 386 and 486 microprocessors). High volume in turn draws third party software vendors into the arena, who now have incentives to write "shrink-wrapped" (take out of the package, install, and use) applications programs.

However, the lack of a single standard version of Unix has so segmented its market that the secondary segmentation problems, such as those that characterize the DOS-based PC market (IBM and clones) pale by comparison. In fact, highly distinct market segments for Unix have emerged, just as DOS and Apple Computer, Inc.'s operating systems have battled for the PC market. This is evidenced by estimates that the Unix market will grow at a 25 to 35 percent annual rate over the next several years, reaching the $60 billion range by 1993, but that about one-third of that will consist of customer services to "fix" incompatibilities.[14]

Some of the larger competitors who had been marketing their own proprietary designs, resisted attempts to set a single Unix standard. They countered with announcements of provisions for compatibility of their respective hardware architectures and operating systems with available communications software from third parties. This approach ostensibly makes the interfaces between the equipment of different vendors "seamless". However, these "fixes" add significantly to overall system costs and thus reduce the attractiveness of Unix-based systems.

In late 1988, UNIX International was formed as a non-profit organization by AT&T, Sun Microsystems Inc., Unisys Corp., NCR Corp., NEC Corp., Control Data Corp., and several other hardware and software vendors to coordinate and promote a single Unix operating system standard. The AT&T-led organization made an important strategic move in February 1989 when it announced that it would not develop any products, take over Unix development from AT&T, or draft specifications for future releases. Instead, the group would rely on its member companies and its newest member -- the X/Open consortium -- to detail the specifications.

X/Open Co. is a non-aligned consortium of hardware systems vendors, including IBM, Digital Equipment Corp., Hewlett-Packard Co., AT&T, Sun Microsystems and others, dedicated to defining standards for a common applications environment. The non-aligned X/Open consortium had been a key arbiter in the Unix standards battle, and thus giving it a prominent role within Unix International had the effect of further enhancing the credibility of both groups.

However, many of X/Open's members were not members of UNIX International and continued development of their own Unix versions (such as DEC's Ultrix and IBM's AIX).[15] Some of these firms are also members of the Open Software Foundation (OSF), similarly established in 1988, which is designing a totally new version of Unix, OSF/1, to run across disparate hardware platforms. OSF/1 is incompatible with AT&T's version.

---

[14]   Estimate supplied by the Gartner Group.

[15]   Grossman [1989, p. 4].

In summary, both OSF and UI are now well-established entities. Thus, the normal evolutionary pattern of standardization is unfolding in which proprietary systems give way to a smaller number of competing standards. In some cases, this leads only to more frustration on the part of buyers who must still make highly uncertain decisions about future market trends. In this example, the problem is mitigated somewhat by the existence of a broadly accepted standards structure composed of X/Open, ISO, and IEEE (Posix standards).

Neither OSF nor UI can afford to stray too far beyond the application programming interfaces that have been established and widely accepted through these standards organizations, and they both work closely with and have members on the various standards committees. The evolutionary pattern should lead eventually to competition based on vendors' architectural strategies for open distributed systems, rather than the current differences in operating system code.

Economic Impacts of Information Technology Standards

Standards have the effect of greatly reducing integration costs. However, as the previous example indicates, when the technology is immature or when market demand is segmented, several "local" defacto standards may coexist for some period of time. Groups of suppliers form around the several variants of the generic technology. In the case of systems technologies such as office automation, firms combine vertically, often through joint ventures to supply the system-level product based on a particular standard.

The success of long-term strategies hinges on a number of other factors: (1) technical success; (2) the ability to forge alliances, not only to accelerate and improve and technology, but to promote advantageous standards; and, (3) the ability to gain market penetration relatively early in a technology's life cycle in order to force, or at least greatly influence, acceptance of advantageous standards.

The evolution of systems technologies, such as that described above for distributed data processing, is driven not only by the technological advances of system components but by the advances in component interfaces. Standardization is the key factor in interface development. The process finally begins to stabilize when the demand side of the market realizes both *flexibility* in purchasing components among different vendors and *economies of scale* in the use certain critical components.

The *strength* of individual standards frequently depends on the existence of standards for other products in the product system. In other words, the greater the *degree* to which a product or product system is *standardized* across its components, the stronger are individual standards. For example, the so-called IBM PC "standard" is really a set of standards for hardware components plus the operating system software. Such "bundling" of standards creates substantial barriers for individual products that are potential substitutes for the already standardized product system elements.

The penetration of computer platform markets by Unix, which is an "unbundled" operating system will therefore depend on the efficacy not only of Unix itself as an operating system but also on the efficacy of its interfaces with other elements of each computer platform it seeks to serve.

At the point in the evolution of computers discussed here, different "platforms" were invading each other's heretofore separate markets, as evidenced by the increasing competition between PCs and Unix-based workstations. The market gave no indication of being able to select a winner for some time, that is, to settle on a single operating system. Applications written for DOS-based (including Windows) or OS/2-based PCs were not directly usable on Unix-based machines. The installed PC base was large enough to induce all types of applications programs, but the slow shift towards Unix in the middle 1980s was insufficient to induce applications developers to convert popular PC programs to run on Unix-based machines.

The above discussion has not included the strategies of foreign computer manufacturers. The Japanese made several unsuccessful attempts to use standardization of operating systems as a strategy for penetrating the U.S. market. Having the necessary standards in place at the appropriate points in time relative to the technology's development can be critical for a domestic industry's international competitive position. International standards exist for many elements of distributed data processing systems, but the huge size of the U.S. market tends to reduce incentives for adherence by U.S. firms.

For example, X.400 is an international standard for exchanging electronic mail (E-mail) across different computer systems. Although its acceptance grew in the late 1980s, U.S. LAN vendors were slow to accept it.[16] Moreover, E-mail vendors who wished to interface with X.400 had to write an interface program (technically referred to as an "application programming interface" or API) to allow their LAN customers to "seamlessly" exchange electronic mail across various networks.

In such situations, if several firms from a competing nation can show compliance with a set of standards, the advantages of interoperability described above accrue to the domestic users doing business with these firms, so that market shares may shift away from domestic suppliers. The huge size of a united European market may make the EC as influential in this respect as the United States has been for the past several decades.[17]

However, decisions to adopt major systems standards, such as those described above, take considerable planning, time and resources to implement. For example, although implementation of Open Systems Interconnection (OSI) through the U.S. Government's GOSIP (Government Open Systems Interconnect Profile) procurement standard was begun in 1990, government agencies were not about to scrap their installed base of computer and communications equipment to be instantly in compliance. Instead, they focused on compliance in future procurements.[18]

Because the U.S. Government is the world's largest single user of computer hardware and software, incentives to private users to

---

[16] Scott and Kramer [1988, p. 4].

[17] Standards appear to be one area where the vaunted Japanese Keiretsu industry structure is a handicap. Because of their size and rigid control of members, interoperability is readily achieved *within* a Keiretsu. However, at the industry level, factionalism has prevented the several competing Keiretsu from agreeing on standards and thereby presenting a united marketing effort in international markets.

[18] GOSIP is an implementation of OSI, which is based on the International Organization for Standards's (ISO) seven-layer network model. This model defines how data is passed around a computer network. Because of the broad international scope of input into the model, the standard has evolved with many options as to how each layer of the network model functions. This flexibility unfortunately can lead to incompatibility, which defeats the entire purpose of OSI. The problem is being solved by complex implementation directives or "profiles" such as GOSIP.

adopt its preferred standards were substantially increased. However, the pattern of response from private-sector computer users was similar to that of government agencies -- a piecemeal approach to adoption (several "layers" of the standards structure at a time) was typically initiated.

Similarly, vendors will often develop "gateways" to translate their proprietary formats into that of the new standard to protect their installed base. The cost of conversion to comply with complex sets of standards such as OSI is substantial. Thus, vendors may convert sequentially over several generations of their product lines to achieve compliance. Another reason for slow adoption of OSI is that implementation directives, such as GOSIP for U.S. Government users, themselves evolve over time. Such standards are so complicated that additional infrastructure, namely compliance testing, is essential for vendors' products. The testing also takes time but, more important, it requires technically acceptable, cost-effective test facilities.[19] This technology infrastructure must be available before significant diffusion of the standard can take place.

Standards are pervasive in many of the emerging technologies which will collectively dominate industrial structures and international trade in the coming decades. They are therefore an essential element of corporate strategic planning and government growth policy. Even though most standards are set voluntarily by industry, a number of them are based to a significant degree on nonproprietary infratechnologies and are competitively neutral elements of industrial activity. Thus, their provision can require a direct government role in the underlying infratechnology research.

Finally, the economic impact of standards in this area is just beginning to be felt. According to one survey, 6% of all U.S. businesses with PCs comprise 64% of the installed base.[20] Thus, the

---

[19]   Conformance testing for standards systems such as OSI is so complicated that it must be accomplished in three stages: (1) simple abstract (static) conformance test relative to a set of technical specifications; (2) conformance to a carefully devised reference model (a well-established functional implementation); and (3) a non-static, *ad hoc* interoperability test in a dynamic multi-vendor environment (where most problems with the particular vendors' product show up). See Cashin [1990].

[20]   *PC Week*, January 21, 1991, p. 49.

diffusion of information technology across the U.S. economy is a long way from complete, and, coupled with the increased use of networks, implies that the demands for interoperability are just beginning.

Infrastructure vs. Proprietary Strategies

One of the best examples of how domination of technology infrastructure can lead to market leadership in dependent applications markets is Microsoft's success in operating systems. Microsoft rose to prominence through DOS, the personal computer operating system that IBM chose for its initial personal computer, the PC, and succeeding generations (the XT, AT and the PS/2). IBM and Microsoft developed a close working relationship, which was mutually advantageous because their competitive assets were complementary. IBM was dominant in hardware which created huge markets for Microsoft's operating system, DOS. Microsoft became dominant in DOS products, primarily through compatibility of its products with IBM. IBM in turn benefitted from Microsoft's increasing expertise in operating systems, which helped IBM and IBM-compatible machines compete with Apple Computer, Inc.'s proprietary operating system, which was superior to DOS in certain attributes.

This relationship worked well for IBM and also for software companies that produced applications software for IBM-compatible microcomputers. However, in 1989 Microsoft introduced a "applications programmable interface" (API) operating system, Windows. This strategy strained Microsoft's relationship with IBM, which was simultaneously developing -- with Microsoft -- a graphical user interface operating system, OS/2, to be used on its current generation of personal computers, the PS/2 line, and subsequent generations. When the market success of Windows seemed assured, Microsoft terminated work on OS/2.

Simultaneously, developers of applications programs complained that Microsoft was using its dominant position in operating systems to expand its share of applications program markets, in large part by using its inside knowledge of development directions being taken by Windows to achieve earlier market entry of its own applications programs. Thus, both IBM and applications software developers had lost competitive position by allowing

Microsoft to succeed in creating a proprietary product out of the next generation operating system.

Because so many products are tied to the direction of technology infrastructure, when one firm gets control of it and sets the defacto standard (in effect, making infrastructure proprietary), the process is destabilizing to the many firms that base their market strategies on it. In this case, a number of small applications software firms took Microsoft at its word that it would develop OS/2 and made substantial investments in development of applications programs to run under this operating system. When Microsoft dropped development of OS/2, to go solely with Windows, several of these small firms went out of business.

Another strategic issue has to do with the *portability* of certain technology between generations of related technology. That is, when standards are *generation-specific*, obsolescence can be a major barrier to the introduction of new technology. This phenomenon is a manifestation of the "installed base" factor. If users have invested heavily in software technology that runs on a particular generation of hardware technology, they will be unreceptive to a new generation of hardware technology, if the installed base of software is not portable to the new hardware.

This situation is one of the main reasons that IBM's OS/2 operating system will have problems achieving significant market penetration. Existing software is not upwardly mobile. In contrast, Microsoft's strategy is *evolutionary* with respect to standards. Windows is compatible with the ten-year-old operating system MS-DOS; and Windows, along with the applications programs written for it, are to be compatible with a new operating system, NT (for "New Technology"), that will replace MS-DOS.

IBM has recognized this strategic problem along with Apple Computer Inc., but the two firms will pursue a *revolutionary* approach. Looking beyond OS/2, IBM and Apple plan to introduce a radically new operating system concept in the mid-1990s, based on a concept known as "object-oriented programming". This software involves building programs from interchangeable blocks of prefabricated computer code called objects. Several potential important advantages will be the ability to accommodate multimedia technology, which will drive the entire personal computer industry over the next decade, and a significantly increased ability to create custom programs. Creating a radically new standard, if successful, can convey substantial rewards to the innovator, but the risks are clearly high as well.

Standards for Automated Manufacturing

Over the past two decades, the partial automation of industrial processes has resulted in significant gains in productivity and quality. However, in the 1990s and beyond, far greater economic benefits will be realized from higher levels of automation. One critical element of automation will be the *total integration* of information transfer. The nations that invest in the capability for total information integration will far surpass those nations that are slow to adapt to this requirement of global competition.

Achieving higher levels of automation means far more than the reduction of labor -- the target of earlier investments in automated manufacturing technologies. Higher levels of automation, based on total information integration, mean the combining of machines and information into a *system* in which highly skilled labor and complex technology -- both hardware and software -- can produce varied, high-quality products in short periods of time.

Such investments will be evaluated by a new set of performance criteria. For example, corporate strategists have adopted as one measure of world-class performance the percentage of time that value is being added to a product during production. According to Hay [1988], "some companies are now saying the target to shoot at is a throughput time of three times the value-added time." That is, value is being added 33% of the time the product is moving though the plant. Typically, according to Hay, only 5% to 15% of the activities associated with a production process actually add value, and "all the value-added activity occurs in less than 1% of the time that it takes to make a product." Such radical improvement will not be possible without automation of the entire manufacturing process.

Automation of the design phase and its integration with the actual manufacturing steps is a key element of the overall value-added objective. Application of the *design-for manufacturing* (concurrent engineering) concept is estimated to account for 5% of the total product cost, but decisions that are made during the design phase can influence 70% or more of the total ongoing manufacturing costs.[21]

Information Integration Strategies. The overall effectiveness of an automated industrial process depends critically on the content, structure, and availability of information in digital electronic form. By definition, the manufacturing sector of the U.S. economy produces products, so product data are clearly one of the most important classes of information. Product data include mechanical, electrical, and structural categories. Participants in the automated industrial process need to contribute to, access, and share vast amounts of product information that are increasingly expressed in computer databases.

Because total automation is a systems approach, its substantial potential effectiveness will only be realized if information can be efficiently moved among and utilized by all elements of the system. However, achievement of this goal has been retarded by several significant shortcomings in the required technology infrastructure. First, different types of equipment from different vendors do not use the same data formats, so that digital data representing products are not interpretable across the stages of the typical industrial process. This is often true even among different types of equipment made by the same manufacturer.

Second, data relevant to the execution of an industrial process are not simply a collection of independent pieces of information. Rather, industrial information acts collectively to describe all the physical and functional aspects of products, their supporting infrastructure, and their interfaces with other equipment. Thus, use of digital product data in the highly automated environment requires standardization at the functional product element level. That is, standard product models are needed.

Companies have two alternative strategies for achieving some limited degree of digital product data sharing:

(1) *Purchase equipment from different vendors, thereby realizing economic benefits from optimal selection of equipment for each*

---

[21]   Gary L. Cowger, executive director, Advanced Manufacturing Engineering, General Motors.

technical function within their individual industrial processes. However, these potential gains can be substantially reduced by the requirement to invest considerable time and money in developing "translators", so that information produced by one category or brand of equipment can be utilized by the other equipment in the system.

(2) *Purchase all categories of equipment from the same vendor.* This strategy reduces (but does not eliminate) compatibility problems; however, it "locks in" the user to that vendor, which can mean high costs over time or suboptimal system configurations and thus lower overall productivity.

It has been argued that vertically-integrated companies, by minimizing external relationships, avoid many of the interfirm communication problems found in more disaggregated industry structures. However, very few companies add all the value embodied in the final product that they present to the marketplace. In fact, even the largest companies use many suppliers and still must communicate effectively with their customers. Between 60% and 80% of major products, such as an airplane, automobile, or ship, is produced by a subcontractor, supplier, partner, or at multiple locations within the same corporation.

Common program language, data format standards, and product attribute models, which collectively standardize the flows of data among elements of the industrial process fall into the category of *technology infrastructure.* Product-related information standards are the *efficiency drivers* of the new systems concepts that are reshaping the above foci of corporate strategies. These concepts, such as total quality management (TQM) and concurrent engineering (CE), require diverse product-related data that can be rapidly transferred within and among companies. Without standardization of the data, the substantial benefits of these systems concepts cannot be realized.

International standards for product data exchange are not only necessary for the normal efficiency reasons, but, for multinational companies competing against single-country firms, the necessity of moving product design data to suppliers and customers in different countries demands standardization across national economic boundaries.

The first major standard of this type was the Initial Graphic Exchange Specification (IGES), for which development began in 1979. IGES is used for the digital exchange of database information among computer-aided design (CAD) systems. In essence, it provides a data format for describing product design and manufacturing information that has been created and stored in a computer-readable form. The standard was necessary because vendors' formats differed, making the transfer of data among CAD systems impossible without the expensive investment in translators.

IGES dealt only with product design systems. Yet, it is extremely complicated and has been evolving over the past decade. In the mid-1980s, the broader problem was addressed of passing digital product data not only among design components but also across the more varied production stage and its supporting management structure.

In the United States, Europe, and Japan, efforts are underway to develop this latter system of standards infrastructure. Because of its complexity and pervasive economic impacts, broad-based cooperative mechanisms with both government and industry participation are being used to develop the standards. Some international cooperation to date has resulted in a single umbrella set of standards -- Standards for Exchange of Product Model Data (STEP). In the United States, the effort to implement STEP is currently called Product Data Exchange/using STEP or PDES. Such national standards efforts are essential to adapt and implement the generic international system of product data standards at the domestic industry level in a timely manner relative to foreign competition and also to maintain the compatibility necessary for global strategies.[22]

---

[22]   An earlier effort, led by General Motors, attempted to establish a Manufacturing Automation Protocol (MAP) as a standard for manufacturing data exchange. MAP was supported by a number of large users of automation equipment. These users saw the dual benefits from MAP of reducing the cost of communicating product data and the cost of being locked into a single vendor's product line. MAP has never succeeded in becoming established, in part because like most standards of this type it is complex and therefore subject to continual change. Even though in mid-1988 major users agreed to "freeze" MAP protocols until 1994, the more recent standards development effort will likely supersede it. See, for example, Bresnahan and Chopra [1990, pp. 105-108].

The substantial potential impact of STEP is indicated in the following comprehensive set of economic benefits that could be realized by any nation that successfully implements this set of standards in a timely manner:

Time to Market. The facilitation of concurrent engineering by digital product data standards will greatly speed up the R&D process by allowing the rapid iteration of design without resorting to paper drawings, prototypes, etc. Efficient transfer of product information further accelerates the overall design process by enabling rapid design changes in response to unanticipated engineering problems that occur after the end of formal R&D. Such problems often occur in early, low-volume production runs and substantially retard scale-up for pursuing larger market shares.

The concept of *just-in-time (JIT)* delivery or production has significant cost implications (for supplier relationships as well as for inside the organization), but the potential benefits will only be fully realized through digital product data sharing. Rapid and simultaneous sharing of digital product data, based on a common computer language, will enable suppliers to respond to a producer's demand for a wider variety of products to be produced on short notice in single, batch, and mass production lots.

Additional costs that are incurred in post-commercialization or market-development can also be reduced. In particular, after sales service has become an increasingly important part of overall corporate strategy. The speed and efficiency of sustaining engineering support made possible by digital product data flows can greatly reduce the time as well as the cost of this activity.[23]

---

[23] The complexity of modern technology has actually increased the burden of the "paper" society, rather than usher in the "paperless" society as forecast several decades ago. Only seamless flow of digital product data throughout the production chain will achieve this goal. The Department of Defense estimates that its version of STEP/PDES (CALS) will do away with the need for enormous amounts of paper, much of which must currently be carried on military vehicles. For example, CALS technology is claimed to enable doing away with 26 tons of weapon systems manuals needed to service a Ticonderoga-class navy cruiser and the more than 1,500 pounds of operation and repair manuals that the crew of a C-17 air transport has to carry with them for emergencies.

Productivity. One of the benefits of product data sharing in terms of leveraging new techniques such as concurrent engineering is greater harmony between design and manufacturing. The impacts on production are less wasted materials and higher production yields -- in other words greater productivity.

The early phase of a new product's production life cycle is typically characterized by low yields, resulting in wasted materials, energy, etc., and thus higher unit costs. Digital product data permit the rapid and efficient recycling of product and process design in response to engineering problems that typically turn up in both the product itself and the production process. With rapid design modifications, the volume of output can be steadily increased, and the adverse consequences of low yields rapidly reduced.

Quality. In addition to increasing the speed and the efficiency of the design-manufacturing relationship, digital product data enable a more rigorous engineering definition for design validation. Edward Demming and other quality assurance experts have argued that about 80 percent of the typical product's defects can be traced to the design stage of the product's life cycle. According to some industry estimates, the concurrent engineering process, facilitated by digital product data technology, can reduce by 50 percent the number of engineering changes required by reliability and maintainability (i.e., "quality") problems. At the manufacturing stage, real-time feedback on process variables, made possible through digital product data, enables the process control necessary to assure higher quality levels.

Flexibility. Quick and varied responses to changing market conditions have been touted as one the most important characteristics of advanced automation systems. This flexibility strategy may be divided into three categories:

> *customer responsiveness.* Technology-based markets are becoming increasingly differentiated because more sophisticated and competitive customers are demanding customized or at least semi-customized products. The responsive manufacturer must build flexibility into both design and production technologies. The capability to quickly alter and validate product designs and then to automatically configure production equipment, along with the production

control and inspection processes, requires digital product data sharing among a wide range of equipment and applications software supplied from a variety of vendors. Moreover, as service becomes a more important component of the overall market transaction, replacing paper manuals and engineering drawings will allow virtually instantaneous corrections and updates to operation and repair instructions.

supplier integration. Because the typical manufacturer actually produces only a fraction of the final product that it delivers to the marketplace, its suppliers must be equally efficient in reacting to rapidly changing demand. Traditional business relationships have been based on a paper trail by which information is distributed serially. In other words, one supplier designs a component, which in turn drives the design of a second component by another supplier, etc., with the manufacturer approving each successive step. Considerable time elapses between initiation of a procurement request and delivery of the desired components. Digital communications and computer storage not only greatly accelerate the exchange of product data between supplier and manufacturer, but allow several suppliers to proceed with the design of their components virtually simultaneously.

industrial networking. In addition to allowing rapid and efficient exchange of design specifications between a manufacturer and its existing suppliers, standardized digital product data also enable a manufacturer to conduct a more efficient bidding process among potential suppliers. Standardized product data models are also essential to reducing the substantial transaction costs in traditional subcontractor bidding for large-firm work, and thus to the participation of small and medium firms.

In an open systems environment in which digital product data can be passed seamlessly among individual pieces of equipment and among companies, maximum operating efficiency is attained at the company level. Moreover, under a multi-enterprise model of competition, maximum competitive efficiency at the industry level is generally obtained when relatively large numbers of suppliers, including small and medium firms, can compete in any one market. This higher level of competition will be possible in the 1990s only by digital product data standards, which allow small and medium companies to participate efficiently at the component levels of markets for systems technologies.

Some large companies have addressed the product data sharing problem internally by standardizing on two or three vendors for a particular class of automation technology (say, computer-aided design) and then investing in the writing of custom translators to convert design data to enable communication among the different vendors' products. While this may minimize costs subject to the constraints of limited flexibility and limited competition among suppliers, it is certainly not the low-cost solution.

And, of course, trying to share product data with suppliers and customers who have each standardized internally on a different set of software presents an even more costly problem. Not only is such an infrastructure inefficient, but it leaves the door open to foreign competitors who collectively have achieved global standards for the critical digital product data models.

The potential competitive impacts of STEP are both widespread and profound. In the short run, implementation of STEP can accelerate investment in a whole range of automation technologies with subsequent increases in productivity growth. In the longer run, a varied spectrum of industrial structures will be possible that include many combinations of small, medium and large firms. Industry structure benefits in terms of increased flexibility will include cooperative ventures that can be quickly created and dissolved as market opportunities dictate.

Such *industrial networking* will create a flexibility that will add a new level of efficiency to an industrialized economy and offers significant advantages over the more rigid networks tied to static industry structures. Rapid and efficient communication of product data at the bidding, design, production, point-of-sale, and after-sales service stages of economic activity will be a key factor in determining global competitiveness in the 1990s and beyond.

Summary

As the above discussion has shown, standards or their absence affect many product and non-product elements of an industry's technology. Moreover, the evolutionary pattern by which the final structure of standards is attained has significant impacts on the fortunes of individual firms, industries, and hence worldwide competitive position. In particular,

(1)   "Open" technology-based product systems have the tremendous efficiency advantage of allowing an entrepreneur to market an improved product or service without having to create a complete vertically- or horizontally-integrated system. Conversely, the user can custom-design a system by choosing components from various manufacturers, with the result that system performance can be optimized with minimum cost.
        The technological innovator that chooses to promote its technology as "open" sacrifices some control over the future direction of the technology and some opportunity to vertically integrate (i.e., to sell "turnkey" systems, with monopoly control over replacement sales). In return, the innovating firm becomes the initial technological leader of a much larger market, one with a greater probability of lasting.

(2)   The existence of standards, while achieving the several important categories of economic benefits discussed here, can have a retarding effect on innovation. For example, if Microsoft, Apple and IBM were freed from maintaining compatibility with existing hardware and software, new generations of system software would evolve at a much faster pace. This phenomenon is one reason why smaller firms appear more innovative, especially with respect to more radical innovations. Success in innovation, however, manifests itself in a large installed base. Once a large customer base is attained, it must be served and, in most cases, this requires an *evolutionary* rather than a revolutionary approach to change.

(3)   Competitive dynamics thus involves a constant battle between firms with large installed bases who want their protocols to be

defacto if not official standards, smaller firms and newcomers to the industry who want true open systems to facilitate entry (and hence an opportunity to innovate), and the demand side of the market which wants the best of both worlds (innovation and compatibility).

Standards are essential to the efficient evolution of most technologies. In fact, to the extent a technology has a systems structure, the lack of an effective set of standards can significantly retard the industry's growth. The computer industry, as analyzed in this chapter, is a good example of the benefits of standards as well as the problems that arise as the standards themselves evolve through several stages. Similar statements can be made for communications, factory automation, etc.

In the early period of a technology's evolution, most firms attempt to dominate markets with proprietary versions of the generic technology. As markets grow and users increase pressure for "open" systems, the competitive dynamics force manufacturers into *partial* standardization in the form of several industry segments with their own standards.

Having a few standards as opposed to a larger number of proprietary product systems barely mitigates the problem for buyers, however. In fact, the failure of expectations for standardization to be realized leads to confusion and reduced demand. Eventually, because no one firm or coalition of firms typically ends up dominating the market, a single set of standards finally evolves.

The costs of letting this process take place *entirely* through market forces can be high, especially when the domestic industry finds that foreign competition has coalesced behind a single set of standards that is not optimal for the domestic industry that was once the world leader in the technology. In fact, efforts are more frequently being made to devise the technical basis for standards through a cooperative mechanism earlier in the technology life cycle.

Industry organizations such the Open Systems Foundation (OSF) and the Corporation for Open Systems (COS) are not only applying this approach to standards formulation, but they are simultaneously developing other infrastructure such as software (operating systems, security protocols, etc.) and test suites for determining conformance to the standards. Such organizations can give the diffusion of a new technology in the domestic industry a significant push forward.

From an economic growth efficiency point of view, the greatest danger is that the appropriate infrastructure, including standards, will lag to the extent that leading-edge users will invest in their own infrastructure, creating an installed base that inhibits a more uniform and widespread infrastructure. In cases such as data processing and communications, demand has become segmented and industry growth has been retarded by large, heavy users of computers, who decided that they could not wait for the evolution of standards. They proceeded to invest in high-cost, private wide area networks.

In conclusion, the central strategic problem -- the timing and content of standards -- is extremely complex and difficult to manage. Diffuse decision making through multi-enterprise market structures pulls innovation and thus provides a rich initial technology base, but the lack of standardization greatly inhibits technological progress through the middle and later phases of the technology life cycle. A concentrated market structure coupled with aggressive government intervention could, superficially at least, solve the problem of insufficient standardization, but creativity would suffer. The answer seems to lie in applying an understanding of how technologies evolve over time and supplying industry consensus standards that fit the particular point in a technology's evolution.

7   Trends in
Technology Infrastructure

*"Wisdom consists not so much in knowing
what to do in the ultimate as in knowing
what to do next"*

Herbert Hoover

     Global technology-based competition is a race with no finish line. The frenzied pace of competing is causing radical adjustments in corporate philosophy, let alone specific strategies. One of the major characteristics of this change process is the increased fuzziness of the previously well-defined corporate boundary. Today, terms such as joint ventures, consortia, strategic partnering, and global alliances are being used with increasing frequency, as industrialized nations attempt to adapt to the new global economic order.

     The most frequently cited factor affecting success in global markets based on new technologies is the commitment to the long run -- both in terms of *planning* and *staying power*. The Japanese have been the most ardent pursuers of this strategic philosophy. However, another factor is at work. The Japanese regard products, markets, and business organizations as interdependent elements of competing. In particular, rather than reject investment in a product on the basis of its profit potential considered in isolation, every product is assessed in the context of its relationships with upstream components and materials and downstream products and systems that use the subject product. The efficiency gain is not so much economies of scale as it is economies of scope over the entire production chain.

Drahalad and Hamel [1990] have argued that the typical U.S. corporate strategy of organizing by strategic business units and basing decisions on whether to internalize production capabilities on least-cost considerations should be rejected and replaced with a technology resource (i.e., core competence) strategy. In this strategic model, technology resources are free to move about the company to take advantage of emerging market opportunities. Embracing such a model would be a move toward the Japanese philosophy.

The focus on core competence rather than on product groups has enabled companies like Canon Inc. to diversify from their original product line, a mechanical camera, to sophisticated electronic and autofocus models, and from cameras to laser printers, fax machines, photocopiers, and video systems. In other words, Canon, like many Japanese companies, has used its core competence in precision mechanics, fine optics and microelectronics to continually expand product lines based on these competencies (horizontal integration), while strengthening the core competencies at all levels of industrial process from components to final products (vertical integration).

In contrast, the U.S. corporate strategy is currently characterized as basing investment decisions on short-term, price-performance considerations, rather than long-term development of core competence. However, this characterization does not adequately portray the strategic deficiency. The more accurate description of the dysfunction is that too many U.S. and European corporations apply price-performance criteria *individually* across lines of business, rather than regarding them as interacting elements of a total rate-of-return strategy.

Another major challenge facing corporations is how to adjust their strategic philosophies to accommodate the fact that a significant portion of what was developed as internal or proprietary technology in the past is now only obtainable in the *required time frame* through a mechanism that shares property rights with another firm, say, through a joint venture, or, even more broadly, through declaring the technology to be infrastructure and organizing an industry-level consortium to produce and disseminate it. Plenty of value remains to be added in the technology life cycle beyond these early phases of the R&D stage, as indicated in Figure 7-1. Applied R&D, production, and market development offer ample opportunity to enhance competitive position. A major problem in today's global markets is to reach the applied R&D stage as a viable competitor.

Figure 7-1

Stages of Technology-Based Economic Activity

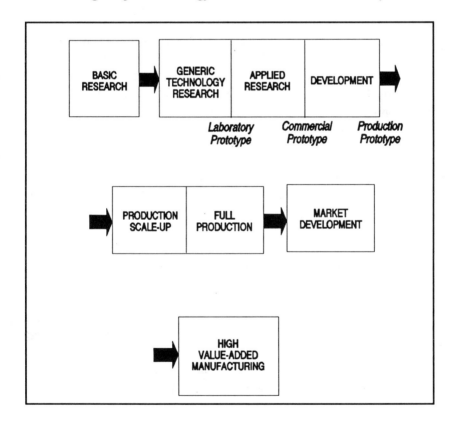

Corporate strategies are going through a process of improving the efficiency with which they implement either a "technology-leadership" or a "fast-follower" strategy. The technology leadership strategy requires the allocation of substantial resources to early-phase technology research. However, depending on the size of the firm, the nature of the technology, and the industry structure, this may mean operating a large central research laboratory (CRL), intensive and regular participation in consortia, CRDAs with Federal laboratories, etc., or, more accurately, some combination of these strategies. For example, companies, such as General Electric, DuPont, American Telephone and Telegraph, etc., pursue a strategy of technology leadership and therefore invest substantial amounts in a CRL.

The fast imitator, on the other hand, relies on relatively long technology life cycles, in which its comparative advantages in applied R&D and product engineering are more effective. TRW, Inc., especially in its automotive product lines, follows a strategy focused on *applied* R&D and thus has no CRL. In other words, TRW does not work far enough toward the "R" end of the R&D spectrum to justify a full-blown CRL facility. A TRW vice president estimates that nearly 80 percent of all technology used by the company is acquired from external sources. In fact, management views the ability to identify, acquire and apply technologies quickly as a major source of TRW's competitive advantage.[1]

The critical point is that neither strategy can be undertaken by a firm as a totally internal effort. The concept of "complementary assets", where some of these assets are accessed outside the firm, is an increasingly important part of corporate strategy. As previously described at length, many of the "external" technology assets come under the general definition of infrastructure.

Making corporate strategy decisions in the face of expanded dependency on technology infrastructure raises new types of risks. In the past, a large firm within an industry could adopt a technology-leadership strategy and implement it, in part through an investment in a central research laboratory, and have to worry only about keeping the technological lead over competitors. As long as this lead was maintained from generation to generation of the technology, the typical market-share distribution over any one life cycle remained acceptable.

---

[1] Lewis and Linden [1990]. This paper provides an excellent analysis of corporate strategies toward central research laboratories.

However, in today's evolving technology-based industry structure, several competitors may gang up on the technology leader by forming a research consortium to "leapfrog" the current generic technology. If the original technology leader continues to rely solely on its internal CRL, it may find its early-life-cycle market advantage eroded away by the consortium. When this strategy is invoked by foreign competitors, the net loss to the domestic industry can be high. This scenario is basically the one that subverted the health of the U.S. semiconductor industry.

Alternative Strategies: Robots vs. Robotics

On September 12, 1990, the last U.S. manufacturer of large, sophisticated robots disappeared, when the Swiss firm Asea Brown Boveri agreed to acquire the robot division of Cincinnati Milacron. The $3.5 billion world robot market is now controlled by five Japanese companies and Boveri. This event is shocking in that a decade earlier robotics was a highly touted, sexy technology that was expected to make a major contribution to a renaissance in U.S. industrial productivity. By now, robots were expected to be an integral component of automated manufacturing processes. Yet, in spite of maintaining the technology lead through the 1980s, the penetration of robots into U.S. manufacturing has been slow compared to Europe and Japan.

Some of the standard economic explanations and rationalizations for lost market share have been offered. On the demand side, many small U.S. manufacturers do not have the technical sophistication to determine their needs for robots or effectively use them once purchased. Moreover, the cost of capital was higher in the United States throughout the 1980s and robots are difficult to integrate into existing manufacturing processes. On the supply side, General Motors' joint venture with the leading Japanese robot manufacturer, Fanuc (GMFanuc) dominates the U.S. market, preventing smaller independent manufacturers from gaining sufficient market share to be competitive.

Clearly, the independent U.S. companies, that had once been investing heavily in robotics R&D and were regarded as the world's technological leaders, never achieved the volume of sales necessary to survive. This industry, as with other U.S. industries, has been criticized for poor market analysis. U.S. firms not only tried to develop the most sophisticated and hence most expensive applications of the generic technology, but they refused or were unable to see the trend in overall factory automation in which the function of *robotics* was increasingly implemented by simpler and less expensive machines.

Instead of expensive stand-alone robots (technically called "universally reprogrammable motion devices"), the majority of automated manufacturing processes incorporated small devices that served the functions of materials handling or positioning. Thus, such devices as pickers, iron hands and manipulators, which the Japanese characterize as robots, were ignored by most of the U.S. industry. American robot manufacturers thought they should sell a million robots at half a million dollars each, while Japanese companies were happy to sell a million at $5,000 each.[2]

Other U.S. companies, however, who view themselves as *equipment* manufacturers (producing machine tools, materials handling, packaging, painting equipment, etc.), add a robotics function (say, a tool changer arm) when it *enhances the overall function* of the piece of equipment in a cost-effective manner. Some industry observers believe that the discrete robot will disappear from the manufacturing environment over time and be replaced by ancillary equipment and add-on devices. Others believe that the automation of design and, in particular, the adoption of concurrent engineering will, by simplifying manufacturing processes obviate the need for sophisticated robots in most applications.

Purists of the free market school will argue that this is simply the natural process of the evolution of markets, with companies that are the fittest, both technologically and managerially, ending up survivors. The problem, as described earlier, is that fewer and fewer U.S. firms are surviving. The question for public policy, therefore, is can infant industries be guided without subverting the efficiency factors of the marketplace. The Japanese have used a whole range of incentives and technology infrastructure support to accelerate and guide their robotics industry.

One of the designated roles of technology infrastructure is the provision of certain types of generic technical and market-related information. Infant industries in the United States that bring new

---

[2]   McCormack [1990, p. 2].

technologies to the marketplace often have structures that are characterized by small, technically-competent firms, that unfortunately initially lack both production and marketing expertise. If the technological and hence product life cycles are long enough, these skills needed for long-term survival can be acquired by enough firms to reach the "critical mass" required for sustained global competitiveness. That is, the industry's internal dynamics coupled with its acquired technology and related managerial assets allow its position to be essentially self-perpetuating over successive technology and product life cycles. However, in the increasingly short "windows of opportunity" that characterize global markets, such skills acquisition by multiple firms are attained only with the assistance of the right infrastructure, as appears to have happened in biotechnology.

One of the roles of technology infrastructure is to provide information on the broad systems context or "paradigm" into which individual companies must "fit" their strategies. With respect to robotics, if the *functional* role had been better thought out by U.S. robotics firms and their customers, the result might have been different.

The proper infrastructure role in such situations is critical. NIST's automated manufacturing research group pioneered the concept of "hierarchical control" for the automated factory, beginning in the late 1970s. This technology infrastructure was a *systems* concept for basically determining the functions of various elements of the automated factory *and* specifying how different pieces of equipment should *interface* with one another.

Had U.S. industry and NIST been more successful at disseminating and applying this generic manufacturing concept, the proper role for robotics might have been implemented. However, the United States is only now reaching a level of appreciation of the importance of having such technology infrastructure play a central role in strategic planning and subsequent investment decision making.

A successful robot depends on applications of a number of generic technologies. They are aimed at the basic tasks that a robot might perform (sensing, selecting an mode of operation, performing some physical task, and turning the work piece over to another machine). To perform a task such as sensing (seeing or feeling) depends on independently developed sensor technology that is useful in other generic technologies/industries as well.

Such technologies, because they transcend a number of industries with somewhat different uses in each industry, tend to suffer from underinvestment -- in part because of a poor understanding of their economic potential, but also because their interfaces with other equipment in the particular production process are not developed, especially in the time frame needed to meet better organized competition.

Moreover, a subactivity such as sensing is much less effective in terms of the robot's overall performance if the data generated cannot be efficiently transmitted to a control computer and the appropriate instructions sent back. Because the control computer and the sensors are made by different manufacturers, communications between the two will be inefficient and thereby greatly decrease a robot's overall productivity, no matter how advanced are each of the two components' generic technologies.

Such communication inefficiencies are now being solved by developing "interface" standards, based on various infratechnologies, which facilitate data flows. When one considers that these interfaces occur between components of the robot, between the robot and other machines, between all machines and the factory-level ("host") computer, and between manufacturing and R&D and marketing, the potential overall productivity impacts of the collection of underlying infratechnologies is easily seen to be substantial.

In summary, the Japanese have correctly viewed the use of robotics as an element of a manufacturing system, rather than as a stand-alone robot which, one designed and built, now goes in search of an application. The stand-alone robot appealed to the American penchant for invention and the entrepreneurial approach to innovation, but while the technology was advanced substantially and continues to have a limited number of applications, the products did not integrate into the broader production system.

Consortia for Cooperative Production?

Chapter 4 analyzed the roles and trends in technology infrastructure produced by R&D consortia such as MCC and SEMATECH in the United States and numerous others around the world. These institutions are providing not only efficiency gains in the conduct of R&D but appear to be having increasing impact on corporate investment strategies. The success in simply establishing SEMATECH lead to an attempt to create a counterpart consortium, known as U.S. Memories, to produce a major class of computer memory circuits, DRAMs. U.S. Memories (USM) was an ambitious seven-month campaign by four U.S. chip makers and three systems vendors to share the costs and risks of re-entering the world DRAM market. However, the effort failed to generate financial support among prospective customers and was abandoned in January 1990.

The attempt to establish USM coincided with a collapse in world DRAM prices and softness in the computer market. This cyclical effect has been cited as the cause of USM's failure. While it may have contributed, the more fundamental factor was the substantial differences that exist in the underlying economics of the R&D and production stages. To put it as simply as possible, the externalities at the R&D stage are typically significantly greater than at the production stage. Economies of scale in production, which often increase as a technology matures, are not sufficient to rationalize cooperation beyond the traditional two-firm joint venture. As a case in point, in 1989 alone 10 joint ventures involving production were formed in various areas of semiconductor product technology between U.S. and Japanese firms.[3]

Downstream users such as computer manufacturers actually prefer to have a number of alternative sources of supply. But, even USM's most enthusiastic sponsor, IBM, decided it could sufficiently hedge against future supply contingencies by licensing its chip technology to other domestic chip manufactures. In other words, in the taxonomy adopted in this book, technology-based products can themselves seldom be rationalized as technology infrastructure and thereby cooperatively produced.[4] In fact, about a month after the demise of the USM effort, IBM announced that it had succeeded in fabricating 16-megabyte DRAMs (a proposed target for USM) on an *existing* production line.[5]

---

[3] "Semiconductor Makers Ready to Call a Truce", *Japan Economic Journal*, January 17, 1990.

[4] Supporters of USM actually claimed in Congressional testimony that the proposed consortium would be "entirely pre-competitive". See Dozier [1989].

[5] See Hooper [1990].

To state this situation somewhat more formally for the policy analyst, *technical* risk during the R&D stage is initially quite high but is successively reduced over time. *Commercial* risk is very high during the early stages of research; but it can be reduced over the later stages of product development, when the product's performance attributes have been specified and reasonably accurate estimates of unit production costs can be made.

In general, once the generic technology has been advanced, medium and even small firms should be able to rationalize pursuing at least some of the potential market applications. At the applied R&D and subsequent production stages, rates of return can be predicted with *relatively* greater certainty and capital markets are therefore more accommodating.

So, why are consortia needed to finance investment in production, given the reductions in technical and commercial risk that typically occur during the R&D stage? Proponents of significant increases in the permitted level of industry concentration at the production stage must make the argument that the minimum efficient scale of *production* is a barrier to individual market entry and even to entry through conventional *joint ventures* (two firms). In the case of DRAMs, this argument is asserted but not substantiated. In fact, the existence of the TI/Hitachi and Motorola/Toshiba joint ventures counter this assertion.

The *cost* of capital can and does have a significant negative impact on what level of investment is "affordable" to a single firm or to a conventional joint venture, but that problem should be solved through policies that lower these costs for the economy as a whole, not through cooperative production.

Finally, proponents of highly concentrated production have not addressed the tradeoffs with respect to the implied reductions in domestic competition and the rejection of vertical integration. Major Japanese electronic firms have cooperated at the research stage in the case of DRAMs, but *not* at the production stage. In the case of U.S. Memories, it would have to be demonstrated that

o   foreign cartel behavior existed, which could not be removed;

o   the economies of scale are not only beyond individual firms, but are beyond joint ventures (which do not require antitrust law changes).

The remaining barriers to inducing capital investment are due to the dynamics of rapidly changing markets, including product refinements, production cost reductions, better service, etc. These barriers can cause unstable cash flows in *individual* markets; but, the resulting commercial (cash flow) risk in any single market is best reduced by vertical and horizontal integration (i.e., more effective linking of firms) across markets, *not* by concentrating production in a particular market.

Evolving Technology Infrastructure Strategies

Possible solutions to the above problems are evidenced by the semiconductor industry. Until recently, U.S. semiconductor chip manufacturers have not shown much interest in diversifying into equipment or materials production. U.S. semiconductor equipment manufacturers are typically small, specialized companies. Lack of diversification, poor relations with their customers (semiconductor chip manufacturers) along with macroeconomic problems such as high cost of capital and financial markets that are not oriented toward high-technology investment led to a steady demise in this industry.

Perkin-Elmer Corporation is a case in point. It had been the technological leader in photolithography equipment. After losing market share to Nikon Corp. and Canon Inc. of Japan for several years, Perkin-Elmer invested a reported $100 million to recapture the technological lead. After becoming the target of a takeover by Nikon, the company sold a majority interest in its electron beam technology division in March 1990 to a coalition of U.S. companies, including IBM and DuPont. In May of that year, it sold a 67-percent interest in its optical lithography division to another coalition, the Silicon Valley Group, Inc. As part of this latter sale, IBM agreed to provide financial support to develop an advanced photolithography stepper and to make substantial purchases of the stepper. SEMATECH awarded a joint development contract to the new company to support development of the new stepper.[6]

The nature of these responses to the demise of a conventional industry structure is important. The combination of cooperative planning, subsidization of R&D, and demand-pull (guaranteed procurement) represent a radical behavioral change for U.S. industry. The ultimate objective is to recapture a needed semiconductor-related industry in order to capture economies of scope and increase the overall efficiency of the domestic production chain. The major lesson here is that the same mechanism used to produce technology infrastructure (coalitions of firms) can be employed to preserve required overall industry structure.[7]

SEMATECH's strategy is to sustain or create one world-class U.S. producer in each major category of chip making equipment, second-sourcing only in special cases where the second firm uses an entirely different tool architecture or represents a particularly high-risk/high-return investment opportunity.[8]

The types of technology infrastructure supplied by SEMATECH are essential to the success of the semiconductor industry. However, other technology infrastructure is required as well. Success in this and other technology-based industries is determined by relative quality, price, and speed of response to changes in demand. All three of these factors are affected by infratechnologies, as defined in Chapter 3. In the R&D stage, ability to understand and manipulate materials through precise knowledge of their properties is essential to both conducting state-of-the-art R&D and communicating the results to managers, venture capitalists, and the financial infrastructure generally.

The semiconductor industry will not invest in the research necessary to characterize these materials because such research derives from a different science and technology base than generic semiconductor product technology. The economies of both scale and

---

[6]   U.S. General Accounting Office [1990, p. 19].

[7]   Equipment suppliers are sometimes called "infrastructure" to the manufacturing industry that they serve, but proprietary products do not conform to the definition of the term as used here.

[8]   Mayer [1990, p. 14].

scope in measurement-related research are typically not captured by a single industry, let alone a single firm. Similarly, as the R&D process proceeds, product characteristics, such as electrical resistance and thermal conductivity in semiconductor device manufacturing, must be accurately measured to determine if the R&D is, in fact, achieving its goals.

At the production stage, the automation of manufacturing to increase both productivity and quality requires numerous types of infratechnology ranging from various sensor technologies to data formatting and communication standards. Finally, the actual transactions in which many thousands of units of a product can change hands require assurances to buyers that performance specifications have been met.

The uncertainty with respect to performance leads to delays in market transactions and, more important, higher transaction costs.[9] The result is slower diffusion of the technology into the marketplace. Both the time delays and higher prices allow foreign competitors a chance to gain market share. These transaction costs can be reduced substantially through standardized test methods. The infratechnologies which are the basis for acceptance testing come from a number of sources, including government laboratories, such as NIST in the United States.

Information infrastructure provides some particularly good examples of industry- and national-level strategy formulation. As the discussion in previous chapters has shown, information technologies collectively constitute a complex and dynamic system that will leverage virtually any industry that incorporates such a system into its technology base. Defining the economic roles and impacts of information infrastructure, as in other areas of technology infrastructure, is a first step in enabling the establishment of institutions and mechanisms for providing it. Such strategy formulation occurs through a number of channels and results in distinctly different strategies being selected.

The genius behind the concept of "networked computing", Robert Kahn, directed the development of the first computer network,

---

[9] Ronald Coase won the Nobel Prize in part for emphasizing the importance of reducing transaction costs. Such costs are particularly important in technology-based trade and hence in determining competitive position. They have been given insufficient attention by economists and policy analysts.

Arpanet. In the absence of a government-managed infrastructure mechanism, Kahn founded the Corporation for National Research Initiatives (NRI) which has performed three infrastructure functions: (1) through industry and government funding, provided a source of funds for academic research on information infrastructure; (2) served as the source of information infrastructure concepts such as the "digital library", "knowledge bank", and "gigabit networking project"; and (3) provided a forum for information exchange among researchers, potential manufacturers, and information users.

    The digital library is a particularly interesting concept. It conforms in ways to the operational philosophy of *incremental* improvement in existing networks, while at the same time drawing on new technology. The cornerstone of the digital library is the "knowbot". Acting as a kind of artificial intelligence librarian, the knowbot's role is to process requests for information and locate the source of that information from a heterogeneous collection of geographically-dispersed networks. This may be as important a technological concept as packet switching, developed by Kahn in the 1960s.[10]

    NRI also follows one of the requirements for private or public institutions that provide technology infrastructure -- remain competitively neutral. Thus, it has turned down opportunities to directly participate with industry in the proprietary stage of the digital library's development. Taking such a step would likely compromise NRI's infrastructure role, which also includes sensitive issues such as brokering intellectual property rights.

    On the hardware side, NRI is coordinating the gigabit networking project which seeks to develop supercomputers capable of sending information at gigabit speeds (more than one billion bytes per second) over fiberoptic cables. These systems must be tested as they are developed, which requires complex test facilities.

    Efficiency in the development of supercomputer networks is enhanced if the companies and universities operating these test beds can exchange information. NRI brings the participants together to compare experiences and to work towards interface and other standards. Thus, NRI acts as a catalyst for institutional and human

---

     [10]   Packet switching made computer networking possible by sending bytes of information from a single source in discrete groups or "packets" rather than in a continuous stream. This concept allowed multiple senders to simultaneously use a network, thereby greatly increasing the network's capacity.

"networking" in order to increase the efficiency of the information infrastructure development.

The networks themselves are, of course, a key element of information infrastructure. ISDN and OSI are the evolving international standards for the multimedia networks of the future. Converting the U.S. information infrastructure to a radically new communications medium (ISDN) in a totally open hardware system (OSI) is a major challenge. Unlike the current set of communications protocols, set by the Department of Defense in its past role as technology leader, the future standards are being driven by an international movement rather than a domestic one, and the primary objectives are economic rather than military.

The hardware elements of the information infrastructure such as high-speed switching systems will require considerable research. So will the software component. The problem is that, as part of a system of technologies, these hardware elements must exhibit "interoperability"; that is, they must be both physically and functionally compatible. This means that both physical and software interface standards must be in place, or the whole information technology revolution will proceed at a snail's pace -- at least in the countries that do not pay attention to and provide the required infrastructure.

Research funding on hardware, public or private, tends to be equipment-specific and self-contained. This leads to compatibility problems. Similarly, software tends to be machine-specific and non-portable. Thus, a critical infrastructure role is to ensure compatibility and interoperability. Every time a major hardware advance is attained, its widespread and efficient use requires a new set of public domain software to perform such infrastructure functions as assuring compatibility across hardware platforms and portability of software among different vendors' versions of the same hardware platform.

For the example, the development of massively-parallel computer systems offers substantial advances in computational speed, but software from other computer technologies does not run on these machines. New software is being written, but unless it is portable across different vendors' machines, the costs will be high enough to significantly retard the development of the domestic market. The cost to software suppliers of writing several semi-custom versions of the same software package coupled with the purchasers' reluctance to tie themselves to one hardware design and the associated proprietary software design will provide significant barriers to market penetration.

Of course, if foreign suppliers agree among themselves on standards and thereby remove these risks (lower the expected costs), they will take market share away from the domestic suppliers.

Note also that basic information infrastructure actually enhances the productivity of its other elements. A variety of public information services will be distributed via such advanced networks as the National Research and Education Network (NREN). Examples include standard reference data, software for reference implementations of communications protocols, and conformance test suites for information technologies. Thus, the original implementation of the information technology infrastructure will actually enhance its further evolution.

Quality

No strategic objective better reflects the multidisciplinary character of new approaches to achieving competitive position in global markets than the objective of quality assurance. Strategies for pursuing the quality objective have changed markedly in the past decade and will continue to evolve in the future.

The increasingly stringent demands for product and service quality mean that quality can no longer be achieved through post-production testing. That is, quality can no longer be "inspected in". This traditional approach results in too much waste due to rejects of final product. Moreover, the increasingly short product life cycles and time-to-market requirements do not permit redesign and second or third production runs to meet specifications. Finally, to attain the levels of quality now being demanded, the desired attributes of quality must be embedded in the product design. That is, they can not be "manufactured in". One job of process control is therefore to assure that *designed in* quality is achieved.

The multidisciplinary content of the technology infrastructure supporting the quality objective is evidenced by the selection criteria for the Malcolm Baldrige National Quality Award, administered by the National Institute of Standards and Technology. For example, IBM's Rochester plant, which manufacturers the highly successful Application System 400 mid-range computer system, did not win this award in 1989, in spite of the superior reliability record of AS/400.

The company set about determining why they had not won and what aspects of their operation needed to be improved. The result was an expansion of quality assurance strategy to what is now called *total quality management (TQM)*. Their efforts paid off, for the Rochester operation was one of the four winners of the coveted Baldrige award in 1990. As important as the prize itself and the consequent public relations benefits were to IBM, of even greater long-run importance was what the application process taught IBM about its internal business operations. In particular, IBM realized that while its emphasis on product reliability had paid off, not enough attention had been given to customer input on problems and design preferences.[11]

Such multidimensional strategies usually require organizational and behavioral changes by companies, as well as purely technical changes. These strategies require top-to-bottom commitment from management as well as the workers who implement changes. This approach, in turn, requires that certain individuals within the organization act as catalysts or "champions" for the new approach. All these ingredients -- commitment, widespread involvement, change agent -- apparently evolved within IBM. In preparing its second (1990) Baldrige award application, IBM made some of the very improvements in quality assurance practice that the Baldrige examiners had suggested the previous year.

An important point is that while technology infrastructure, in this case quality assurance practices, can be developed and made available to industry, the mechanism selected to accomplish the transfer or "diffusion" is as critical as the content of the infrastructure itself. In the above example, IBM put significant resources into winning the award. They studied the application process forward and backward, interviewed examiners, and rehearsed questions they thought would be asked. In the process, they learned and implemented total quality management practices that might have taken years to acquire under their previous strategies.

Because the pursuit of quality is a multidisciplinary strategy, requiring virtually an entire company's involvement, technology infrastructure support must be equally multi-faceted. Progress in designing and implementing quality assurance strategies has varied

---

[11]   Skrzycki [1990, p. H1].

from firm to firm and from industry to industry, and, in fact, from nation to nation. The reasons for these variances are complex, but essential to understand if both the private sector and the supporting infrastructure are to combine to achieve an economy-wide level of quality assurance that is competitive in global markets. One thing is certain, any nation that does not commit substantial resources to quality improvement will fall ever farther behind in terms of competitive position.

Even as TQM is being embraced in industrialized nations, such as the United States, the Japanese are beginning to move beyond it to a "Zero-Defects Management" concept, which allegedly is based on "drastically different principles and methods".[12] Overall, the drive towards quality improvement in Japan continues. According to the Union of Japanese Scientists and Engineers (JUSE), which manages the Deming Prize for Quality, investment in quality training programs is increasing relentlessly -- even though Japan is the acknowledged leader in product quality.

Quality as an Element of Corporate Strategy

As part of its strategic planning for providing quality assurance infrastructure support, the National Institute of Standards and Technology (NIST) has conducted analyses of quality investment practices in U.S. industry.[13] These analyses have examined investment patterns -- how these patterns have changed over the past decade, and how U.S. strategies compare to major foreign competitors in two important industries: semiconductors and optical fibers.

Quality was defined in the early 1980s in a rather generalized manner -- conformance to specifications and/or fitness for use. The NIST study confirmed that this traditional definition of quality is outmoded. The responses of the firms surveyed, revealed a trend

---

[12]   See Drucker [1991].

[13]   See Quick, Finan & Associates [1990]. The optical fiber industry portion of this study is summarized in Link, Quick, and Tassey [1991]. Portions of the semiconductor industry analysis are in Finan [1990].

toward the view that a contemporary definition cannot stop with stating only a "bottom-line" objective.

However, such evolution of strategic philosophy varies greatly among industries. For example, the survey responses in the NIST study indicate that the optical fiber industry tends to accept the traditional definition to a greater degree than does the semiconductor industry. The greater degree of competition from the Japanese in semiconductors appears to have been a factor in forcing the more rapid evolution of quality assurance philosophies in this industry compared with U.S. industry in general.

The working definition of quality is becoming broader in that service factors are included along with product specifications. Moreover, the typical definition is now more operational- or organizational-oriented in that concepts such as *continuous improvement* and *prevention* are increasingly the dominant drivers of quality assurance strategies.

This more dynamic view of quality assurance is reflected by the fact that *continuous* improvement is sought in service levels, delivery, product value-added, and production capability. Operationally, this evolution is evidenced by a change from the narrow focus on product defects to one of *total quality performance* (management decisions, customer interface, vendor interface, and total quality control).

An appreciation of the radical change in the content of quality as a strategy variable can be gained by noting the four stages through which quality assurance strategies have evolved over the past decade:

> *Stage 1: Inspection and Verification.* This approach consisted simply of inspecting some or all units of a production run. Because inspection occurred *after* production, the rate of rejects was not diminished rapidly and total wasted resources over the product life cycle were high.

> *Stage 2: Appraisal.* After-production inspection broadened in the early 1980s into an emphasis on measurement, evaluation, and auditing of final product quality as well as ensuring that purchased components and materials conformed with quality standards and performance requirements.

Stage 3: Prevention. While the appraisal stage, unlike inspection, resulted in some feedback that changed certain specific aspects of a firm's production activity, the concept of *prevention* changed management philosophy in a comprehensive way. This change involved major new concepts such as designing quality into the product, application of statistical process control techniques to manufacturing operations, and shifting the responsibilities for quality assurance to the operating organizations.

In the firms applying this concept of prevention, separate dedicated quality-assurance units actually decreased in size and changed their function from direct responsibility for quality to conducting audits and recommending overall quality-related strategies to operating units.

Stage 4: Total Quality Management (TQM). This approach seeks to emulate completely the Japanese management philosophy on quality assurance. It incorporates all the elements of prevention, but goes beyond changes in particular organizational units and functions to make quality assurance the responsibility of all levels of management and employees. In addition, relationships with vendors and customers are integrated into the operational strategy.

In the semiconductor case study, almost all the firms interviewed reported that they are currently in the prevention stage or applying some form of the TQM approach.

Trends in Quality-Related Expenditures

Based on the survey responses received from the U.S. semiconductor companies in the NIST study, it was estimated that 20 to 35 percent of the *total* annual budgets of U.S. semiconductor companies in 1988 were devoted to achieving acceptable levels of quality. For the industry as a whole, that translates into $3.7 to $6.5 billion in that year. These *quality-related* outlays increased four-fold in absolute terms over the past decade. In relative terms, quality-related investments in this industry have grown at a faster rate than the industry overall and faster than investment in R&D or capital expenditures for equipment and structures.

Table 7-1

Objectives of Quality Assurance Strategies in the Optical Fiber Industry

Objective	Average Percentage of Quality Expenditures by	
	U.S. Firms	*Foreign Firms*
Improving Product Performance	28	17
Reducing Attribute Variability	15	18
Increasing Product Reliability	17	16
Decreasing Need for Service	5	11
Increasing Product Life	5	6
Improving Manufacturability	31	15
Other (Education/Training)	4	5

Annual expenditures toward achieving quality by all firms in the optical fiber industry were estimated to have increased from an average of 13 percent of their total budgets in the early 1980s to an average of 18 percent in 1988-1989 (a 37 percent increase). A second survey of foreign optical fiber producers' allocations for quality showed that these expenditures increased from 7 percent of total budget in the early 1980s to an average of 12 percent in 1988-1989.[14] The substantially larger relative investments by U.S. firms may be a major factor in their continuing dominant share of the world market.

The greater product homogeneity of the optical fiber industry compared with semiconductors allowed meaningful data to be collected on company expenditures for specific *objectives* of the overall quality strategy. Six functional objectives of quality strategies were identified and data collected on relative expenditures for each (the expenditure allocations do not sum to 100 percent because they are averages across respondents).

The survey of foreign optical fiber manufacturers tried to determine if any substantial differences exist compared to U.S. firms with respect to the composition of expenditures on quality assurance by functional objective. The results, shown in Table 7-1, indicate that foreign producers distribute expenditures more evenly across functional objectives. In particular, whereas U.S. firms show an

Table 7-2

Quality Assurance Expenditures by Major Budget Category for the Optical Fiber Industry

Budget Category	Average Percentage Allocated to Quality by	
	U.S. Firms	*Foreign Firms*
Operations	19	4
Capital	27	6
Research and Development	27	9
Overhead	22	5

---

[14] The NIST study estimated that foreign firms responding to the survey account for roughly 25 percent of sales by all foreign manufacturers.

emphasis on *improving product performance* and *improving manufacturability*, the percentages allocated by foreign firms to those two objectives are approximately half the U.S. level.

Data were also collected from domestic and foreign optical fiber firms on expenditures for quality assurance within major budget categories. Table 7-2 compares relative allocations in terms of four major budget categories. In all four budget categories, U.S. firms spend three to four times as much on a percentage basis on quality assurance as do foreign competitors. This finding is compatible with the observation that the U.S. industry is pursuing the broader objective, increasingly observed in U.S. manufacturing industries as a whole, of "building quality in" through both product design and control of the production process -- i.e., through a *concurrent engineering* process.

In both industries studied, the trend over the past decade has been toward increasing investment in *non-technical* aspects of quality improvement, such as training and analysis of overall systems efficiency. Simultaneously, there is increasing investment in *service* quality (time to delivery, technical assistance to customers, etc.) as a key to gaining market share instead of product quality (on the assumption that everyone has to meet the same product quality standards).

The Importance of Measurement Investments

As noted above, U.S. semiconductor firms responding to the NIST survey indicated that they allocate between 20 and 35 percent of their total budget to quality assurance. Of these quality assurance expenditures, an estimated 15 to 40 percent is measurement-related.[15] For the optical fiber industry, an average of 27.5 percent of U.S. firms' *total expenditures for quality* is allocated toward measurement. The comparable average percentage for foreign producers surveyed is 19.4 percent.

Much of the measurement technology used by industry is supplied by sources outside of individual companies. NIST is a major

---

[15]   Thus, between 3 and 14 percent of the total outlays of the industry is estimated to be allocated toward measurement technology for quality assurance.

source of this infratechnology. Respondents to a survey of individuals in semiconductor firms with measurement-related responsibilities rated the importance of quality-related information from NIST as 4.1 on a scale running from 1 (not important) to 5 (very important).

When asked to specify ways in which NIST could further enhance its support for quality-related information, respondents cited "research cycle time" (timeliness) as an area where improvement would be beneficial. Several firms stated that they would prefer some sacrifice of depth for speed. Such responses undoubtedly reflect the increasing competitive pressures that are shortening technology and product life cycles, thereby making timeliness relatively more important. New generations of semiconductor devices are measurement-intensive and have few, if any, of the measurement requirements met when first developed. At least some firms in this industry want NIST to focus more on measurement for the test/assembly/fabrication stages than on the earlier stages such as product design.

Such statements are compatible with broader industry-wide trends towards increasing emphasis on *process* technology. More specifically, these preferences likely are derived from efforts towards achieving more rapid (even "perpendicular") build up to full production and high yields, shorter and more flexible production runs, and more efficient quality assurance procedures for market transactions. For example, one respondent remarked that "investment in measurement is increasing rapidly...[and] it takes hours to test a part today". Such statements reflect the tremendous competitive pressures that exist in most high-technology industries to produce and deliver high-quality parts, virtually on demand. Taken as a whole the survey responses show that the content of the need for measurement technology support varies greatly over the life cycle of each generation of product, so that planning for delivery of this type of technology infrastructure will require considerably more effort in the future.

Industry Structure and
Quality-Related Strategies

Many industries produce critical intermediate products that are inputs into final products and systems of products. That is, these products affect the overall performance and reliability of downstream products and final product systems. Thus, they may be thought of as "enabling" technologies in the sense that the competitive positions of a number of downstream industries are significantly affected by the quality of these technologies and the products based on them.

Continuing with the above examples, the semiconductor and optical fiber industries have large capital-intensive firms that are pursuing large-volume markets for commodity-type products. A distinguishing feature is that the semiconductor industry also has many small firms and hence more firms in total than the optical fiber industry. This is due to the existence of product market niches which are relatively less capital-intensive than the large-volume commodity product lines (represented most prominently by memory circuits in semiconductors and by most of the production of optical fibers). The role of quality varies depending on the market niche.

Smaller firms, particularly in the semiconductor industry, emphasize product quality as a *distinguishing feature* of their product strategy. Larger firms, which focus on high-volume, commodity products that typically require more capital-intensive production processes, tend to regard product quality as a *minimum requirement* for competing. This is because the more homogeneous the product, the more difficult it is for firms to differentiate themselves in terms of *product* attributes. These larger firms integrate quality assurance techniques directly into their production processes to a greater extent than do smaller firms pursuing niche markets. In effect, such investments by competitors tend to neutralize each other's investments in quality, and product quality therefore becomes a *minimum* requirement for competing. These large firms instead display relatively greater emphasis on *service* quality as a means of distinguishing themselves from competitors.

In the optical fiber industry, the size of a firm does not appear to be a particularly important factor in implementing quality assurance strategies. Of the six functional objectives of a quality-enhancing strategy for which expenditure data were collected in the NIST study (see Table 7-1), only two (increasing product reliability and decreasing need for serviceability) showed any significant correlation with size and market share.

Future improvements in quality assurance by U.S. firms may hinge on further progress in integrating the various organizational elements within a company. For example, the NIST study found that on average only a modest link exists between R&D technical support and the growing efforts in non-technology (basically non-equipment) activities for quality improvement. The study went into great detail on the comprehensive organizational and technological strategies for increasing both productivity and quality. Pioneered and continually improved by the Japanese, these strategies -- concurrent engineering, Total Productivity Maintenance (TPM) and Total Quality Management (TQM) are clearly *systems* concepts and therefore require change by the entire firm *and* its external environment.

Organizationally, most U.S. semiconductor firms have not fully integrated technology infrastructure such as measurement-related activities with quality-related strategies. Individuals with responsibility for measurement are typically located in a different part of the firm (a measurement lab or a R&D-related unit) from those responsible for quality assurance. NIST staff, for example, primarily interact with and support the measurement and R&D units. This situation did not appear in the case study of the U.S. optical fiber industry. The survey responses by individuals with responsibility for quality assurance indicate that NIST has been a valuable source of quality-related information, used by a majority of firms in the industry. The implication is that different organizational strategies can mean different degrees of access to technology infrastructure.

The final point with respect to the relationships between quality-related strategies and industry structure has to do with the interactions with other industries. U.S. semiconductor firms have clearly had to undergo substantial strategic changes in response to increasing global competition. U.S. semiconductor firms' domestic customers (such as computer firms) were educated by Japanese semiconductor suppliers with respect to new potential levels of quality performance. American companies have to respond to this "learned" demand for higher quality or simply disappear as viable competitors. In responding, U.S. firms have had to overcome a tradition of arms-length relationships with their suppliers and customers. The Japanese, on the other hand, have a tradition of cooperation, facilitated in major segments of their economy by the organization-linking *Keiretsu* structure.

By studying and then emulating the Japanese strategies for quality, U.S. firms have begun to (1) broaden their definitions of quality to include virtually all business activities (R&D, production, marketing) and (2) include in the implementation of quality assurance strategies their interactions with both customers and suppliers. These interactions are with suppliers of raw materials and intermediate goods to increase quality on the input side and with customers to increase output (final product) quality.

The changing nature of industrial technologies is partly responsible for these changes in strategy. For example, the increasing complexity, not only of individual products, but systems of products, has meant that some types of defects (such as low quality) can only be reproduced once the product is integrated into a system. In such cases, defects can only be identified and dealt with through cooperation between users and suppliers. Also, an increasing proportion of defects in products such as semiconductors are not reproducible at all -- again requiring cooperation to optimize product design and overall quality assurance practice. The net result has been to increase the effective integration of the vertical structure of the electronics industry.[16]

In comparing the U.S. and Japanese semiconductor industries, it is clear that independent of the degree of vertical integration, Japan's leadership in quality has derived from a significant number of quality-driving end-markets and major product groups that force technical improvements enhancing quality in other product groups. The early integration of quality into the business strategy influenced both the organization of their businesses and also their management style. The implementation of that strategy tended to focus on three areas: line operator training, automation of production lines, and improvements in equipment. External relationships with equipment and materials firms also facilitated achieving higher quality assurance goals.

More extensive feedback of quality-assurance data between vendor and customer and greater exchange of information on product requirements and specifications are two aspects of the external relationships in the Japanese semiconductor industry that are qualitatively different from those in the U.S. industry. Today, many U.S. firms are making great efforts to emulate Japanese quality

---

[16] Some analysts have argued that lack of vertical integration in the U.S. semiconductor industry has contributed to a slower rate of adaptation to the new order of global competition (see Tassey [1990] and Chapters 4 and 5). The concept of *multi-enterprise integration*, introduced in Chapter 3, is an industry structure alternative to the Japanese *Keiretsu*. SEMATECH and MCC have promoted initial elements in this "model" of integration.

strategies in semiconductors. The NIST study found that "differences in design of the overall strategy are not that large. Firms in both countries define their quality strategies differently from the classic definition of quality that focuses on 'fitness for use'. Where differences are still evident is in the techniques used to implement quality-assurance strategies." In other words, the content of *management practice* infrastructure differs between the two nations.[17]

In analyzing the composition of quality assurance strategies and their interaction with industry structure, the pronounced differences in the strategies of individual firms must not be overlooked. Otherwise, one-dimensional infrastructure policies can be mistakenly pursued, at the expense of the advantages of pluralistic competition.

This reality was reflected in the findings of the NIST study in which a series of statements were presented to industry respondents who were then asked to agree or disagree. While answers to many of the questions were highly uniform, those questions that reflected "strategic choice" elicited a wide range of responses. For example, respondents were asked to agree or disagree with the statement "Quality activities are guided primarily by what competing firms are doing with their product/process strategies." The responses ranged from mild agreement to strong disagreement.

This diversity reflects the fact that some firms view themselves as competing through *product innovation* and therefore through an industry leadership strategy, while other firms compete as *fast imitators* coupled with emphasis on product improvements and superior *process* technology. In other words, this second group competes relatively more on the basis of product cost and quality in a reactive mode. Yet other firms emphasize the *service* quality aspects of competition. As previously described, most large semiconductor firms *currently* believe that service quality is the key way to be differentiated from other vendors. However, this emphasis may be indicative simply of the particular phase in the technology/product cycle as well as reflective of the overall adjustment taking place in the industry's previously narrow approach toward quality assurance.

---

[17]   Recent NIST strategic planning and proposed Congressional legislation have included *management practice* as an explicit element of technology infrastructure.

Different strategies also lead to derived demands for different quality-enhancing technologies. For example, semiconductor memories -- especially DRAMs -- have been the dominant "technology driver", especially for the major Japanese semiconductor producers, over the past 15 years.[18] However, DRAMs principally drive process and manufacturing technology. Other aspects of semiconductor technology, such as design and test, are not impacted by DRAMs to the same degree. Thus, there is a set of quality-assurance issues related to non-memory, logic products, that cannot be addressed by using DRAMs as the technology driver.[19]

Technology-driver products are important because the management disciplines developed to support them are gradually applied across other segments of the firm's organization. The technology driver, therefore, tends to be the pacing product with respect to establishing quality-related management practices. Thus, the existence of multiple technology drivers within one global market argues that different product and related quality strategies may be pursued successfully.

In summary, quality is a complex, multifaceted strategy that requires participation of every element of a corporation and its suppliers and customers. Many of its elements therefore have the characteristics of technology infrastructure. The trends in strategies towards quality assurance can be summed up by the following:

(1) many technology-based firms are moving away from product-only strategies for improving quality toward integrated or systems-level practices such as *concurrent engineering* or *total quality management* that involve the entire firm and even extend beyond

---

[18]   The term "technology driver" refers to a product family, within a larger set of product families deriving from the same generic technology, which has both sufficient market scale and continuing requirements for application of leading-edge technology that it significantly influences or "drives" the technology for the other product families.

[19]   See Finan [1990] and Hobday [1990]. Competitive position in ASICs, for example, is much more dependent on design automation and sophisticated testing algorithms than is the case for DRAMs, whose competitive position is highly dependent on fabrication technology.

corporate boundaries to interactions with suppliers and customers;

(2) from one-fifth to one-third of the total budgets of firms in technology-based industries are allocated to quality assurance activity, with measurement an important component of these investments;

(3) for larger firms producing high-volume, commodity-type products, *product* quality has become a *minimum* requirement for market entry with competition centering more on *service* quality, while smaller firms pursuing niche markets continue to emphasize product-related attributes of quality improvement to distinguish themselves from competitors;

(4) contrary to commonly-voiced opinions, U.S. firms are not hopelessly behind foreign competitors, and several technological and operational tracks exist within a single industry for developing and implementing successful quality assurance strategies; and,

(5) like most elements of technology-based competition, competitive levels of quality assurance require long-term investments by both industry and institutions supplying technology infrastructure.

Clearly, an increasing percentage of the world's industries recognize that competing on the basis of quality is a do-or-die proposition. Consequently, self-motivation in terms of devising and implementing new strategic approaches to quality improvement is essential to long-term success. In the long run, however, the ability of an industry to compete successfully may also depend on what the NIST study refers to as the contributions of "external" organizations (i.e., technology infrastructure). The study suggests that Japan may simply have more of such infrastructure to offer its firms. This would seem to be true for Germany and some other European countries as well. Thus, over time, the advantage of an efficient technology infrastructure which creates, consolidates, and transfers certain types of widely used information, including much that is related to quality improvement, may make a decided difference.

The competitive environment is now evolving towards systems approaches such as TQM, CE, and JIT inventory management. The ultimate applications of these concepts extend beyond the boundaries of the firm. Motorola, which won the Malcolm Baldrige National Quality Award in 1987, has progressively reduced its supplier base from 25,000 firms in the mid 1980s to 6,000 in 1990 with continued reductions targeted.[20] To Motorola, this supply management strategy is essential in order to have partnering relationships with its suppliers, rather than confrontational ones. As the National Quality Award criteria sift into the U.S. business culture, more firms will adopt systems approaches based on close external interactions. An important policy question is how fast is this "cultural" change taking place.

Unfortunately, this "transition" period for U.S. industry has lead to a proliferation of quality systems that has become a nightmare for suppliers. Unlike Japan, which has standardized on a set of homogeneous quality standards derived over several decades, the more recent U.S. effort is much farther back on the evolutionary ladder. Catching up requires promoting, catalyzing, and leveraging a process towards a uniform set of standards for assuring quality -- a technology infrastructure role to which government can contribute through multiple information dissemination channels that, in the United States, are just being established.

Future Infrastructure Roles

In Chapter 3, a conceptual model of technology-based competition was presented, which shows how the complexity of the

---

[20] As a winnowing function, Motorola has insisted that all of its suppliers adopt the National Quality Award criteria and pushes them to apply for the award, primarily as a learning experience. In 1990, 66 of the 97 companies that applied for the Baldrige Award were suppliers to Motorola. Executives from these companies participate in Motorola training programs and now receive a 95-question "self-scoring quality system" that enables companies to rate themselves with a high degree of precision and consistency across companies. Motorola auditors visit its suppliers to give advice on how to improve the assessment. See McCormack [1990].

typical industrial technology requires a holistic strategy on the parts of both government and industry. This strategy includes the traditional role of private firms in which proprietary technology applications are developed for specific markets, but it also includes the newer roles for multi-firm and industry-government cooperation to provide the generic technologies and infratechnologies that are critical to achieving and maintaining competitive position. The model in Chapter 3 emphasizes the many important linkages among industry and government at the various stages of the technology-based economic process, and thereby highlights the leverage points in the technology life cycle that are critical to an industry's success in global markets.

This model is represented as essentially linear, in order to focus on infrastructure roles at each major stage in the economic process. However, feedback loops have been introduced in the last several decades through such organizational concepts as *total quality management* and *concurrent engineering* and such technical concepts as *flexible computer-aided manufacturing*. In the coming decade, the linearity characteristic of economic activity will continue to recede. It will replaced by a much more simultaneous concept of economic activity. Such a model is hinted at in its infancy by concepts such as concurrent engineering and the primitive initial integration of CAD and CAM, but as the various feedback loops increase in number and the technology and product life cycles continue to shorten, sequential activity as currently conceived will become less and less a characteristic of the economic process.

This evolution of technology-based economic activity and the implications for changes in a firm's organization and an industry's structure are indicated in Figure 7-2 (identical to Figure 3-6). The linear and self-contained process (Figure 7-1) isolates individual elements of the firm and allows only slow learning. The Japanese solved this problem by substituting simultaneity for linearity within internal organization processes and by creating new forms of infrastructure to improve firm-to-firm interaction. The internal changes are based around a *systems* approach to economic activity. Processes such as concurrent engineering, total quality management, and total productivity maintenance require total organization participation in simultaneous information exchange.[21]

Figure 7-2

Evolution of Manufacturing Organization and Strategy

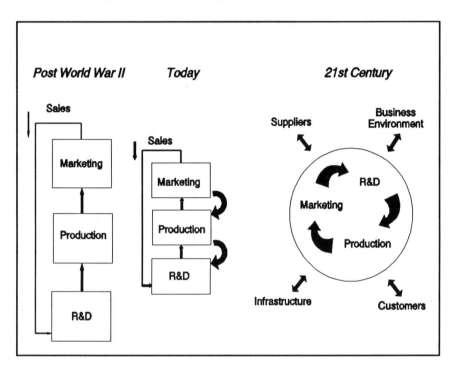

With respect to external linkages, Japanese companies pioneered common approaches to improve communications, product flow, and product performance. These linkages between supplier and industrial customer are now being copied and, in fact, improved upon by U.S. companies. Large American companies have allocated

---

[21] As an example of the importance the corporate world has come to attach to such systems concepts, in the 11 years from 1978 to 1989, 8,424 people from 96 countries came to Japan to study Japanese "total quality control" at the Japanese Union of Scientists and Engineers (JUSE). See Shiba [1989].

considerable resources to disseminating such information to their suppliers. In the case of large companies, the number of suppliers reaches the thousands. As previously discussed, some companies, such as Motorola, Inc., have gone beyond simple information transfer to instructing suppliers in how to conduct quality assurance audits.

In the late 1980s, the foci of such infrastructure dissemination in the United States were timely delivery mechanisms and internal quality assurance practices. More recently, information has been developed and disseminated on such transaction-related activities as receiving and inspection. Technology-based products have very complex performance specifications. Although compliance standards are developed to handle such transaction problems, learning to implement these standards can be technically and organizationally demanding. Thus, some companies have taken the initiative to spread information on compliance standards, packing information, standard packaging, and return-of-defective-product procedures.

In high-volume, technologically complex product areas such as semiconductors, distributors have taken the lead in counseling suppliers. For example, Hamilton/Avnet Electronics now holds an annual suppliers conference, from which exchanges of information have lead to innovations in implementation of quality assurance and transaction efficiency procedures such as audits of suppliers. Whereas Motorola's audits of its suppliers attracted the most attention, Hamilton/Avnet has promoted "distributor" audits of its suppliers (which includes Motorola) in order to assure its downstream customers and thereby reduce its own transaction costs. Furthermore, to reduce the redundancy that occurs when several firms conduct audits of the same supplier, third-party auditors have been proposed to consolidate several redundant supplier or subcontractor audits into one objective third-party review.

These and other trends discussed in earlier chapters are leading towards a much more simultaneous model of the major stages in technology-based economic activity. Within the firm the evolutionary process is quite similar across nations. However, among firms the alternative paths are quite different -- ranging from rigid organizational integration (Keiretsu-type) to multi-enterprise integration concepts.

Summary

A major strategy shift occurred in many industrialized nations during the 1980s -- a greatly increased emphasis on quality as a strategic objective. The total organization approach to quality assurance and, even more recently, the extension of these concepts to the multi-enterprise level has set the stage for the advent of the multi-enterprise model of economic activity in which simultaneity replaces linearity as the primary characteristic of technological change within and among firms. This evolutionary trend is being "enabled" by the relentless advance of systems technologies from factory automation to telecommunications. These technologies have a strong information infrastructure base.

Analyses of evolving strategies toward the strategic objective of improved quality lead to the generalizations that (1) major changes are occurring in the substance of investment strategies for quality assurance, (2) the scope of these strategies is the total organization and even the multi-organization level (i.e., at the systems level), and (3) in spite of these common trends, strategies still differ by company, by industry, and even by country.

In the 1990s, corporate strategy will continue to evolve beyond the integration of the productivity and quality objectives to include a third major strategic objective, *flexibility.* New production technologies and the supporting technology infrastructure will therefore be designed around these three strategic factors. In particular, growth strategies in many nations will increasingly emphasize

* *cooperative research* -- will become an increasingly important factor in determining the time required to bring new technologies to market, with the approximate pre-competitive line typically falling at the end of generic technology research, but with occasional extensions to the later phases of R&D;

* *competition* -- will be encouraged above the pre-competitive line, which means rejection in most cases of cooperative production at the industry level (on the other hand, joint ventures, usually two firms, will be an increasingly viable strategy for combining

complementary assets, including production assets, to handle rapid changes in the dynamics of the technology life cycle);

*   *vertical* and *horizontal integration* -- will increase, but through *information infrastructure* as the important long-term strategy for achieving multi-enterprise integration, rather than the more rigid organizational integration of Japan's *Keiretsu*.

This chapter has discussed some of the major strategic issues that involve technology infrastructure. Strategy does not exist by itself but within the confines of organizational and industry structures. Both strategy and structure must then be integrated with the supporting technology infrastructure. The next chapter will discuss the directions that this critical integration may take.

8 Corporate Strategy and Government Policy

"Some things have to be believed to be seen"

Ralph Hodgson
(English Poet)

Many recent reports and statements by industry groups have called for similar divisions of effort between industry and government in restoring U.S. competitiveness. For example, a report by the National Academy of Engineering stated that

"U.S. public policy should acknowledge the need for a stronger public role in support of generic technological capabilities for the benefit of the nation, and establish credible mechanisms for translating this commitment in principle into specific actions."[1]

However, the United States is behind several of its major competitors in adopting the needed consensus model of technology-based competition, which is essential to drive both private-sector strategy and government policy. In fact, it has only recently begun to

---

[1] Lee and Reid, editors [1991, p. 81].

collect the data necessary to apply such a conceptual framework for a national economic growth strategy. For example, in 1987, when the first major government allocation of funds to an R&D consortium (SEMATECH) was being considered (a decade behind a similar effort by the Japanese), the opposition to such "massive" government intervention in private markets cited, among other objections, the proposed $100 million-per-year government contribution.

During this period, a Congressional Budget Office analysis tabulated all existing programs for semiconductor technology research and found that U.S. Government expenditures were already $529 million.[2] In other words, misconceptions, lack of data for decision making, and lack of a general consensus on industry and government roles abound.

Changing R&D Funding Patterns

The United States spends more on R&D than the next four countries combined. Yet it continues to fall behind competitors. Major reasons are that U.S. R&D investment is not sufficiently directed at civilian applications and allocated through the right

Table 8-1

Non-Defense R&D as a % of GNP

Country	1988
United States	2.0
Germany	2.6
Japan	2.9

Source: National Science Foundation [1990]

---

[2]   Webre [1987, p. 60].

mechanisms. A majority view is that Germany and Japan currently have the most productive and generally successful economies in the world. The reason for their competitive advantage is indicated in part by Table 8-1 which shows that their economies are 45-55 percent more *civilian* R&D-intensive than is the United States.

A major problem facing any industrial nation that allows itself to fall behind is that it must run *faster* than competitors in order to catch up. In the United States, macroeconomic policies, such as the R&D tax credit, have been implemented. While definitely helpful, their primary point of stimulus is where one would expect -- at later-phase proprietary R&D. Underinvestment remains in the early-phase generic technology research.

Table 8-2

Manufacturing Sector R&D and Capital Expenditure Trends in the United States and Japan

YEAR	R&D/Capital Expenditures	
	United States	Japan
1980	0.26	0.62
1982	0.31	0.74
1984	0.35	0.83
1985	0.34	0.91
1986	0.40	1.17
1987	0.41	1.26

Source: Japan: MITI for capital investment, Prime Minister's Office for R&D; United States: Council of Economic Advisors for capital investment, NSF for R&D.

Equally ominous is the difference in importance between Japan and the United States that is being attached to manufacturing R&D as the future driver of competitive advantage. Using ratios of

R&D to capital investment as an indicator of this relative commitment, Table 8-2 shows the tremendous efforts by the Japanese to achieve a knowledge-based economy. In recent years, Japan's manufacturing sector has actually been spending more on R&D than on plant and equipment.

Fumio Kodama, Director of Japan's National Institute for Science and Technology Policy, first observed this shift in emphasis on R&D. He concluded that the change represented a permanent transformation of the Japanese corporation from "a place for producing things to a place for producing knowledge".[3] Kodama calls this transformation the "techno-paradigm shift". Whereas the period 1975 to 1985 was an era when technological development served economic growth, from that point on an era has evolved in which economic growth serves technological development -- as indicated by the fact that R&D investment exceeds capital investment.

His paradigm shift may sound counter-intuitive to most economic growth analysts, who will correctly assert that economic growth is the ultimate objective. In fact, the R&D/capital investment ratio may shift back to less than unity in Japan at some future date. However, Japan's conceptual model of technology-based competition, with its longer time horizons, correctly addresses the explosion of new technologies that is occurring in the 1990s. At such times, which may only occur at the beginnings of long-term technology cycles or eras, the nations that make the appropriate levels and types of investment in both technology and technology infrastructure will be the big winners.

In the post-war period in the United States, the Department of Defense has been the major source of funds for many areas of *technology* research. DoD R&D is credited with the development and/or accelerated application of a number of commercially important technologies. However, more and more frequently, arguments are being made that these *spin-offs* have been much smaller in overall effect than projects funded by competitor nations that have *commercialization* as the primary objective.

In fact, today, the commercial version of a particular technology frequently leads the defense version. Increasingly, therefore, technology is moving in the reverse direction; that is, *spin-*

---

[3]   Kodama [1991].

ons are being observed -- adaptations of commercial technology to
military applications.

This trend is occurring because commercial markets are global
and large. The result is multiple sources of new commercial
technology and thus more rapid rates of technical change. Moreover,
competition for global markets is multidimensional in that at least
several product attributes besides absolute performance (quality, cost,
serviceability, compatibility with other products, etc.) now determine
market success to a greater extent than in the past. Consequently,
commercially-oriented R&D (both government- and industry-funded)
is becoming similarly broad in terms of attributes pursued. As global
commercial markets have grown to enormous size, so has the relevant
R&D. The overall result has been rapid progress across several
product attributes in an increasingly large number of technologies.

Defense technology, on the other hand, has been relatively
more focused than commercial technology, emphasizing product
performance and de-emphasizing other attributes. In addition to this
strong emphasis on performance, the relatively small size of most
military markets has contributed to the lack of attention in the past to
commercially-important attributes, particularly unit cost.

Therefore, defense technology requirements are increasingly
moving towards and, in fact, being derived from commercially-targeted
technology. This trend is reflected in the "U.S. Technology Policy"
statement, issued by the White House (OSTP) in September 1990. It
states that in continuing to provide for a strong defense technology
base, "special emphasis needs to be placed on...using commercial
products".

To this end, the concept of *dual-use* technology research has
been proposed to provide an efficient funding approach to the
increased integration of the two sectors' technology needs. This
concept is, of course, feasible only if the required research can be
designed to meet the needs of both the defense and commercial
sectors. Sufficient technology overlap occurs if (1) the two sectors
require the same general level of technical sophistication *and* (2) the
sets of performance attributes and their relative importance in both
sectors' applications are approximately the same. In cases where one
sector's technical requirements are less than the other's, a spinoff
from the sector setting the technology pace will have to occur.

An example of the difficulty in achieving dual-use technology
research is the VHSIC program. This program has been highly

successful in achieving its military objectives, but it has spawned relatively few commercial applications. VHSIC was designed both to develop components which suited identifiable military needs and to ensure their rapid insertion into military systems, an emphasis reflecting the fact that it has typically taken 10-15 years to adapt commercial semiconductor technologies to military applications.[4] The need for such a program had become critical because the pace of technological change in the commercial market had become more rapid than in the military area.[5]

From the civilian technology perspective, it was envisioned from the outset that VHSIC would have commercial benefits, but these potential spinoffs were viewed as incidental to the fundamental military thrust of the program.[6] The divergences between the VHSIC program and the Japanese semiconductor projects were clear. The Japanese projects have placed heavy emphasis on the development of commercial device prototypes and process technologies that can be used in low-cost, mass production of future applications -- semiconductor devices for commercial markets.

The VHSIC research, on the other hand, emphasizes the development of customized devices which deliver a desired level of performance in specific military systems. VHSIC research with respect to semiconductor design has emphasized fast turnaround time from design to production (to permit rapid insertion into military systems).[7] Because this singular focus satisfied military requirements, state-of-the art chip performance, yields, and production cost -- all crucial factors in the commercial market -- were given little attention.

In contrast, SEMATECH represents a radical departure, for the United States, from this past practice. It is the first U.S. attempt at an industry-led, public-private partnership to promote national commercial objectives. SEMATECH's first target was semiconductor

---

[4]   National Materials Advisory Board [1982, p. 14].

[5]   Howell *et al* [1988, p. 118].

[6]   The National Materials Advisory Board [1982] stated that "The VHSIC Program should not be misconstrued as the Federal Government's attempt to counter foreign competition in integrated circuits."

[7]   Howell *et al* [1988, p. 120].

processing technology. By cooperatively advancing this technology, the industry was in effect greatly expanding the scope and content of the technology infrastructure which can be drawn upon by all firms to develop their custom applications. This is a marked departure from the independent tracks taken by the VHSIC contractors. Moreover, in 1990, SEMATECH expanded the scope of its efforts to provide more infrastructure support to the semiconductor manufacturing equipment and materials industries. This step was significant in that it included programs for information transfer (planning, technical performance data, and competitive analysis) as well as research support.

Of the six categories of semiconductor equipment tracked by VLSI Research, Inc., only in one category, metrology, did U.S. firms increase their share of world markets between 1983 and 1988.[8] It may not be a coincidence that metrology is one area where commercial technology infrastructure support has been regularly supplied by the U.S. Government (one of NIST's primary missions is to provide U.S. industry with metrology infrastructure). The amount of resources allocated to measurement-related technologies by NIST, which are then provided to these firms, has been small compared to the typical DoD research project. However, the fact that the NIST research was targeted at the *commercialization* needs of that industry greatly increased the economic impact.[9]

For the foreseeable future, even in a period of declining defense dollars, the Department of Defense will direct a sizeable portion of the total federal investment in new technology and technical talent. DoD spends around $38 billion per year on R&D and is a first buyer of nearly $100 billion per year in goods and services. Nearly one-third of U.S. scientists and engineers are employed in military-related activities and more than 10% of factory workers are engaged in defense production. About 20% of the

---

[8] U.S. General Accounting Office [1990, p. 18].

[9] This differential effect from focusing support on economic activity is also reflected in NIST's record of winning a large number of R&D 100 awards (given annually by *Research & Development Magazine*). Over the past 15 years, NIST has won 71 awards to rank third on the cumulative winners list and first among federal laboratories. 41 of the 71 award winners were subsequently commercialized by private firms.

manufacturing and plant facilities in the U.S. are engaged in military-related work.

Thus, the policy objective should be to maintain maximum spin-offs from targeted defense research and dual use from other research. As the levels of funding for these two sectors adjust to changing priorities, criteria will evolve for determining opportunities for dual-use technology research, as will procurement criteria for determining when defense use of off-the-shelf commercial technologies is feasible.

Funding issues that have to do with industry-government cost sharing will become increasingly important in the United States, as more resources are allocated to early-phase R&D with commercial objectives. Much has been said in earlier chapters about "pre-competitive generic technology" research. In particular, the importance of cooperative research has increased as a mechanism for accelerating this phase of R&D. However, even though generic technology as a discrete phase in the R&D process has certain unique externality characteristics, it is not homogeneous. Rather, it displays a range of risk levels. Consequently, the degree of risk pooling between government and industry varies across projects.

Generic technology research, where the time involved is particularly long or where the technology is loosely connected at best to existing industry structures, will have to have significant contributions in both funding and conduct from government laboratories. In other cases, intermediate time horizons and some degree of matching between projected applications of the technology and existing industry structure should result in more equal cost sharing. Cost sharing between industry and government in many nations varies greatly, reflecting estimates of the variances in time and capturability variables. Finally, at the other extreme, generic technology research with *relatively* short time-to-completion estimates and projected applications for existing industry structures is typically funded entirely by industry -- either through consortia or by single large firms.

No formula exists for calculating cost sharing, and protracted debates between industry and government over projections at any point in time can only be self-defeating. For example, in March 1991, the Department of Energy announced a 10-year research program on continuous fiber ceramic composites. DoE's plan called for industry cost sharing of 10 percent in the first year of the program and 20 to

30 percent over the next four years. In the succeeding five years, industry cost sharing would have to be at least 50 percent.[10] DoE is implicitly projecting progressive reduction in technical risk to allow increasingly certain technical and commercial outcome forecasts by industry and hence greater projected capturability of the overall benefits from this technology. The industry, through the U.S. Advanced Ceramics Association, argued for full government funding on the grounds that the risk was too high at the program's initiation to forecast the rate of technical progress implied in the DoE plan. An iterative planning approach could be considered in such cases, adjusting cost sharing as research progress is made.

New Funding Strategies

For most categories of technology infrastructure, some government role has been identified for its provision and diffusion. It is a fact that any contribution by government that has differential effects across industries constitutes a subsidy. Subsidies have a negative connotation in some countries such as the United States, even though they exist in profusion. The reason for this view of subsidization is the fact that the largest subsidy rates are found either in declining industries or in certain "non-industrial-growth" areas such as housing or farming (which employs only about three percent of the labor force).

Smaller subsidies are given for the classic economic rationale of market failure. Markets "fail" when they do not allocate resources to their most efficient use, often because the owner of those resources cannot capture the full return or, more accurately, a return (adjusted for risk) which is above those from alternative investments. Research and development is one of the classic examples. The earlier in the life cycle, the more difficult is capturability and hence the greater is the underinvestment. Economic theory argues that a properly designed subsidy can increase economic efficiency by offsetting such market failures.

Based on the limited data available for international comparisons, the United States ranks last among 19 OECD countries

---

[10] See Crawford [1991].

in terms of rates of subsidies for industry.[11] But, as this book has gone to great lengths to point out, the result of not dealing efficiently with market failures relating to technology investment is relentless loss of competitiveness and hence standard of living. The efficiency issues are, therefore, the *identification* of market failures and the *selection and management* of appropriate technology infrastructure to remove them. The fact that Japan and Germany also have low industrial subsidy rates implies that a strong efficiency factor can be developed and applied.

Industry subsidies used to be frequently rationalized on the basis of achieving economies of *scale*, in particular, to enable "breathing space" in which an infant domestic industry could get established and attain minimum threshold size for efficient operation relative to established foreign competitors. In today's technology-driven markets, many of which are not particularly capital-intensive, (at least for extended portions of their life cycles), economies of scale are not the only important source of market failure. In fact, many of today's market failures are the lack of attainment of economies of *scope.*

The fact that U.S. Government spending accounts for approximately 36-37 percent of GNP compared to an average of about 40 percent for all OECD countries and 48 percent for European countries may imply some potential to increase spending on technology infrastructure. On the other hand, interest payments have risen from about 8-9 percent of Federal expenditures in the 1970s to almost 17 percent in 1990.[12] In fact, the U.S. Government spends about 22 percent of GNP; but, after allocating most of this amount for defense, social security and other entitlements, and net interest, only

---

[11] See Ford [1990]. Subsidy rates to industry were calculated as a percent of value added for the year 1985. Data were available only for direct grants. These rates ranged from less than one percent for the United States to almost eight percent for Sweden. Japan and Germany were at the low end of the range. Based on data for 10 EC countries, Ford estimated that when other major categories of subsidy were added, the subsidy rate would approximately double.

[12] OECD [1990, pp. 63-66].

3.7 percent of GNP is left for so-called *civilian* expenditures, including technology infrastructure.[13]

Whatever the available resources, mechanisms for funding technology infrastructure must be constructed and the criteria for selecting among them determined. If all "technology goods" were either "purely public" or "purely private", assignment of funding responsibility would be easily resolved. However, many so-called "quasi-public" goods exist, many of which fall in the category of technology infrastructure.

As a case in point, the National Institute of Standards and Technology (NIST) provides U.S. industry with a wide range of measurement technologies, data, and related services. These "infratechnologies" leverage the productivity and quality of industry's own investments in R&D, plant and equipment, and marketing. Hence, the scope of NIST impact on the economy is very broad and critical to competitiveness objectives. The variety of NIST contributions and the economy-wide scope of its industry clients have historically caused difficult planning problems. One of these problems is the determination of funding responsibility between NIST and industry.

The funding by NIST of basic measurement research, as with basic research generally, is not controversial. However, many of the measurement methods, test methods, calibration techniques, etc., require some generic and sometimes even applied research in order to meet the needs of particular economic sectors. Carrying this infratechnology research through these several stages raises the question of how much of this research should be funded by the benefiting industries.

The issue is not should NIST *conduct* the research. Within the scope of a wide range of measurement-related research, NIST has the unique ability to efficiently carry out and disseminate this research. Rather, the issue is how much, if any, of a particular research project should industry *fund*.

---

[13] This breakdown does not, of course, allow for that portion of defense R&D spending which is applicable to commercial investment. However, as pointed out earlier, the "spillover" of defense technology into civilian applications has been declining and therefore contributes less to the civilian technology base than in the past.

Before global competition became a major economic policy problem for the United States, the *time* taken to develop a particular measurement-related infratechnology was not an especially important concern. Elements of the needed infratechnology (say, a measurement method) appeared over a relatively extended period of time in a largely ad hoc manner from some combination of industry and NIST contributions. At some point, NIST may have assimilated the technical elements of the method and an industry standards committee promulgated the desired standard. In cases where industry could supply little or none of the needed infratechnology, NIST proposed a dedicated research program to Congress. Several years frequently elapsed before NIST received funding and could proceed to conduct the research.

As the intensity of global competition increases, the pressure to initiate and complete research programs in a more timely fashion makes the ad hoc approach to NIST-industry cooperation in producing the needed infratechnology less and less acceptable. Such research must now be undertaken earlier in a technology's life cycle in order to help domestic industries beat foreign competition to market. Because firms are concentrating on developing new products and production methods earlier in a technology's life cycle, the private sector may actually be under-investing in nonproprietary technologies to a greater extent than in the past. This situation leads to an argument for greater government funding in certain categories of technology infrastructure.

What makes planning, including funding determinations, more difficult is that the trends described above have created many "grey" areas between these public and private technology components. That is, numerous generic and applied technologies, such as those underlying automated manufacturing, contain both public and private components that are *inseparable* from a research perspective. Thus, neither pure measurement research nor pure product or production technology research can be conducted in isolation of the other to the extent possible in the past.

Moreover, the portions of a particular technology that should be considered either in the public domain or the responsibility of the private sector differ from industry to industry. These differences occur not only because of variances in the intrinsic natures of technologies but also because of variances in industry structure and the maturity of the technology (emerging versus established).

Where resources have permitted, NIST has made progress in assuring the timely provision of these *"mixed"* technology components by assessing technological and economic trends in cooperation with its industry partners. One direct result has been a substantial increase in its *collaborations with industry* (approximately 500 separate collaborations were in place at the end of 1988, ranging from individual guest workers to multi-firm consortia). These cooperative arrangements amount to joint funding of much of this mixed technology.

Adapting to Globalization

Assignment of roles between government and industry for the conduct of R&D and a distribution of funding responsibilities reflect an overall concept of global competition. A major philosophy in the Japanese economic strategy is the treatment of technology-based competition as a systems problem. Over several decades, the Japanese have continually advanced the implementation of this philosophy with great success. Their long-term increases in productivity and quality testify to this.

In contrast, the American cultural trait of emphasizing individualism in economic activities creates a grain into which the cooperation and integration necessary for a systems approach, especially with respect to technology infrastructure, have difficulty penetrating. Strategic concepts that the Japanese have either invented or taken the lead in advancing such as just-in-time delivery, total quality management, concurrent engineering (or design for manufacturing), and the man-machine interface are systems concepts. While these strategic concepts were evolving in Japan, U.S. industry somehow forgot most of what Mr. Ford had taught it.[14]

---

[14]   It often pointed out with some irony that Americans such as Edward Demming taught the Japanese much of their original knowledge of quality control, cycle times, inventory management, and other competitiveness techniques in the 1950s, while U.S. companies ignored this wisdom. In fact, American knowledge of today's requirements for global competitiveness may go back much further. As pointed out by Schonberger [1986], "By 1914, [Ford's] Highland Park facility was unloading a hundred freight cars of materials a day, and the materials flowed through fabrication, subassembly, and final assembly back onto freight cars. The product was

The Europeans originated the true global corporate philosophy. In describing a concept called "the globalization of technological innovation" or GTI, Riccardo Petrella of the Commission of the European Communities stated that "a pure 'business strategy' for GTI is an 'archaic' solution. GTI demands a geo-technical, geo-economic, geo-political and geo-cultural strategy." This philosophy has been translated into a strategy of *global* visions and actions and of *local* industrial bases, foci, and structures.[15]

In implementing these global strategic concepts, different attitudes toward technology evolved. For example, the majority of U.S. manufacturers have pursued automation primarily as a means of reducing costs. For the Japanese manager, cost reduction is only one of a number of objectives of automation, and not the primary one at that. Japanese corporations invest in automation to increase quality and, in fact, to produce products that could not be manufactured in any other way. They can set and achieve such objectives partly because they plan farther into the future, over several generations of the technology.

By regarding long-range strategic planning as having a significant infrastructure element, the Japanese Government (MITI) can lead an industry-government effort to develop consensus long-range plans or "visions". These visionary statements guide the formulation of more focused industry and individual corporate strategic plans.

Without such collaborative statements of future direction, economies become mired in *status quo* technologies. For example, in many industries, future generations of product technologies will not be able to be manufactured by current production technologies. The needed manufacturing processes do not just include new technology but require new management techniques and practices and even wholesale organizational change. Such major changes in behavior occur very slowly without some sort of collective catalytic action.

To provide such a catalyst to their domestic industries, the Japanese, the Germans, and others have developed a sophisticated view of the roles of technology infrastructure in the improvement of

---

the Model T and the product cycle was 21 days. At River Rouge, about 1921, the cycle was only four days -- and that included processing ore into steel."

[15]   Petrella [1988].

the science and technology base *and* in the provision of associated management practice. The Japanese, in particular, have explicitly stated the following roles:[16]

1) production and distribution of science and technology information;
2) development, installation, and provision of machines and equipment;
3) capital and material for research;
4) development, preservation, and supply of generic technology resources;
5) research support functions; and
6) intellectual property rights.

To implement such a comprehensive technology infrastructure policy, a nation needs mechanisms for

1) funding civilian R&D;
2) conducting civilian R&D, particularly generic technology and infratechnology research;
3) comprehensive and rapid diffusion/transfer of research results;
4) removing technical, financial, and transaction barriers to commercial applications of new technology; and
5) providing technical, managerial, and market information needed for global market penetration.

Today, for the first time, such lists are beginning to appear in U.S. Government strategy documents and Congressional legislation. Long-range planning between industry and government is increasingly called for. The Europeans have begun to establish similar global strategies.[17]

---

[16] "S&T R&D Infrastructure Guidelines Presented", *Kagaku Kogyo Nippo*, December 6, 1989, p. 1.

[17] The U.S. Office of Science and Technology Policy issued its technology policy statement in September 1990 (see Executive Office of the President [1990]). It provides rationales and objectives for a "U.S. Technology Policy". The Council of the European Communities [1990] issued a similar document in April of that year.

Opportunity to "catch up" may be somewhat greater than the conventional wisdom believes. As much as Americans examine and laud Japan, the Japanese economy has some potentially serious structural problems that will become more evident as the decade of the 1990s progresses.

For example, the structure of corporate wealth in Japan is concentrated in the Keiretsu -- at the expense of the majority of Japanese firms that are outside and subservient to these agglomerates. The Japanese Government has continued to condone this economic structure for the same reasons that most governments find structural change difficult: (1) something that worked in the past is very difficult to let go of, even in the face of mounting evidence that change is required, and (2) vested interests evolve that resist change.

Japan is a culture of consensus-building and face saving. While this has worked well on the way up the economic ladder, now that they are a leading economic force in the global market place, some of the weaknesses in this approach are just becoming apparent. For example, consensus building in Japan takes place within this skewed, Keiretsu-dominated industrial structure, which appears to have placed significant limits on creativity for many Japanese firms. Moreover, the huge Keiretsu have resulted in a degree of factionalism that has prevented critical infrastructure such as standards from being promulgated at the industry and national levels.

Although the Japanese have done many things right, they have also benefitted greatly from the uneven trade patterns that the Keiretsu have maintained with the rest of the world, particularly with the United States. As inequities are removed, these sectors will not be able to carry the entire Japanese economy to the extent that they have over the past several decades. Moreover, the majority of the Japanese economy is increasingly demanding a larger share of the economic rewards. The reallocation of wealth that this trend implies will act as an additional drag on Japanese performance.

One of the most curious aspects of the United States' halting and piecemeal approach to formulating a comprehensive set of roles for needed technology infrastructure is the reluctance to think and act in collegial manner. The concept of planning, *per se*, seems difficult to accept. Tom Peters and some other analysts of business strategy have argued that strategic planning is actually harmful. They cite "evidence" that high-technology companies make successful business decisions based on "intuition" and "feel".

Of course, what is being captured here is *short-term* success based on acquisition of a particular generation of a technology and successfully applying it in specific markets. Let intuition try to guide a company over time through several generations of a technology and, even more so, through the transition to radically new technologies. Such an approach fails miserably.

The United States is in the early stages of rejecting the conventional economic model that portrays competition as consisting of individual firms with tight and rigid boundaries around them, so that competition among firms is 100 percent through all stages of the economic process beyond basic research. The government role in this traditional model is regarded as largely *environmental.* What must be substituted is a role in which government is responsible for contributing to pre-competitive phases of technology development and to other supporting infrastructure -- both technological and managerial. Thus, in addition to adapting to the need for broad systems strategies, technology-based economies must add a *complementary technology asset* strategy in which industry and government plan for the cooperative provision of a number of technology infrastructure elements.

Successful examples of strategies based on the paradigm of the post-war era can be found around the world in particular industrial sectors. For example, in comparing the Italian and German economies, Michael Porter [1990a] observes that

> "in industries where Italian companies are world leaders -- such as lighting, furniture, footwear, woolen fabrics, and packaging machines -- a company strategy that emphasizes customized products, niche marketing, rapid change, and breathtaking flexibility fits both the dynamics of industry and the character of the Italian management system. The German management system, in contrast, works well in technical or engineering-oriented industries -- optics, chemicals, complicated machinery -- where complex products demand precision manufacturing, a careful development process, after-sale service, and thus a highly disciplined management structure. German success is much rarer in consumer goods and services where image marketing and rapid new-feature and model turnover, are important to competition."

The reason why some industries prosper while others do not within the same economy is that the interactions between industry structure, technology infrastructure, and corporate strategy vary significantly across technologies and hence industries. Under a "single-stage" strategy, as fits most industrialized nations to a significant degree, the successful matching of appropriate combinations of these three factors with the needs of particular industries occur only for a limited set of industries. More important, the competitive advantage attained through such narrowly focused strategies is increasingly more difficult to maintain.

Such strategies are the context for Porter's explanation of why the ceramic tile industry prospers in Italy, while the printing press industry prospers in Germany.[18] Unfortunately, the status of these heretofore successful industries, depending for a continued competitive advantage on a particular (and often randomly assimilated) combination of these factors, will become more precarious over time. The evolution of the German technology infrastructure is one of the most successful examples of the traditional single-stage model and explains why the German printing press industry is not an exception but rather typical of that nation's economy. The Germans have put more effort into developing technology infrastructure, high-quality production methods, and associated global marketing strategies than have most other European nations.

However, in the current decade and beyond, even a highly efficient single-stage strategy will not work. Much of the change currently underway in Japan, Europe, and the United States is the provision of the technology infrastructure needed for a "multi-stage" competitive strategy *and* its application to *many* industrial sectors.

When a nation consciously undertakes the establishment and implementation of technology infrastructure that efficiently supports a broad industry structure and adaptable sets of corporate strategies that address all three major stages of the economic process, then a far larger percentage of that nation's industries will attain and sustain competitive advantage.

---

[18] A "single-stage" strategy refers to attaining a competitive position through a focus on one stage in the economic process. See Tassey [1991].

An Expanded Technology Infrastructure

Areas of new policy initiatives are required in part because economies of both scale and scope have increased at several stages in the typical technology-based industry. The externalities that result from these conditions lead to systematic underinvestment by the private sector. This underinvestment is particularly pronounced in technological elements such as generic technology and infratechnology and in processes such as technology transfer and information dissemination.

The portfolio approach to supporting an economy's technology base, while gaining the advantage of diversification, will also require considerable resources. Even though most of this support will be focused on early-phase technology research, which is relatively less expensive than the applied research and development phases, minimum scales of investment by an economy exist for each technology. Thus, only the number of technologies should be pursued for which sufficient resources can be provided to achieve the research, diffusion, and private-sector investment needed to achieve a competitive position in the global market.

Obviously, a "list" of emerging technologies can be generated more easily than a set of effective support programs. The European Community (EC), after several years of rapidly expanding cooperative research programs across an ever widening range of technologies, is beginning to question its ability to achieve this minimum scale research requirement for all of them. Arguments are now being made to concentrate more resources in a smaller number of megaprojects such as JESSI, HDTV, and Cooperation for OSI Networking in Europe (COSINE).[19]

These infrastructure strategic thrusts will combine, as indicated in Figure 8-1, to greatly leverage an economy's rate of growth. Many of these infrastructure elements have been discussed individually, but the point here is to indicate their collective action across the three major stages of technology-based economic activity.

---

[19]   See, for example, "Evaluation Committee Advises New Course: 'More Eureka Funding for Megaprojects'", *COMPUTABLE* (Dutch), April 12, 1991.

Figure 8-1

Infrastructure Impacts on Competitive Position

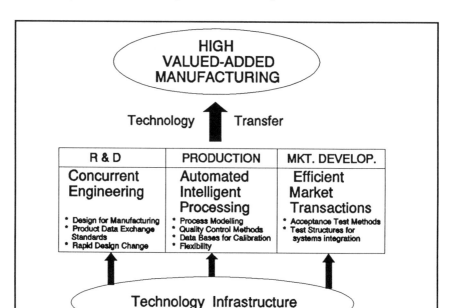

To successfully achieve these objectives, the weak links (i.e., market imperfections) and the subsequent leverage points in the disaggregated technology growth model presented in Chapter 3 (Figure 3-2) must be identified and appropriate policy objectives and mechanisms designed. The complexity of the range of policy objectives is indicated in Figure 8-2. The disaggregated technology model is used to show the leverage points in the typical technology-based industry, where government policy can attack an externality or other market imperfections.

This representation is clearly a much more microeconomic view of the government role, than has been the accepted philosophy in the either the traditional economic literature or past government growth policy. However, these infrastructure elements are not only essential to global competitiveness, but they must be developed and used in an integrated manner as part of a larger economic system. In essence, Figure 8-2 represents a shift toward a needed balance in the United States between macroeconomic and microeconomic growth policies.

Figure 8-2

Growth Policy Objectives

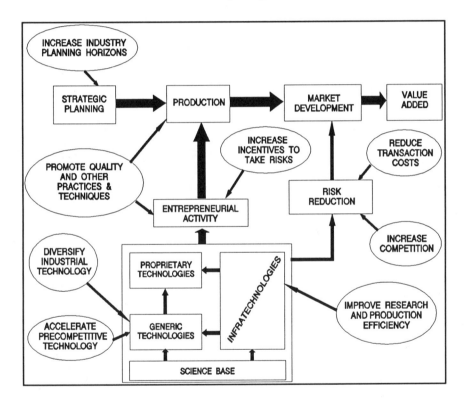

Effective policy also requires that *objectives* be transformed into efficient *mechanisms*. Examples of mechanisms and their points of leverage on the process of technology-based competition are shown in Figure 8-3. Actually, most of these objectives have been stated and the associated mechanisms have already been created, at least in embryonic form. The major problems now are refinement, expansion, *and* integration.

Moreover, in the United States, some of the needed technology infrastructure has been effectively designed and used in a few industries such as aerospace, agriculture, and biotechnology. The increasing technological content of virtually all industries will require technology infrastructure synthesized from the lessons of these past successes and also from the successes of foreign competitors.

Figure 8-3

Growth Policy Mechanisms

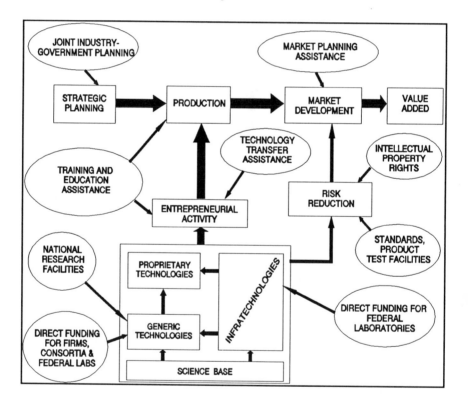

The implication is that large economies and "blocks" of smaller ones will have to design and manage their technology infrastructures as *portfolios* of generic technologies and supporting infratechnologies. This approach is necessary to ensure a diverse and timely technology base that will stimulate higher levels of investment by domestic industries and that can be drawn upon by industry as it develops and markets specific applications. The content of technology infrastructure will vary somewhat from technology to technology because of differences in such factors as the intrinsic nature of technologies and industry structure. This last fact is simply part of the management problem.

Growth policy will also have to address the fact that the position of the "pre-competitive" line will vary somewhat within the early phases of technology research among a nation's portfolio of emerging technologies, and thus so will the content of government support. Assessments of such conditions are complex, but nations that compete effectively in global markets are making and acting upon such assessments.

Other categories of market imperfections exist because of cultural and institutional biases towards information sharing and technology transfer. Government must act as a facilitator in information flows among the economy's firms. Such a role will be required not only in the conventional sense of technology transfer, but in the dissemination of holistic organizational methods such as total quality management that embody the systems concepts still foreign to much of the world's industries.

Thus, the increasingly global scope of investments in technology and capital will drive world economic expansion in the 1990s. However, the distribution of the benefits of this growth among nations is highly uncertain. More investment in civilian technology infrastructure should begin to turn the U.S. technology base towards a more globally competitive structure.

However, change is almost always slow. After several years of relatively intense debate over technology-based competitiveness and some movement toward the type of *portfolio*-based model of managing technology infrastructure that is proposed here, many continue to label such evolution as "industrial policy" -- interpreted to mean "picking winners and losers" and thereby subverting the free market. For example, the *Wall Street Journal*, in commenting on OSTP's critical technologies report stated:

"Recently, the White House's science office put together a report
naming 22 technologies as crucial for economic prosperity -- a clear
example of trying to pick technological winners"[20]

Labeling the identification of 22 broadly-defined technologies,
which cover virtually the entire technological base for the 1990s, as "a
clear example of trying to pick winners and losers" is a "clear example"
of an oxymoron. It shows the substantial gap that still exists between
the conventional wisdom and the realities of global technology-based
competition.

To make the transition to a globally-competitive infrastructure,
further modification of U.S. institutions that provide technology
infrastructure will be required. Currently, the Federal laboratory
system conducts state-of-the-art generic technology research, and the
remaining levels of the institutional structure (regional technology
transfer centers and extension programs) are dedicated to technology
transfer only, with little or no applied research.

However, the resulting early-phase technology advances are
typically not transferable to most of industry, without applied research.
In other industrialized nations, this more applied research is
supported by a second tier of government or government-sponsored
laboratories/institutes (for example, the Fraunhofer Institutes in
Germany). Attempting pre-competitive generic technology research
and applied research within the same research institution is a difficult
management operation, which is why most nations separate the two
roles institutionally.

Furthermore, new technology infrastructure strategies will have
to be built around the radically different ways by which economic
activity will be conducted in the 1990s. The proliferation of the
computer or, more accurately, information networks is already
changing both industry strategy and structure. More broadly, the
systems nature of new technologies, such as manufacturing
automation, imposes significant new management burdens on firms.
A study by Jaikumar [1986] received a lot of attention because it
revealed that investment by U.S. firms in flexible automation systems
(FMS) was much less productive than comparable investment by
Japanese firms. The reasons had to do with a poor understanding by

---

[20]   Davis [1991, p. A16].

the U.S. firms of the generic concepts of the intended uses of such automation.[21]

Had any significant technology planning structure been in place in the early 1980s, these concepts might have been identified and disseminated. In the 1990s, technical information infrastructure is finally evolving, although still not with the scope and intensity necessary. Such information -- economists would call it "disembodied technology" -- consists not only of planning information relevant for investment decision making, but of techniques, methods, processes, and technical data bases that have become so important in the systems approach to effectively utilizing technology.

Strategic Issues in Industry-Government Interaction

In the United States, the idea of cooperation between government and industry was foreign for much of the post-World War II period. Only in the mid-1980s, when U.S competitive positions had deteriorated in a significant number of industries, were attempts made to establish cooperative mechanisms -- first, among individual private-sector firms, and, second, between industry and government. But, as in any other area of economic activity, a wide range of alternative modes of cooperation present themselves with a comparably wide range of efficiencies. To be effective, such cooperation must include development of decision-relevant information.

A Japanese response to this needed selection process derives from Genichi Taguchi's "design of experiments" approach that combines engineering and statistical methods to optimize product and process design. A major objective is to minimize losses by reducing variability in the production process. The concept of experimentation as a device for accelerating progress has several advantages. One

---

[21]   In his study of U.S. and Japanese metal-working companies with advanced FMS technology, Jaikumar found that the average U.S. plant produced ten parts, with an average production volume of 1,727 per part. The average Japanese plant turned out 93 parts with an average production volume of 258. Moreover, the Japanese plants introduced 22 new parts for every one introduced by the U.S. plants. In other words, the Japanese used FMS not just to reduce unit labor costs, but to achieve true "flexibility" in their production structures -- thereby providing customers with more product variety (i.e., greater economies of scope were captured).

advantage is low risk. By characterizing an attempt at a new approach as "an experiment", the onus of failure is largely removed, thereby increasing the willingness to assume risk. This approach also encourages multiple approaches, because the limited scale of an experiment permits several alternatives to be tried within available resources.

Another aspect of the Taguchi method that is relevant for the interface between industry strategy and technology infrastructure is the fact that this approach focuses on *both* "controllable" factors and external factors that cannot easily be controlled.[22] The rapid pace of global technological change greatly increases the need for efficiency at *all* stages of the economic process. Not only does this mean that more of a firm's technology base will have to be developed externally, but also that the efficiency of the process by which this external technology (i.e., technology infrastructure) is produced will have to be improved.

A goal of the Taguchi approach with particular relevance for technology infrastructure policy is to design in "robustness" -- minimizing its sensitivity to factors beyond the control of those managing it. A robust process is one that yields consistently high quality in the target time frame. When cooperative research first began to be used in the United States in the mid 1980s, both the quality variable and time variable were major problems to this mechanism's effective use.

"The power of the Taguchi method lies in its ability to arrive at a greatly improved design or production process in a short time, using only a relatively small number of experiments".[23] The focus on timing as a competitive variable is one of the main driving forces behind cooperative research in the early phases of the R&D process. The Japanese demonstrated this clearly in their VLSI project in the late 1970s. The Europeans adopted this philosophy of industry-

---

[22]   The Taguchi method was developed for the control of production process, with a major objective being to minimize losses by reducing variability in the process. This means controlling internal factors (those which a company can largely control on its own, such as process temperature and pressure settings) and also external factors (such as variations in material inputs and the conditions under which an end product might be used).

[23]   Ronald M. Fortuna [1990].

government cooperation for generic technology research in a major way in the mid-1980s, and the United States has brought up the rear by beginning to implement this model in the 1990s.

The point is that the critical contributions to industrial technology from various possible forms of industry-government cooperation can only be perfected quickly through conscious and critically evaluated experimentation with the numerous alternative mechanisms available. Achieving this level of efficiency in policy/strategy development requires a nation to accurately and explicitly define the respective roles of its private sector and its technology infrastructure.

As the United States belatedly attempts to catch up in this area with its major competitors, it is bound to suffer from an incompletely worked out model of global technology-based competition that enables the effective assignment of these roles. For example, the United States has correctly concluded that it must re-orient its national laboratory system towards more direct support of commercial technology. The Technology Transfer of 1986 was a major legislative effort to help effect this adjustment. However, this Act and subsequent policy initiatives, reflect an incomplete understanding of appropriate roles.

To provide a mechanism for accelerating technology transfer to the private sector, the 1986 Act gave national laboratories the ability to form Cooperative Research and Development Agreements (CRDAs) with industry. CRDAs are formal agreements in which a firm or firms provide funds to a government laboratory to perform specific applied research, which is designed to build upon existing generic technology or infratechnology already developed by the lab. The laboratory may provide staff and facilities but no funds.

Basically, this is contract research with property rights to the resulting technology assigned to the funding firm. This firm may participate jointly in the R&D or conduct a parallel internal project to quickly pick up the government laboratory's contribution. Most CRDAs are with a single firm, making the content of the research considerably more proprietary than what the government laboratory would normally undertake. Proponents of this mechanism have been delighted with CRDAs for just this reason -- more proprietary research means a higher probability of direct market applications.

Ignored in such thinking is that the laboratory, as a public institution, is charged primarily with producing *non-proprietary* elements of an industrial technology -- generic technology and infratechnology. The greater the pressure to undertake CRDAs, which tend to target applied research, the more of available resources (staff and facilities) will be allocated to proprietary research for a single firm.

Not only does this re-allocation compromise the laboratory's primary mission, but it runs the risk of alienating the remainder of the industry that competes with the one firm participating in the CRDA. It is easy to imagine a CRDA producing a significant technological breakthrough, the benefits of which are captured by the one participating firm. Competing firms suddenly realize that they are now at competitive disadvantage due to a technological advance subsidized by a national laboratory.

The argument that the opportunity to form CRDAs with the laboratory is open to competitors has little merit because the target of the agreement is proprietary technology. Unlike pre-competitive generic technology research, little incentive exists to develop an applied technology simultaneously with competitors.

These potential pitfalls have been largely ignored as CRDAs have been seized upon as a "major mechanism" for improving the "productivity" of federal laboratories. By 1991, U.S. Government agencies were aggressively pushing the formation of CRDAs by their laboratories. Counts of CRDAs formed began to appear as an implicit, if not explicit, measure of an agencies "success" in commercializing federal technology.[24]

Pressures are also being applied to national laboratories to generate more royalties, which means the labs must adjust their current highly public-good generic technology and infratechnology research agenda to take individual projects further toward the applied end of the R&D spectrum. This shift in research focus is necessary in order to generate not only patentable results, but patents that will be attractive to industry to license. It is not that CRDAs are a poorly

---

[24] *New Technology Week* has had numerous articles on CRADAs. Workshops have been formed to counsel companies on identifying opportunities and negotiating CRADAs. See, for example, McCormack [1991].

conceived policy mechanism. The basic problem is that a single federal laboratory cannot perform two conflicting roles efficiently.[25]

In both Germany and Japan, the two roles -- generic technology research and applied research -- are assigned to separate institutional mechanisms. Both nations pursue generic technology research through industry-led consortium mechanisms, as well as in government laboratories. In Japan, the typical scope of a generic technology research consortium (MITI/AIST's Next Generation Industries Program and Large-Scale Projects) is somewhat broader than in Germany (the Federal Ministry for Research and Technology (BMFT)'s Direct Project Support for Market-Oriented Technologies Program). Japan's national laboratories focus on research requiring large-scale instrumentation and large capital investments.

Europe as a whole has adopted a similar conceptual model in which generic technologies are funded through separate institutional mechanisms from those for applied research. The European Community (EC) encourages pre-competitive generic technology research through programs such as ESPRIT for information technologies and BRITE/EURAM for advanced materials and processing technologies.[26]

With respect to managing the design and conduct of technology infrastructure research programs, Japan uses an arduous consensus-building process to define the research agenda, while Germany uses a more streamlined approach to select its smaller but more numerous projects.[27] Government laboratories may

---

[25] Another example of mixing roles within the same institutional entity is DARPA's equity investment in Gazelle Microcircuits Inc., a small company working on gallium arsenide semiconductor technology. Although approved by Congress, taking on the role of venture capitalist was a major departure from DARPA's long-standing, successful role of funding primarily early-phase technology research, and predictably led to strong objections within the Administration.

[26] ESPRIT is the European Strategic Programme for Research and Development in Information Technology and BRITE/EURAM combines the Basic Research in Industrial Technologies in Europe and European Research in Advanced Materials programs.

[27] Another difference is that for Japanese research projects for particular technological areas, selection and management are coordinated by trade associations, while in Germany a government manager performs these roles.

participate in these consortia, in which the research is conducted at
the facilities of the individual participants and the results shared. The
important characteristics of this mechanism are generic technology
objectives, multiple-firm participation, and shared research results.

For more applied R&D, which still has a public good element
but is somewhat more focused on specific market applications, Europe
relies on EUREKA, a pan-European umbrella research consortium of
19 countries, in which the EC is one participant. EUREKA sponsors
applied research through "industrial consortia to develop marketable
new technologies".[28] Thus, EUREKA complements the EC research
programs. With respect to individual countries, both Japan and
Germany use different institutional mechanism called (in Germany) a
"contract research organization" (CRO). Although CROs share costs
and benefits like other mechanisms, the selection process puts more
emphasis on market factors, and the CRO managers play a larger role
in selecting research topics. The Fraunhofer Society, for example,
focuses on applied research and obtains approximately 70 percent of
its funds from contract research.[29] The results of contract research
are owned by the funding company.

However, some underlying "core" (generic) technology
research is performed in German CROs to support the applied R&D.
This research is typically performed in the Fraunhofer institutes as
multi-client projects and is co-funded by the German Government and
a portion of the payments from contract research. Intellectual
property rights in this latter case are shared across all participating
firms. Other German firms sponsoring contract research also benefit
indirectly from the increased expertise of the institute staff.

Japan supplements its basic consortium mechanism, which
focuses on generic technology research, with a form of state venture
capital, called the Key Technology Center, in which the government
provides about 70 percent of the funds. Instead of assigning
responsibility for project segments to each member of the consortium,
the consortium itself assumes responsibility for the entire task. In this
case, the government has a recoupment objective. It eventually sells

---

[28]   Mitchell [1990].

[29]   U.S. National Science Foundation [1986, pp. 17-22].

its shares in the project and the participating firms then own the intellectual property rights.

The United States has no explicit set of institutional mechanisms comparable to those in Japan and Germany, or the EC for that matter. Private institutions such as Battelle perform applied R&D for industry clients, but their is no mechanism for government financial support. As a result, CRDAs are being pushed to fill the gap.

The Industry-Government Interface

One of the most important requirements for an effective technology-based growth strategy is the incorporation of the time element into strategic planning and role assignment. The dynamics of technology-based competition are such that relatively small amounts of resources, applied at the right points in the technology life cycle, can have substantial leverage. Chapter 4 argued that this is the case for cooperative research, for example.

However, western economic thinking still has too great a *static* component to it. Even when reasonably direct analysis of the Japanese experience is undertaken, the importance of dynamics is underestimated. For example, a study by Crow and Nath [1990] of technology strategy development surveyed Japanese firms to determine the relative importance of government policies on corporate strategic planning. They concluded that "government influence, at least individual policies, are not critical influences in technology development planning offices in corporate Japan", and "individual government policies in Japan play a secondary role compared with the individual corporation's internal plan and general market forces".

The fact that most private firms will state that their internal technology development strategy is more influential than government policy is tautological. Moreover, industry will habitually take a shorter time horizon and therefore not respond initially to some government policy initiatives. However, Crow and Nath do perceive, at least at a very general level, that some sort of significant environmental effect on corporate strategic planning is at work in the Japanese economy when they state that such their conclusion "overlooks the national goals, which may be the dominant feature of the Japanese approach".

In fact, the Japanese "approach" is much more microeconomic than the setting of national goals. The provision of information as well conventional technology infrastructure leads to more effective decisions in a more optimal time frame at the industry level. The survey results in the Crow and Nath study show that for a number of generic policy mechanisms, more than 50 percent of the Japanese firms responded that these mechanisms had a positive influence on their technology development strategies. But it is the *collective* influence of individual government policies that is the key factor. This is the main message of Figures 8-1 and 8-2.

Summary

Government influence on private-sector strategic planning can be substantial early in the technology life cycle, but then typically declines. This early support, whether it be strategic planning information, support for cooperative research, research at national laboratories, technical support for standards, etc., can impart advantages in terms of research efficiency, technology diffusion, timeliness, etc. If these efficiency gains only advance eventual commercialization by domestic firms relative to competitors by a short period of time, the resulting advantages in competitive position in terms of first-to-market, installed base, stimulation of investment in downstream industries, etc. will make a significant difference in long-term economic success.

However, industry-government interactions in terms of joint planning, cooperative research, standards development, technology transfer, etc., take place to varying degrees over the entire technology life cycle, not just in early-phase technology research -- at least if long-term competitiveness is to be maintained. The Japanese are now even planning the obsolescence of technology life cycles in order to achieve optimal phasing in of the next generations. Such apparent attempts at "control" will once again offend and bewilder western economic planners. However, one thing is certain: the potential impacts of such strategies cannot be ignored. Change in both private-sector investment and government infrastructure strategies will continue in all parts of the global economy, and intelligent responses must be forthcoming.

9 Infrastructure Strategies in an International Economy

"Make things as simple as possible, but no more so"

Albert Einstein

Paul Macrae Montgomery, a well-known bond market analyst, has said that any attempt to understand the bond market -- or any other market -- without intermittent study of human emotions is doomed to failure: "The study of economic behavior is a subset of the study of human behavior".[1]

Much, although certainly not all, of financial market analysts' efforts is aimed at short-term changes in market trends. In this area of forecasting, one can understand the importance of analyzing "emotions" or the psychology of market participants. However, as the forecasting or planning horizon lengthens, Montgomery and others

---

[1]   See Queenan [1991, p. 11].

admit that psychology becomes less important; that is, *fundamentals* take control.

Given the focus of this book on long-term trends and the strategies and policies that affect them, it might seem paradoxical at first to argue that long-term performance of a technology-based economy is not totally the result of conventional fundamentals. However, the discussion at many points, especially Chapters 3 and 8, argues that long-term economic success derives to a significant extent from a "higher-order" fundamental -- namely, a *philosophy* of what a technology-based economic system should look like. This philosophy manifests itself in a conceptual framework that identifies major roles for government and industry, their linkages and interfaces, and metrics for assessing performance.

Differences in overall philosophy are clearly evident among industrialized nations. The Japanese understood the process of technology development well enough several decades ago to emphasize certain inter-firm mechanisms such cooperative research, sharing of technical knowledge intelligence, and more general cooperation in planning through interlocking multiple-firm (*Keiretsu*) industry structures. Moreover, they evolved a philosophy that competitive position depended upon excelling at *every* stage in the technology-based economic process. Thus, in addition to the R&D stage, they emphasized quality and productivity in production and an iterative marketing strategy that placed great emphasis on developing product designs for large markets. Finally, they promote diversification of technology investment ("fusion") across both related and unrelated markets, thereby maximizing the realization of economies of scope.

The United States does not yet have a similarly comprehensive strategic, institutional, and philosophical basis from which to organize itself for effective long-term participation in global markets. Although some progress has been made, initiatives have been largely tentative and taken as isolated steps, rather than as elements of an integrated strategy based on a consensus economic growth philosophy. While this situation is not surprising, given the substantial change required of U.S. society, rapid and fundamental adjustment is essential.

As adjustments to corporate strategies and government policies are made, the systems nature of the typical industrial technology and the consequent systems approaches to providing these technologies in a timely manner will have to become a central element of economic philosophy. It is the lack of such a conceptual basis for formulating and executing economic strategy that led to poor performance in many industrialized nations over the past several decades.

No area of industrial technology has lagged more for lack of a systems approach than technology infrastructure. The several reasons for this situation are (1) technology infrastructure is a set of disparate elements that, to the casual observer, do not appear to be linked in any functional way, (2) the institutions that provide this infrastructure are consequently not functionally linked, and (3) the adoption of a systems approach requires, among other things, a long-term and multidisciplinary model for policy planning and implementation.

Increasingly strong competitive positions will be the reward of those nations or blocks of nations that adapt to the requirements for global competition by adopting the correct philosophical directions and setting up the required policies and supporting institutions.

The Changing of the Tide

The essential *first step* in achieving national competitiveness is the development of a broad consensus on the need to improve technology development and diffusion throughout the U.S. economy. The *second step* is the agreement on roles for government and industry in implementing this consensus.

As with the previous worldwide industrial revolution, major shifts are occurring in both the technologies that underlie industrial activity and in the *organization* of this activity. These dual phenomena, which typically occur in major economic upheavals, result in shifts in economic power among industries and even entire nations. Nations around the globe are moving rapidly towards the formulation of new strategies, based on complementary roles for industry and government, which will determine where the centers of economic wealth will be under this new economic order.

One of the most remarkable aspects of the current pattern of evolving technologies and industry structures is their almost completely opposite character from the industrial revolution. In the latter, the advent of mass production techniques and economic infrastructure, such as improved transportation, enlarged markets and made economies of scale possible.

Today, the reverse is taking place. Flexible, highly precise automated manufacturing is allowing large markets to be addressed as a collection of small, individualized segments. To be successful within this context, a nation must supply the infrastructure that not only helps bring forth the generic technologies that provide the basis for addressing large global markets, but also supply the infrastructure that enables the many diverse market segments to be addressed simultaneously.

Even though elements of these strategies will vary from nation to nation and from trading bloc to trading bloc, several critical elements are common to all *successful* strategies. These elements revolve around the nature of the core technologies driving economic change and the requirements for new industry and government behavior. The analyses undertaken in this book indicate that cultural and management change are harder to implement than technical change. Moreover, the former holds back the later, so that decisions to adopt new technology, even if such decisions are possible within the old order, are likely to be incomplete, late in coming, and generally ineffective.

But the essence of the major changes required in economic growth policies, including those for the technology infrastructure, has continued to evade too many Americans. In a *Business Week* editorial, Gary S. Becker, noted University of Chicago economics professor, supported the findings of economists at the University of Pennsylvania, lead by Robert Summers, that small nations do at least as well as large nations over extended periods of time.[2]

What is particularly relevant in their argument is the observation that the growth rates of large countries are held back by regional factionalism and jockeying of special interest groups for subsidies and favorable regulations. Smaller nations, on the other hand, are considerably more homogenous, and, by specializing in a few industries have been able to attain comparable rates of per capita growth.

Of course, as this book has labored at length to point out, not all large nations have succumbed to factionalism or to an adherence to a single-stage growth strategy. As for medium and small nations, some have recognized that their economic future requires them to

---

[2]   See Becker [1990, p. 20].

access the economies of scale and scope inherent in the emerging technologies that will dominate the global markets of the next century. It is revealing that Becker cites exports of fruits and vegetables by Chile, small arms from Israel, textiles from Mauritius, and oil from Kuwait as examples of "successful" specialization by small countries.

If Chile is satisfied to remain an agricultural economy, with the certain low relative standard of living, or if Mauritius can continue to export textiles into global markets in competition with nations that are increasingly relying on automation of both textile design and manufacturing, or if the demand-supply relationship remains favorable in petroleum for decades to come, etc., then these nations may continue to hold their *relative* positions in terms of per capita income.

But the increasing importance of technology in determining global market shares, the necessity of adopting a portfolio model of technology-based growth, and the greater role of a supporting technology infrastructure argue that small countries will remain far down the economic ladder, if they remain isolated from both common markets and the technology infrastructure that can only be provided by economic cooperation.

The complementary asset approach to defining industrial growth strategies is based on recognition of several key factors: (1) technology and market life cycles are shrinking due to intense global competition and the increased efficiency with which individual nations and blocs of nations are implementing these complementary roles; (2) the early phases of a technology's development are *pre-competitive* from a global strategy perspective, meaning that government has a major role at these phases; (3) the overall efficiency of the economic process requires a number of *competitively neutral* infratechnologies that facilitate every stage from R&D, through production, and finally marketing; and, (4) technology transfer must be rapid and widespread, requiring specialized, permanent institutions.

In the industrial nations making the most successful transitions to the new competitiveness requirements, national laboratories play a major role in responding to each of the above four factors. The high risk of early-phase (generic technology) research, the competitive neutrality of infratechnologies, and the highly nonproprietary character of technology transfer mandate a significant role for government laboratories or institutes, because they have the unique facilities, skills, and *public* perspective necessary to rationalize these types of technology investments.

The Japanese have greatly advanced the process of integrating complementary competitive assets in technology-based growth. Specifically, they have combined appropriate industry structures with both internal and external sources of technology, expertly selecting various combinations of sources according to a range of efficiency factors. The external sources of technology and other elements of technology infrastructure are particularly well integrated with corporate strategy. Similarly, their financial infrastructure is particularly efficient in supplying low-cost, patient capital.

The Japanese have been appropriately characterized as fierce competitors in a free-market sense that offends many western nations, but one might expect them to become somewhat complacent in the face of their extremely positive economic performance. In fact, as a MITI policy statement on economic objectives for the 1990s states, "If we simply look at the numbers, there is no question that Japan has left a trail of superior economic performance".[3]

However, the tone of the MITI document from which this quote (translated) is taken is just the opposite. It begins by stating that "rapid changes in the international order and the increasing uncertainty over the future are causing increased anxiety. Now, more than ever before, the extensive changes and unprecedented fluidity demand creative and deliberate responses". Later on, the same document states,

> "The challenges of the 1990s include creating a vital industrial structure that can respond flexibly to changes in the values and needs of the people, eliminating gaps between developing new industries, rationalizing or converting low-productivity industries, and fostering small and medium size companies -- the source of the energy which drives the Japanese economy. Science, technology, and information will be keys to success. Work must be done to promote science and technology and to expand Japan's information capabilities."[4]

---

[3]   From MITI's statement on international trade and industrial policy for the 1990s. See Ministry of International Trade and Industry (MITI) [1990, p. 1].

[4]   MITI [1990, p. 8].

This general statement leads to more specific statements of national policy objectives for the 1990s, including the objective of significantly increasing government funding of R&D:

> "The enormous risks, the long lead times, and the broad range of
> applications of new technology require that the national
> government play a large role in technology and drastically expand
> its support of R&D with the aim of increasing government funding
> of R&D to about 1% of GNP.[5]

The relentless push by Japan towards an increasingly technology-based economy is further evidenced by the substantial relative increase in R&D expenditures by Japanese firms over the decade of the 1980s from about 1.5% of sales to 2.6%.

But the burning question is: Do the United States and other technology-based economies have the capacity to develop and execute effective long-term strategies, as evidenced by the Japanese? The past several decades do not provide much encouragement. After a severe economic shock caused by the OPEC oil embargo in late 1973, a comprehensive energy policy to secure a greater degree of energy independence was developed by the United States. But in 1981, most of the programs resulting from these policy objectives were scrapped, consumer behavior regressed, and the overall rate of progress on energy conservation declined significantly. In 1990, the United States continued to use 1.5 to 2.5 times as much energy per dollar of GDP as other industrialized nations.

The confrontation with Iraq reawakened the debate. A *Wall Street Journal/NBC News* survey found that 80 percent of voters favored conservation. However, when specific measures were suggested, the results were quite different. 57 percent opposed the construction of additional nuclear power plants and 62 percent of Americans opposed taxing gasoline to encourage conservation, even though U.S. consumers pay far lower prices for gasoline than in other industrialized nations. James Schlesinger, President Carter's energy secretary stated that "this is a society that has powerful antibodies against a consistent and persistent energy policy. The *Wall Street*

---

[5] MITI [1990, p. 35]. Japan's non-defense R&D expenditures funded by government were 0.55% of GNP in 1988.

Journal concluded that "in the end, Americans will demonstrate once again their chronic unwillingness to suffer short-term pain for long-term gain".[6]

The Policy Process

A major part of the problem is the lack of systematic policy development apparatus which would begin, as does Japan's MITI, with a "vision of the future". The Technology Administration (TA) was created in the Department of Commerce in 1989 to upgrade the civilian S&T policy capabilities of the Federal Government as part of an increased response to "the competitiveness problem". But, this organizational unit has not been sufficiently funded to permit the full range of technology-based growth policy analyses needed for comprehensive and sustained policy development and management. The majority of its staff was drawn from other units in the Department, when new skills were also needed. Moreover, the traditional domination by macroeconomic policy elements in the Office of Management and Budget (OMB), the Council of Economic Advisors, (CEA), and the Treasury have resisted attempts by the TA and the Commerce Department as a whole to design and implement a microeconomic policy role.

Other microeconomic policy units within the Federal Government suffered from different but equally crippling dysfunctions. The Office of Science and Technology Policy (OSTP), headed by the President's Science Advisor, has made an effort to upgrade and expand its range of policy activities from purely scientific or "high" technology to include the broader range of technology, economic, and other competitiveness-related issues. However, the fact that OSTP is staffed largely by individuals on temporary assignments from industry, academia, and other Federal agencies prohibits continuity, institutional memory, and other attributes for sustained and effective policy analysis.

The National Science Foundation (NSF) used to conduct basic technology and innovation policy research, which at least provided a knowledge base for more applied policy analyses elsewhere. But, in

---

[6]   Rosewicz [1990].

the mid 1980s, NSF was largely restricted to funding policy analysis in the area of university research, effectively removing it from the broader S&T growth policy arena.

One of the major dysfunctions in the technology-based economic growth process is the schism between the technology and economic infrastructures. The Japanese have done an amazingly good job of fusing the two into a single strategic policy framework. In other countries, particularly the United States, the S&T infrastructure has traditionally been separate from the economic infrastructure.

The economic infrastructure has therefore largely ignored the role of technology and, in particular, the complexity of the infrastructure support required to produce new technology *and* get it into the marketplace. The technology infrastructure, on the other hand, has looked upon technology objectives as end points, rather than intermediate inputs in an economic process. The result in this latter case has been to pursue overly complex technical objectives, including megaprojects with little economic relevance, *and* to fail in communicating technology infrastructure needs to the economic policy community.

What is Required?

Agriculture once permeated our economy and our culture. Recognizing its importance, the United States established a very effective infrastructure which helped make this U.S. industry the most productive in the world. Today, agriculture absorbs only three percent of the labor force, with technology-based manufacturing and services having replaced it as the dominant drivers of economic growth. Growth in employment, productivity, quality, exports, income, and, ultimately, the standard of living is now very diversified and technology dependent. The question is, therefore, will the United States, marshal the financial resources, management and labor skills, and infrastructure support to achieve the high and sustained rates of growth achieved in agriculture when it was the economic driver?

Government is not simply a *supplier* of some of the elements of an industry's technology base, it is also an *integrator* among the various suppliers: itself, industry, and academia. The Japanese have evolved this philosophy to the greatest extent, through concepts such as technology fusion.

In the United States, however, the majority of analyses of the "competitiveness problem" have focused on what worked well in the past, why the U.S. competitive position has declined, and who might be to blame. While these exercises have been important as the first step in "problem solving", logical, comprehensive, and integrated prescriptions for new strategies, including adaptations from the experiences of other nations, are the essential second step. Most of these analyses have failed to address this latter step to any significant degree.

Recently, however, some substance has been infused into individual problem areas. Numerous proposals have been offered for revamping the U.S. educational system. Proposals are slowly being developed and implemented for improving the production of technology infrastructure such as generic technologies, infratechnologies, standards, etc. But less progress has been made in integrating these elements into a system which is itself an integral part of the overall economic system. Until the United States begins to think, plan, and act in systems terms, effective technology-based economic growth policy will not be forthcoming.

In general, some fundamental changes in philosophy, policies, and institutions will be required. How, then, can the need for a systems approach to all stages of the technology-based life cycle and the derived need for cooperation of varying types and degrees be rationalized within a market-based economy, where the efficiency gains from competition are well-established?

First, we must accept the premise that all economic players are better off by recognizing and behaving as if their own economic well being is tied to the well being of their fellow economic players. This is simply a re-definition of the meaning of self interest, as originally stated in "the invisible hand" principle of Adman Smith.[7]

Second, we must accept the complexities of technology-based economic markets. Among these is the fact that the typical technology-based industry has significant infrastructure elements, which are "common" or "public" goods and therefore must be produced, as well as used, collectively. Third, other infrastructure -- in

---

[7] Another phrase, "the hidden foot" (coined by Burton Klein) is equally applicable in today's global marketplace. That is, in addition to responding to economic incentives (the invisible hand), firms, industries and nations must constantly be alert to aggressive competition (the hidden foot).

particular, education -- that must be in place to not only produce but to use technology must be given much higher priority.

The ultimate challenge for a modern economy, then, is to promote creativity and innovativeness, which in the past has been largely an individualistic effort, while at the same time capturing the longer-term efficiency gains achieved through cooperation among economic agents, where this approach is the efficient one. The economic history of the past several decades reveals many attempts by national economies to achieve steady growth on one or the other of these two basic elements. Now, in the 1990s and beyond, we will see attempts to combine the two elements into a single framework for global competitiveness and economic growth.

Both corporate strategy and government policy are slowly evolving in the direction of this dual-element growth model. The major problem is that the current evolutionary pace in the United States and other nations may not be sufficient to maintain a position of economic competitiveness. Surely, those nations that do not adapt to this new economic order will decline in economic stature.

In order to achieve long-term economic growth and sustained increases in the standard of living, a technology-based growth strategy must be adopted which recognizes the recursive relationship between private-sector economic activity and the supporting technology infrastructure. That is, as each of these two major elements grows over time, it provides signaling or feedback to the second, which, in turn, helps the first one perform more efficiently. Within this economic structure, however, several strategies must be implemented:

o   a diversified value-added strategy encompassing all three major stages of economic activity -- R&D, production, and marketing;

o   early-phase R&D (generic technology research) must be treated as a key activity of combined public-private efforts;

o   As a technology matures and the derived markets increase in size and number of global participants, an evolutionary trend toward some type of vertically-integrated industry structure will be required; facilitating this process requires specific types of

information infrastructure that allow rapid and efficient
communication among independent firms to improve
management practice and to substitute for
organizational integration (i.e., mergers) when the
market determines to evolve that way;

If it is possible to sum up the myriad of technological,
economic and policy issues that affect technology-based growth, it
might be the following. Technological change as a major factor in
global economic growth is a systems phenomenon. Nations have by
and large tried to focus on specific elements of the technology-based
economic system and, as a result, have failed or will fail to sustain a
competitive position in the world economy. The movement is now
towards operating domestic economies with (1) the *entire* production
chain as the major strategic target, and (2) progressive diversification
of a technology -- first across related and then "fused" applications
(production chains).

In formulating and implementing technology infrastructure and
other growth strategies, no nation should think that its existing
economic structure and behavior is the ultimate economic system.
Japan has experienced enormous economic success for several
decades because it has addressed more of the elements of a
competitive technology-based economy than have other nations. The
Japanese have excelled at advancing and extracting the benefits from
the successive generations of technological life cycles that make up the
longer-term major technology cycles, which originated elsewhere in the
world through radical technological change.

The transition from one major cycle to the next is
characterized by major bursts of innovativeness and entrepreneurial
activity -- an element in which the United States has excelled. These
outpourings of technological innovativeness have spawned periods of
tremendous economic growth worldwide. The problem is that pure
entrepreneurial activity, defined as product-oriented strategies
confined to the individual firm, is by itself increasingly ineffective as
major technological life cycles mature.

The *Keiretsu*, now envied by many Americans and Europeans,
may be too rigid to accept sustained entrepreneurial and innovative
behavior. Yet, its advantages in providing patient capital and
cooperation throughout the production chain are now legend.
Moreover, its ability to work cooperatively, not only among its own

members but with the broader government-supplied infrastructure has achieved tremendous efficiency advantages over most of the typical technology life cycle. The German economy has had great success by emphasizing this last element.

In the long run, however, current national strategies will be inadequate. Instead, future success will be attained by the evolving economic systems that simultaneously incorporate and capture the advantages of the several sets of economic elements.

At the most general level of characterizing the major factors determining an industry's global competitive position, technology infrastructure can be listed along with private-sector competitive behavior and industry structure as the three "pillars" of competitiveness. If any one of these three is deficient in some major way, long-term economic success is not likely. Making sure that they are not deficient requires long-term planning and persistent implementation of these plans, revising them continually in response to changing technological and market trends.

Technology, like physical capital, is an asset, or rather a collection of interrelated assets -- to be accumulated steadily over time. Such a stock of technology capital will also continually depreciate. Successful economic use of technology requires a integrated approach in which individual assets are regarded as part of a larger economic system. The proposition that technology can be acquired through intermittent efforts or by focusing on one or two elements of an industry's technology base is a prescription for competitive failure.

Above all else, a philosophy of global competition must be adopted which stresses a *multi-stage* strategy. A singular focus on being innovative or being efficient in production or being expert in marketing will not achieve long-term success. Thus, competing in global markets requires a *systems* view. This perspective is implemented at three levels: the firm, the industry, and the sector or nation. Strategies for all three are *leveraged* and *integrated* by technology infrastructure. It serves as both a building block and a catalyst for technology-based economic activity.

As Dwight D. Eisenhower once said, "Plans are worthless, but planning is essential". Clearly, the dynamics of global competition will ensure that strategic objectives and the mechanisms for pursuing them will change continually ("plans are worthless"). However, because economic success over time will be determined by the overall efficiency of national strategies ("planning is essential"), a nation that does not do its planning well will have it done by others, and probably not to its liking.

Bibliography

Abegglen, James C. and George Stalk, Jr. [1985], *Kaisha: The Japanese Corporation*. New York: Basic Books, Inc.

Becker, Gary S. [1990], "Actually, Small-Fry Nations Can Do Just Fine", *Business Week*, (October 1).

Bird, Jane [1991], "Britain Picks Wrong Way to Beat the Japanese", *Science*, vol. 252 (May 31), p. 1248.

Blinder, Alan S. [1990], "There Are Capitalists, Then There Are Japanese", *Business Week* (October 8), p.21.

Bloch, Eric [1991], *Toward a U.S. Technology Strategy: Enhancing Manufacturing Competitiveness* (The Manufacturing Forum, Discussion Paper No. 1). Washington, DC: National Academy Press (February).

Bresnahan, Timothy F. and Amit Chopra [1990], "The Development of the Local Area Network Market as Determined by User Needs", *Economics of Innovation and New Technology*, vol. 1, no. 1 (July), pp. 97-110.

Bromley, D. Allan [1991], "Research and Development in the President's FY 1992 Budget", testimony before the U.S. House of Representatives, Committee on Science, Space, and Technology, February 20.

Burke, James [1978], *Connections*. New York: Little, Brown and Company.

Bylinsky, Gene [1990], "Turning R&D into Real Products", *Fortune* (July 2).

Cantwell, John [1989], *Technological Innovation and Multinational Corporations*. Oxford, UK: Basil Blackwell.

Charles River Associates [1981], *Productivity Impacts of NBS R&D: A Case Study of the NBS Semiconductor Technology Program*. Gaithersburg, MD: National Bureau of Standards.

Charles River Associates [1982], *Analysis of the Role of the National Bureau of Standards in Supporting Industrial Innovation and Growth*. Gaithersburg, MD: National Bureau of Standards.

Cashin, Jerry [1990], "Test Suites Rolling Out to Ensure 'Open' Systems", *Software Magazine* (August).

Coffee, Peter C. [1988], "Don't Be Surprised If IBM Has the Last Laugh", *PC Week*, vol. 5, no. 44 (October 31).

Council on Competitiveness [1990], *Japanese Technology Policy: What's The Secret?* Washington, DC.

Council on Competitiveness [1991], *Gaining New Ground: Technology Priorities for America's Future*. Washington DC.

Crawford, Mark, [1991], "Healthy Boost In Ceramics Budget Isn't Enough To Please Industry Researchers", *New Technology Week* (March 18).

Crow, Michael M. and Shrilata Nath [1990], "Technology Strategy Development in Japanese Industry: An Assessment of Market and Government Influences", *Technovation*, vol. 10, no. 5 (July): pp. 333-346.

Council of the European Communities [1990], "Council Decision of 23 April 1990: concerning the framework programme of Community activities in the field of research and technological development (1990 to 1994)" (90/221/Euratom/EEC).

Dalton, Donald H. and Phyllis A. Genther [1991], "The Role of Corporate Linkages in U.S.-Japan Technology Transfer" (NTIS PB165571). Washington, DC: U.S. Department of Commerce (March).

Dataquest [1991], "U.S. Companies Top List for Strategic Alliances" (summary of report by the Whorton School of Business), *Research Newsletter*, February.

David, Edward E. [1987], *Report of the White House Science Council Panel on Semiconductors*. Washington, DC: Office of Science and Technology Policy, Executive Office of the President.

David, Paul A. and Shane Greenstein [1990], *The Economics of Compatibility Standards: an Introduction to Recent Research* (CEPR Publication No. 207). Stanford, CA: Center for Economic Policy Research (June).

Davis, Bob [1991], "White House, Reversing Policy Under Pressure, Begins to Pick High-Tech Winners and Losers", *The Wall Street Journal* (May 13).

Dertouzos, Michael L., Richard K. Lester, and Robert M. Solow [1989], *Made in American: Regaining the Productive Edge*. Cambridge, MA: The MIT Press.

Dozier, Kimberly [1989], "Debate Rages Over Need for Production Consortia Exemptions", *New Technology Week* (October 2).

Drahalad, C. K. and Gary Hamel [1990], "The Core Competence of the Corporation", *Harvard Business Review*, May-June.

Drucker, Peter [1991], "Japan: New Strategies for a New Reality", *Wall Street Journal*, October 2.

Ernst and Young [1990], *Biotech 91: A Changing Environment*. San Francisco.

Executive Office of the President, Office of Science and Technology Policy [1990], *U.S. Technology Policy*. Washington, DC (September 26).

Executive Office of the President, Office of Science and Technology Policy [1991], *Report of the National Critical Technologies Panel*. Washington, DC (April).

Ferguson, Charles [1990], "Computers and the Coming of the U.S. Keiretsu", *Harvard Business Review* (July-August), pp. 55-70.

Finan, William F., *A Comparison of Japanese and American Approaches to Quality in the Semiconductor Industry*. Research Triangle Park, NC: Semiconductor Research Corporation (February).

Flamm, Kenneth [1988], *Creating the Computer: Government, Industry and High Technology*. Washington, DC: The Brookings Institution.

Ford, Robert [1990]. "The Cost of Subsidizing Industry", *The OECD Observer*, October/November, pp. 5-7.

Fortuna, Ronald M. [1990], *Total Quality: An Executive's Guide for the 1990s*. New York: Dow Jones-Irwin.

Fransman, Martin [1991], *The Market and Beyond*. London: Cambridge University Press.

Germon, Claude [1986], "La normalisation, cle d'un nouvel essor", *la Documentation Francaise* (report to the Organization for Economic Cooperation and Development), Paris, France.

Glickman, Norman J. and Douglas P. Woodward [1989], *The New Competitors: How Foreign Investors are Changing the U.S. Economy*. New York: Basic Books, 1989.

Government-University-Industry Research Roundtable and Industrial Research Institute [1991], *Industrial Perspectives on Innovation and Interactions with Universities*. Washington, DC: National Academy Press (February).

Graham, Edward M. and Paul R. Krugman [1989], *Foreign Direct Investment in the United States*, Washington, DC: Institute for International Economics.

Griliches, Zvi [1958], "Research Costs and Social Returns: Hybrid Corn and Related Innovations," *Journal of Political Economy* vol. 46 (October), pp. 419-431.

Griliches, Zvi [1964], "Research Expenditures, Education, and the Aggregate Agricultural Production Function," *American Economic Review* vol. 54: pp. 961-974.

Grossman, Evan [1989], "AT&T to Remain at Unix Helm, Group Says", *PC Week*, vol. 6, no. 5 (February 6).

Guilder, George [1988], "The Revitalization of Everything: The Law of the Microcosm", *Harvard Business Review* (March-April), pp. 49-61.

Hay, Edward J. [1988]. *The Just-in-Time Breakthrough.* New York: John Wiley & Sons.

Herbert, Evan [1989], "Japanese R&D in the United States", *Research*Technology Management* (November-December), pp. 11-20.

Heurteaux, Michel [1991], "ESPRIT and RACE Programs: European R&D in Its Third Phase", *Electronique International Hebdo* (French) (February 21).

Hill, Christopher T. [1991], "New Manufacturing Paradigms -- New Manufacturing Policies?, *The Bridge*, Vol. 21, No. 2 (Summer).

Hobday, Michael [1990], "Strategies for the U.K. Semiconductor Industry: Lessons from the Alvey Program", *Technovation*, vol. 10, no. 3 (May).

Hooper, Laurence [1990], "IBM says It Built 16-Megabit Chip on Existing Line", *Wall Street Journal*, February 14.

Howell, Thomas R. *et al* [1988], *The Microelectronics Race: The Impact of Government Policy on International Competition.* Boulder, CO: Westview Press.

Iversen, Wes [1990], "Information Systems: Tying It All Together", *Industry Week*, vol. 239, no. 16 (August), pp. 20-30.

Jaikumar, Ramchandran, [1986], "Postindustrial Manufacturing", *Harvard Business Review* (November-December), pp. 69-76.

Japan Ministry of International Trade and Industry (MITI) [1990], *International Trade and Industrial Policy in the 1990s: Towards Creating Human Values in the Global Age* (summary prepared by MITI's Overseas Public Affairs Office). Tokyo, Japan (July 5).

Japanese Industrial Standards Committee [1990], *Recommendations for a Long-Range Plan for the Promotion of Industrial Standardization* (June 5).

Jenks, Andrew [1990], "Reston Networking Whiz Kahn Leads National System Effort", *Washington Technology* (December 6).

Johnson, G. Patrick [1990], "Summary of First Report on the State of Science and Technology in Europe", *ESN Information Bulletin* (report no. 90-02). New York: Office of Naval Research, European Office (February), pp. 23-35.

Katzman, Martin T. and Donald W. Jones [forthcoming], "Cooperative R&D Viewed from the Theory of Clubs: An Application to a Federally Sponsored R&D Consortium".

Kenney, Martin and Richard Florida [1991], "How Japanese Industry is Rebuilding the Rust Belt", *Technology Review* (February/March), pp. 25-33.

Kodama, Fumio [1991], *Analyzing Japanese High Technologies: The Techno-Paradigm Shift*. London: Printer Press.

Krugman, Paul [1990], *The Age of Diminished Expectations*. Cambridge, MA: The MIT Press.

Landau, Ralph [1988], "U.S. Economic Growth", *Science*, vol. 258, no. 6 (June), pp. 44-52.

Lee, Thomas H. and Proctor P. Reid, editors [1991], *National Interests in an Age of Global Technology* (Report of the National Academy of Engineering, Committee on Engineering as an International Enterprise). Washington, DC: National Academy Press.

Lewis, William W. and Lawrence H. Linden [1990], "A New Mission for Corporate Technology", *Sloan Management Review* (Summer).

Link, Albert N. [1981], "Basic Research and Productivity Increase in Manufacturing: Additional Evidence", *American Economic Review* (December).

Link, Albert N. [1987], *Technological Change and Productivity Growth*. London: Harwood Academic Publishers.

Link, Albert N. [1991a], *Economic Impacts of NIST-Supported Standards for the U.S. Optical Fiber Industry: 1981-Present*. Gaithersburg, MD: National Institute of Standards and Technology.

Link, Albert N. [1991b], *Economic Impact on the U.S. Semiconductor Industry of NIST Research in Electromigration*. Gaithersburg, MD: National Institute of Standards and Technology.

Link, Albert N. [1991b], *Economic Impact of NIST Research on Electromagnetic Interference*. Gaithersburg, MD: National Institute of Standards and Technology.

Link, Albert N. and Laura L. Bauer [1989]. *Cooperative Research in U.S. Manufacturing: Assessing Policy Initiatives and Corporate Strategies*. Lexington, MA: Lexington Books.

Link, Albert N. and John Rees [1990], "Firm Size, University Based Research and Returns to Scale", *Small Business Economics*, vol. 2, pp. 25-31.

Link, Albert N., Perry Quick, and Gregory Tassey [1991], "Investments in Product Quality: A Descriptive Study of the U.S. Optical Fiber Industry", *OMEGA: The International Journal of Management Science*, vol. 19, no.5, pp. 471-474.

Link, Albert N. and Gregory Tassey [1987a], *Strategies for Technology-Based Competition: Meeting the New Global Challenge*. Lexington, MA: Lexington Books.

Link, Albert N. and Gregory Tassey [1987b], "The Impact of Standards on Technology-Based Industries: The Case of Numerically Controlled Machine Tools", in H. Landis Gabel, editor, *Product Standardization and Competitive Strategy*. Amsterdam: North Holland.

Link, Albert N. [1991], "Investments in Infratechnology as an Indicator of Technological Advancement: An Exploratory Study", Report to the National Science Foundation (SRS-9012402).

Lynn, Leonard H. [1985]. "Technology Transfer to Japan: What We Know, What We Need to Know, and What We Know That May Not Be So?" in Nathan Rosenberg and Claudio Frischtak (editors), *International Technology Transfer: Concepts, Measures, and Comparisons.* New York: Praeger.

Maggs, William [1991], "Industry Taking Advantage of Cooperative Research Agreements with Labs," *New Technology Week* (January 14).

Mansfield, Edwin *et al* [1977], "Social and Private Rates of Return from Industrial Innovations," *Quarterly Journal of Economics* vol. 91: (May), pp. 221-240.

Mansfield, Edwin *et al* [1982]. *Technology Transfer, Productivity, and Economic Policy.* New York: Norton.

Mansfield, Edwin [1988a], "Industrial R&D in Japan and in the United States: A Comparative Study," *American Economic Review*, vol. 78, pp. 223-228.

Mansfield, Edwin [1988b], "Industrial Innovation in Japan and the United States," *Science*, vol. 241, pp. 1769-1774.

Mansfield, Edwin [1991], "The Social Rate of Return from Academic Research", *American Economic Review*, vol. 81.

Mayer, Jeffrey L. [1990]. *SEMATECH 1990: A Report to Congress by the Advisory Council on Federal Participation in SEMATECH.*

McCormack, Richard [1990]. "Gone: Large U.S. Makers of Large Robots", *New Technology Week*, vol. 34, no. 38 (September 24).

McCormack, Richard [1990]. "Quest for Quality Slashes Motorola's Supplier Base," *New Technology Week*, vol. 4, no. 47 (November 26).

McCormack, Richard [1991]. "Bush Administration Presses for Results in Federal Technology Transfer Efforts", *New Technology Week*, vol. 5, no. 21 (May 20).

Mitchell, Dean L. [1990], "The Evolution of 'Europe 1992'", *ESN Information Bulletin* (report no. 90-02). New York: Office of Naval Research, European Office (February), pp. 3-5.

Murray, Alan and Urban C. Lehner [1990], "Whatever U.S. Scientists Discover, the Japanese Convert -- Into Profit", *Wall Street Journal* (June 25).

National Academy of Engineering [1990]. *National Interests in an Age of Global Technology*. Washington, DC (November).

National Advisory Committee on Semiconductors [1991], *Toward a National Semiconductor Strategy: Regaining Markets in High-Volume Electronics* (Second Annual Report, two volumes). Arlington, VA: The National Advisory Committee on Semiconductors (February).

National Institute of Standards and Technology [1991], *Measurements of Competitiveness in Electronics* (NISTIR 4583). Gaithersburg, MD.

National Materials Advisory Board [1982]. *An Assessment of the Impact of the Department of Defense Very High Speed Integrated Circuit Program*. Washington, DC: National Academy Press.

OECD [1990a]. *OECD Economic Surveys: United States*. Paris: Organization for Economic Cooperation and Development.

OECD [1990b]. *Industrial Policy in OECD Countries*. Paris: Organization for Economic Cooperation and Development.

Peck, Merton J. [1986], "Joint R&D: The Case of Microelectronics and Computer Technology Corporation," *Research Policy*, vol. 15, pp. 219-231.

Peterson, W. [1967]. "Returns to Poultry Research in the United States," *Journal of Farm Economics* vol. 49: (August) pp. 656-669.

Petrella, Riccardo [1988], "The Globalization of Technological Innovation, Strategy and Options", paper presented at the National Conference of the Advancement of Research on "America and the Globalization of Technological Innovation", Rancho Mirage, California (October).

Porter, Michael [1990a]. "The Competitive Advantage of Nations", *Harvard Business Review* (March/April).

Porter, Michael [1990b]. *The Competitive Advantage of Nations.* New York: The Free Press.

Prestowitz, Clyde V. Jr., Alan Tonelson, and Robert W. Jerome [1991], "The Last Gasp of GATTism", *Harvard Business Review* (March/April), pp. 130-138.

Queenan, Joe [1991], "Exotic Indicators", *Barron's*, June 3, pp. 10-11.

Quick, Finan, and Associates [1990], *U.S. Investment Strategies for Quality Assurance (NIST Planning Report 90-1)*, prepared for the Program Office, National Institute of Standards and Technology, Gaithersburg, MD.

Reich, Robert B. [1991a], "Who Is Them?", *Harvard Business Review* (March/April), pp. 77-88.

Reich, Robert B. [1991b], "Up the Workers", *The New Republic* (May 13).

Robyn, Dorothy [1989], "Buying America", book review of *The New Competitors: How Foreign Investors are Changing the U.S. Economy* by Norman Glickman and Douglas Woodward, in *Issues in Science and Technology*, Fall 1989, pp. 88-89.

Rosewicz, Barbara [1990]. "Crisis in Mideast Unlikely to Break Americans of Their Deep-Rooted Addiction to Imported Oil," *The Wall Street Journal*, August 23, p. A16.

Ross, Ian [1989], *A Strategic Industry at Risk: Report to the President and the Congress from the National Advisory Committee on Semiconductors*. Washington, DC.

Samuels, Richard J. [1989]. "Cooperation and Conflict in Science and Technology," *The JAMA Forum*, December 1989.

Schlesinger, Jacob M. [1991], "Sharp, Under Attack by U.S. Regulators, to Build Laptops' Thin screens in U.S.," *Wall Street Journal*, February 22, p.B5.

Schonberger, Richard J. [1986]. *World-Class Manufacturing: The Lessons of Simplicity Applied.* New York: The Free Press.

Scott, Karyl and Matt Kramer [1988], "LAN Vendors Ponder Uniting to Develop Common X.400 API", *PC Week*, vol. 5, no. 44 (October 31).

Sheridan, John H. and John Teresko, "Open Systems: Gateway to a New Computing Age", *industry Week,* (April 15), pp. 25-56.

Shiba, Shoji [1989], "Universal Quality," *Look Japan* (October), pp. 32-33.

Skrzycki, Cindy [1990], "Behind Big Blue's Blue Ribbon," *The Washington Post*, December 16.

Sheridan, John H. [1990], "World Class Manufacturing" *Industry Week* (July 2).

Schlender, Brenton R. [1988], "Motorola Gets Unix Computers to Run IBM-Compatible Software", *Wall Street Journal* (November 2).

Spencer, Linda M. [1989], *Foreign Investment Barriers: Where America Stands Among its Competitors.* Arlington, VA: Congressional Economic Leadership Institute.

Spiegelman, Lisa L. and Madeline Epstein [1989], "Concerns Mount as EISA Nears Market", *PC Week*, vol.6, no. 4 (January 30).

Stowsky, Jay S. [1989], "Weak Links, Strong Bonds: U.S.-Japanese Competition in Semiconductor Production Equipment" in Chalmers Johnson, Laura Tyson, and John Zysman, eds., *Politics and Productivity: The Real Story of Why Japan Works.* New York: Ballinger Publishing Co.

Taft, Darryl K. [1988], "People Still Seen as No. 1 Challenge for Technology", *Government Computer News* (April 1).

Tassey, Gregory [1982], "Infratechnologies and the Role of Government," *Technological Forecasting and Social Change*, vol. 21, pp. 163-180.

Tassey, Gregory [1986], "The Role of the National Bureau of Standards in Supporting Industrial Innovation," *IEEE Transactions of Engineering Management*, vol. 33 (August).

Tassey, Gregory [1985], "The Technology Policy Experiment as a Policy Research Tool", *Research Policy*, vol. 14, pp. 39-52.

Tassey, Gregory [1989], "Industry and Government Strategies for Product Quality", *International Journal of Technology Management*, vol. 4, no. 2, pp. 189-203.

Tassey, Gregory [1990], "Structural Change and Competitiveness: The U.S. Semiconductor Industry", *Technological Forecasting and Social Change*, vol. 37, pp. 85-93.

Tassey, Gregory [1991], "The Functions of Technology Infrastructure in a Competitive Economy", *Research Policy*.

Tatsuno, Sheridan [1989a], "Japan: From Imitator to Innovator", *New Technology Week* (October 2).

Tatsuno, Sheridan [1989b], "Japanese Manufacturing Proving That Creativity Can Be Learned", *New Technology Week* (December 18).

Technology Review [1990]. "Rethinking the Military's Role in the Economy: An Interview with Harvey Brooks and Lewis Branscomb" (August/September), pp. 55-64.

Tewksbury, J., M. Crandall, and W. Crane [1980], "Measuring the Societal Benefits of Innovation," *Science*, vol. 209 (August), pp. 658-662.

U.S. Department of Commerce [1990], *Emerging Technologies: A Survey of Technical and Economic Opportunities*. Washington, DC: Technology Administration.

U.S. Congress, Office of Technology Assessment [1990], *Making Things Better: Competing in Manufacturing*, OTA-ITE-443. Washington, DC: U.S. Government Printing Office, February.

U.S. Congressional Budget Office [1987], *The Benefits and Risks of Federal Funding for SEMATECH*. Washington, DC: The Congress of the United States (September).

U.S. Department of Commerce, Bureau of Economic Analysis [1989], *Foreign Direct Investment in the United States: 1987 Benchmark Survey, Preliminary Results*. Washington, DC (July).

U.S. Department of Commerce, Bureau of Economic Analysis [1990a], *Foreign Direct Investment in the United States: Operations of U.S. Affiliates of Foreign Companies, Preliminary 1988 Estimates*. Washington, DC (August).

U.S. Department of Commerce, Bureau of Economic Analysis [1990b], *U.S. Foreign Direct Investment Abroad: Operations of U.S. Parent Companies and their Foreign Affiliates*. Washington, DC (July).

U.S. Department of Commerce, International Trade Administration [1990], *The Competitive Status of the U.S. Electronics Sector: From Materials to Systems*. Washington, DC (April).

U.S. Department of Commerce, Bureau of the Census, [1989, 1990] *Annual Survey of Manufacturers*. Washington, DC.

U.S. Department of Commerce, Technology Administration [1990], *Emerging Technologies: A Survey of Technical and Economic Opportunities* (Spring).

U.S. Congress, Congressional Budget Office [1990], *Using R&D Consortia for Commercial Innovation: SEMATECH, X-Ray Lithography, and High-Resolution Systems*. Washington, DC (July).

U.S. Congress, Office of Technology Assessment [1990], *Helping America Compete: The Role of Federal Scientific & Technical Information*, OTA-CIT-454. Washington, DC: U.S. Government Printing Office, July.

U.S. General Accounting Office [1990]. *SEMATECH's Efforts to Strengthen the U.S. Semiconductor Industry* (report to the Committee on Science, Space, and Technology, House of Representatives). Washington, DC: GAO/RCED-90-236 (September).

U.S. National Science Board [1989], *Science & Engineering Indicators -- 1989*. Washington, DC: U.S. Government Printing Office (NSB 89-1).

U.S. National Science Foundation [1991], *Survey of Direct U.S. Private Capital Investment in Research and Development Facilities in Japan* (NSF 91-312). Washington, DC.

U.S. National Science Foundation [1990], *Research and Development in Industry: 1988* (NSF 90-319, Detailed Statistical Tables). Washington, DC.

U.S. National Science Foundation [1988], *The Science and Technology Resources of Japan; A Comparison with the United States*. Washington, DC.

U.S. National Science Foundation [1986], *The Science and Technology Resources of West Germany: A Comparison with the United States* (NSF 86-310). Washington, DC.

VLSI Research, Inc. [1990], *The VLSI Manufacturing Outlook*. San Jose, CA.

Waldman P. and P. Carroll [1988], "Unisys Joins AT&T, Sun Microsystems In Effort to Standardize Unix System", *Wall Street Journal* (March 9).

Zachmann, William [1988], "AT&T Counterattacks; OSF Overreaches Itself", *PC Week*, vol. 5, no. 44 (October 31).

Zachmann, William [1989], "OSF Lives Up to Promises With Motif User Interface", *PC Week*, vol. 6, no. 3 (January 23).

Zachmann, William [1990], "Quick End to Unix Wars Falls on OSF's Shoulders", *PC Week*, vol. 18 (May 7).

Zraket, Charles A. [1989], "Dual-Use Technologies and National Competitiveness", *The Bridge*, vol. 19, no. 3 (Fall).

Subject Index